Guided
by
Performance

Guided
by
Performance

Building Stronger Bridges
between Learning, Curriculum,
and Assessment

Michele Pahl Monson *and* Robert J. Monson

SECONDARY

Zephyr
Press ®
REACHING THEIR HIGHEST POTENTIAL
Tucson, Arizona

Guided by Performance
Building Stronger Bridges between Learning, Curriculum, and Assessment
Secondary

Grades 6–12

©1998 by Zephyr Press
Printed in the United States of America

ISBN 1-56976-081-0

Editors: Veronica Durie and Stacey Shropshire
Cover design: Daniel Miedaner
Design, typesetting, and production: Daniel Miedaner

Zephyr Press
P.O. Box 66006
Tucson, AZ 85728-6006
1-800-232-2187
http://www.zephyrpress.com

Library of Congress Cataloging-in-Publication data are available.

Contents

Preface

Teaching is a creative and challenging endeavor. Drawing upon knowledge of content, a repertoire of pedagogical skills, and observations of the learning process, teachers craft educational experiences to support learners in their classrooms. Far from an exact science, teaching requires the artful blending of knowledge, skills, and observations of student performance in an interactive, dynamic, and challenging classroom context.

Given the complex nature of the task, it is important that teachers be supported in their efforts to improve the learning environment. Although support can come from many sources, the current landscape is cluttered with educational innovations and standards for educational practice, making it difficult to chart a definitive course for educational improvement. Conscientious educators feel the need to respond to current trends in educational practice; in reading educational journals, teachers encounter a wide range of innovative approaches that they want to implement in their classrooms. Researchers and consultants promote educational innovations; in an effort to learn about these new approaches, teachers attend a variety of workshops and training sessions on programs designed to promote student learning. In addition, local school districts, state departments of education, and national professional organizations hand down standards in all of the content areas. Multiple innovations and a surfeit of standards compete for attention, time, and resources. Juggling innovations and standards in classrooms makes it difficult for teachers to make connections in ways that result in improved student learning. For teachers, the goal is to be creative in implementing innovations, responsive to standards for educational practice, and responsible for improving student performance. Support for teachers should enable them to achieve this goal.

This publication is based upon our efforts to provide support to creative educators in a variety of educational settings. Our combined experiences in administration, professional development, and teacher education have prompted us to consider the implications of multiple innovations and educational standards for teachers' work at the classroom, school, and district levels. In this work, we share a framework for making educational decisions by focusing on student performance. We encourage teachers to use student performance data as guides for charting a course to educational improvement.

Introduction
Building a Bridge

Building a bridge between learning, curriculum, and assessment revolves around the critical examination of student work. Through assessment strategies that promote the close observation of student learning, we can investigate and improve the effectiveness of our curriculum. In this book, we craft a series of opportunities for close observation; we call these opportunities "performance assessment packages" and use them to create a forum through which teachers can examine work generated by their students.

Each performance assessment package includes a classroom implementation guide for the teacher and task descriptions and cover sheets for students. The classroom implementation guide contains performance criteria and curriculum notes. Each cover sheet includes a matrix for indicating the aspects of performance addressed in the package and an evaluation format for documenting individual student performance. The packages are targeted at benchmark grades used in the majority of standards documents produced at the national, state, and local levels. In the first volume, we've targeted a primary benchmark grade (3) and an intermediate benchmark grade (5); in this volume, we've targeted a middle school benchmark grade (8) and a high school benchmark grade (11). Packages are numbered sequentially within their sections, but the numbers do not indicate a level or progression; students can complete package 5 without having completed packages 1 through 4, for example.

Beyond sharing a uniform structure, the assessment packages share common characteristics and reflect a philosophical orientation. The packages utilize curriculum-centered, standards-referenced, and classroom-based assessment strategies. Each package centers around a curriculum topic or technical product that is typical for that grade level and addresses curriculum standards that have been identified for the grade level. In addition, the assessment packages are designed to encourage teacher reflection, inform instruction, and enrich classroom learning experiences; they are subjective, open to multiple interpretations, and readily adaptable to any classroom setting. Designed to engage teachers and students in an exploration of learning, the packages are based upon classroom projects that provide natural opportunities to evaluate student learning. Although these assessment packages are not designed for large-scale performance assessment, they represent the kinds of approaches used by many states in performance testing programs. In fact, several of these performance assessment packages have been adopted by the State of Minnesota and aligned with their Graduation Standards and the Profile of Learning. The assessments are provided to schools as models to use in the documentation of student performance. Using these packages will help prepare teachers and students for the demands of statewide performance testing.

In developing these packages, we've learned a great deal about our own educational philosophy. The packages are a reflection of our beliefs about how students learn, about how best to design curriculum to support student learning, and about how to design the best methods for assessing what it is that students have learned. We've used the "four I's" as a starting point for designing each of the packages; the packages are integrated, inquiry based, interesting, and integral to classroom instruction. What do we mean by these terms?

Lately, we've been working a great deal with integrated models for curriculum development by trying to make connections among content areas. In order to make these connections, we've been designing curriculum units that are based upon a unifying theme. The assessment packages in this book represent the kinds of work we expect students to be able to produce at the end of a thematic experience. In each of the packages, students are asked to demonstrate proficiencies in at least two curriculum areas. In addition, each package requires that students demonstrate the integration of knowledge and skills through performance. We've decided to emphasize integration for two reasons. First of all, learning requires integration; that is, after learning something, the learner is able to draw upon knowledge and skills and apply them in appropriate ways and at appropriate times. Secondly, we have been addressing a multitude of curriculum standards at the state and national level. By viewing them in an integrated fashion, we look for opportunities to combine curriculum areas and assess curriculum standards representative of several disciplines. We believe professional organizations who publish curriculum standards intend to help us understand each discipline in greater detail; we do not feel that it is their intent to promote the teaching of these standards in isolation. In fact, it is unrealistic to assume that such isolation could be accomplished; our decision to integrate disciplines in each of these assessment packages is pragmatic and grounded in the practical realities of the classroom.

In addition, we've based our packages upon an inquiry-based model for curriculum development. Learners need strategies for asking questions, gathering information, recording and analyzing this information, formulating answers, sharing the results with a variety of audiences, and making applications and connections. Once they acquire these strategies, they can use them in a variety of learning and work experiences. As you read through the assessment packages, you will see that our approach is based upon the research cycle (see figure I-1); in whole or in part, the assessment packages engage students in asking and answering questions. This "quest to know" is at the heart of learning and it flows throughout the assessment packages in this book.

We feel that the assessment packages are based upon content, processes, and products that students will find interesting. Because we are suggesting that students spend a great deal of time working on these packages, we've attempted to pick topics that appeal to students, have relevance to their lives, and will

challenge them to perform at high levels. When we field test the packages, students often report that they "worked hard" on something that they "will remember" in the future. To us, this is high praise indeed. Students long to be challenged by rigorous work that will inspire learning with lasting relevance to their lives. Our best ideas for performance packages come from working with and talking to students about the kinds of learning experiences that matter to them.

Finally, we've built packages that are integral to classroom instruction. That is, we have not tried to develop performance assessments that conform to the measurement demands of large-scale performance assessment (Linn 1993) used for accountability purposes; in this forum, we are not concerned with technical issues regarding validity, fairness, comparability, or generalizability. We are concerned with teachers in classrooms and have tried to develop performance assessments that are part of the substance of classroom life—in all its subjective, challenging, engaging, and endearing glory! Each of the packages is predicated upon a high level of teacher involvement in the assessment process; we believe that this involvement will inform instruction, improve the learning environment in the classroom, and improve curriculum at the school or district level.

Throughout the book, we allow our definition of student performance to guide us as we make observations about student learning and assess the effectiveness of our curriculum. In chapter 1, we describe how we've arrived at our definition of student performance and how we've incorporated it into an assessment matrix. In chapter 2, we explore the process of creating assessment packages based upon our definition of performance. In chapter 3, we examine the use of these packages to yield information about student performance that can be used to make decisions at the classroom, school, and district level. Chapters 4 and 5 contain the classroom implementation guides and cover sheets for benchmark grades 8 and 11, respectively. Finally, in chapter 6, we share closing thoughts and reflections. Throughout, we share a process for building stronger bridges between learning, curriculum, and assessment.

Figure I-1. What is inquiry?

What is Inquiry?

The Research Cycle

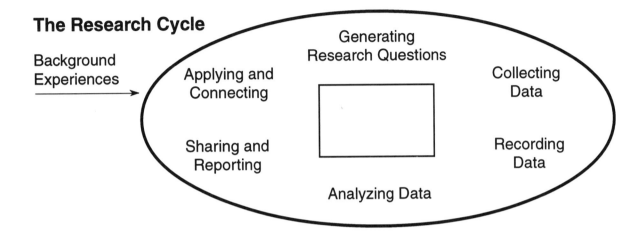

1
Learning and Performance

What do we want students to know and to be able to do? If we are to use student performance as a guide, we need to share common expectations for student learning and develop a shared definition of "student performance." This process involves engaging in a dialogue with other educators about the meaning of performance in various educational contexts. With several teachers, we have been working on the implementation of performance assessment packages for the Minnesota Graduation Standards and the Profile of Learning in school districts. We documented discussions as part of a study of implementation efforts. In the following examples, two teachers discuss their efforts to define, support, and assess student performance in their classrooms:

Although we had been working for over a week on the final project, I still wasn't sure that all of the students understood the material or the skills. Unit tests used to give me a sense of what they knew, but I never had any sense of what they could do with the knowledge—other than use it to fill in the blanks! Looking at the state standards and assessments, it is clear that students are going to have a hard time getting away with only being able to regurgitate facts. I'm convinced that working on these final projects is good for the kids . . . It is a logical extension of what we're doing in class and it gives them meaningful preparation for the state assessments. But I wish I felt more confident about using class projects for assessment purposes.
—Grade 5 teacher

Lately, I've come to understand that my goal is to provide opportunities for these students to meet standards. If I do what I've always done, I have to admit that I'm not always providing those opportunities. I need to get more specific with myself about how I'm actually going to make it possible for students to learn and demonstrate each standard. If it's not part of what

I normally do, I'll have to develop a new instructional approach. I can't take it for granted that I'm getting to all of the standards . . . I just don't think it's fair to the students to make that assumption about my teaching. If students aren't meeting standards, I think we need to be critical of our own curriculum and willing to make changes. It isn't productive to spend time trying to find excuses; I want to be part of the solution.
—Grade 11 teacher

One of the most exciting outcomes of the movement to establish educational standards has been a heightened level of discourse about what constitutes effective performance in the various disciplines. Like that of the teachers quoted above, we want our definition to be informed, in part, by the curriculum standards associated with the various content areas. But we believe a more comprehensive definition of performance is required. As we discuss the meaning of performance, we will be building a performance assessment matrix that serves as a concrete manifestation of our definition of student performance; it will become the basis upon which we will build assessment packages.

The Meaning of Performance: Building a Matrix

Where should we begin? To our way of thinking, performance implies concrete demonstrations of understanding and the use of productive habits of mind in authentic contexts. Defining performance requires that we ask ourselves questions about the content knowledge, content skills, cognitive strategies, and task management strategies that we expect students to be able to demonstrate within an authentic role and through the development of an authentic product. In this chapter, we discuss some of these questions and potential sources for finding answers.

What Content Knowledge and Content Skills Will Students Demonstrate through Performance?

When we think about the information, specific concepts, and concrete facts that we expect students to know, we are considering the content-knowledge component of student performance. If we ask students to discuss the factors that contributed to the United States' Declaration of Independence, to demonstrate an understanding of the concepts of force and motion, or to list the major events in the life of Thurgood Marshall, we are requiring performance in the area of content knowledge.

In contrast, when we think about the processes, procedures, and skills that we expect students to be able to do, we are considering the content-skill component of student performance. If we ask students to perform a laboratory experiment, conduct an oral history interview, or solve a mathematical problem using manipulatives, we are requiring performance in the area of content skill. However, unlike content-knowledge standards that outline what students should know in the various disciplines, content-skill standards focus on what students should be able to do with that knowledge. Obviously, declarative and procedural standards are linked; students cannot perform adequately without knowledge.

Curriculum standards help us to identify the kinds of content knowledge and content skills that we should be factoring into our definition of student performance. At the national level, the efforts of professional organizations to set standards have yielded numerous documents (see appendix); in fact, in some curriculum areas, multiple documents have been produced by various organizations. Testing organizations (NAEP, ACT, SAT, and ETS) produce tests and performance assessments that are based upon objective assessments of content knowledge and skills. At the state level, forty-eight states have initiatives aimed at the identification of curriculum standards; only Iowa and Wyoming appear to have refrained from participating in a standard-setting effort (Gandal 1996). Locally, many school districts have either developed their own curriculum documents or have adopted curriculum materials that address specific aspects of content knowledge and content skills in the various disciplines. Clearly, there is no shortage of documents outlining a wide range of standards in a variety of content areas.

The majority of standards documents contain both declarative and procedural standards; depending on the discipline, content knowledge and content skill are represented in different proportions. In their analysis of the national curriculum documents, Robert J. Marzano and John. S. Kendall (1996) make observations about the percentages of declarative and procedural standards contained in each document; see table 1.1 for their findings. When reading the standards documents, it is easy to distinguish content knowledge from content skills. As the following examples illustrate, declarative standards describe content knowledge using key words such as *know* and *understand*:

Table 1-1. Marzano's and Kendall's Findings

Subject Area	Declarative Standards	Procedural Standards
Science	92 percent	8 percent
Mathematics	49 percent	51 percent
Geography	98 percent	2 percent
Language arts	24 percent	76 percent
History	97 percent	3 percent

- "The student understands how Mesopotamia, Egypt, and the Indus valley became centers of dense population, urbanization, and cultural innovation in the fourth and third millennia BCE" (National Center for History in the Schools 1996, 141).
- "As a result of their activities in grades K–4, students should develop an understanding of: properties of earth materials, objects in the sky, changes in earth and sky" (National Research Council 1996, 130).

These standards can easily be distinguished from procedural standards contained in the same documents, which include key phrases such as *be able to, know how to,* and action verbs:

- "The student engages in historical analysis and interpretation. Therefore, the student should be able to . . . challenge arguments of historical inevitability" (National Center for History in the Schools 1996, 66).
- "As a result of activities in grades 9–12, all students should develop abilities of technological design" (National Research Council 1996, 190).

Teachers need to make decisions about the foundation of content knowledge and content skills that they will expect students to demonstrate. For this purpose, teachers should draw upon the curriculum standards in place in their educational setting, which may mean basing decisions about content on published sources, instructional materials, local curriculum guides, state curriculum frameworks, specifications from testing organizations, or national standards documents. Throughout this book, we'll be using a variety of examples of content knowledge drawn from national curriculum standards as a focus for our assessment packages; although the standards for content knowledge will vary from package to package, they will all be referenced to the national documents appearing in the appendix. With respect to the content skills associated with various disciplines, we will select a consistent foundation of skills to guide our development of assessment packages. In doing so, we will demonstrate that the standards we assess can come from a number of different sources—national standards documents,

published sources, instructional materials, and testing organizations. Taken together, they reflect our definition of *content skills.* Specifically, we drew upon the following publications to construct our performance assessment matrix for designing performance assessment packages:

- **Literacy:** Fabio 1994
- **Mathematics:** National Council of Teachers of Mathematics 1989
- **Science:** Hogan 1991
- **Social Studies:** National Council for the Social Studies 1994
- **History:** National Center for History in the Schools 1996
- **Visual Arts:** National Art Education Association 1994

The performance assessment matrix, with a space for inserting specific content knowledge standards from local and national documents and with a listing of the content skills associated with each area, is included in figure 1-1. We've used standards from these documents because they reflect our own understanding of the content skills associated with the various disciplines. Obviously, modifications can be made in the design of this matrix; in fact, they should be made to correspond with the standards in place in any educational setting. For example, in working with a variety of educational organizations, we have adapted the matrix to reflect individual state standards or to reflect the curricular program in place at individual schools. Figure 1-2 illustrates how content skills can be adapted to reflect state standards. The literacy column has been changed to reflect Massachusetts State Department of Education (1977) language arts standards and the science column has been changed to reflect the scientific method inquiry standard in Minnesota's High Standards in the Profile of Learning (Minnesota Department of Children, Families, and Learning 1996). Figure 1-3 lists additional content skills you may want to address.

In making decisions about the matrix, you need to consider specific content skills that you are interested in observing through performance and make the skills explicit by including these skills on the matrix. You may want to consult a comprehensive source that lists standards from a variety of content

Figure 1-1. Content skills in the performance assessment matrix

Performance Assessment Matrix

Package Title:

Curriculum Area:

Package:

Student: _____

Content Knowledge

Content Skills

Literacy	Mathematics	Science	Social Studies	Visual Arts
Reading	Problem solving	Defining questions	Acquiring information	Creating
for aesthetic response	Communication	Forming hypotheses	*reading*	*conceptual skills*
for information/understanding	Reasoning	Investigating	*study skills*	*production skills*
for critical analysis/evaluation	Connecting	Observing	*reference skills*	*evaluation skills*
Writing	Estimation	Monitoring	*technical skills*	*application*
for response/expression	Numeration	Measuring	Organizing/Using information	Responding
for social interaction	Computation	Keeping records	*thinking skills*	*descriptive skills*
for information/understanding	Data analysis	Transforming records	*decision-making skills*	*analytical skills*
for critical analysis/evaluation	Measurement	Collaborating	*metacognitive skills*	*valuing skills*
Listening	Patterning/Relating	Interpreting information	Relationships	*application*
for response/expression		Integrating information	*personal skills*	
for information/understanding			*group interaction*	
for critical analysis/evaluation			*social/political participation*	
Speaking			Historical thinking	
for response/expression			*chronological thinking*	
for social interaction			*historical comprehension*	
for information/understanding			*analysis and interpretation*	
for critical analysis/evaluation			*historical research*	
			issues and decisions	

Figure 1-2. Revised performance assessment matrix to accommodate state standards

Performance Assessment Matrix

Package Title:
Curriculum Area:
Package:
Student: _____

Content Knowledge

Content Skills

Language Arts		Mathematics		Scientific Methods		Social Studies		Visual Arts	
Use discussion rules		Problem solving		Identify and formulate a question		Acquiring information		Creating	
Question, listen, contribute		Communication		conduct a literature review		reading		conceptual skills	
Perform and present (oral)		Reasoning		define a problem		study skills		production skills	
Acquire and use vocabulary		Connecting		formulate a hypothesis		reference skills		evaluation skills	
Apply structure and conventions		Estimation		design an experiment		technical skills		application	
Analyze dialect of English		Numeration		Gather information		Organizing/Using information		Responding	
Analyze origin of English		Computation		use tools and methodology		thinking skills		descriptive skills	
Use strategies to decode words		Data analysis		record data		decision-making skills		analytical skills	
Identify facts and ideas		Measurement		perform an experiment		metacognitive skills		valuing skills	
Apply genre and theme		Patterning/Relating		Handle data		Relationships		application	
Apply elements and structure				apply appropriate technology		personal skills			
Provide evidence from text				apply statistical processes		group interaction			
Analyze author's style				analyze data/make generalizations		social/political participation			
Compare and contrast works				replicate experiment		Historical thinking			
Interpret meaning				consider alternative results		chronological thinking			
Write with focus, ideas, and detail				formulate new questions		historical comprehension			
Revise for content and organization				compare findings		analysis and interpretation			
Edit for conventions				use evidence to support ideas		historical research			
Use effective learning strategies				develop conclusions		issues and decisions			
Use effective research strategies				Communicate results					
Use criteria for self-assessment				report findings					
				summarize results/conclusion					
				self-reflect/generalize					

Figure 1-3. Possible alternative content skill areas

Additional Content Skill Areas

Arts	Health	Physical Education	Civics
Dance: Demonstrates	Health Promotion	Competence in Movement Forms	Defining and Understanding
movement and choreography	Disease Prevention	Proficiency in Physical Activity	*government at all levels*
meaning, culture, and history	Access of Health Information	Development of Motor Skills	*basic values of democracy*
critical and creative thinking skills	Practice of Healthy Behaviors	Design of Personal Fitness Programs	*basic principles of democracy*
Music: Demonstrates	Reduction of Health Risks	Identification of Benefits and Costs	*responsibilities of government*
singing and performing	Analysis of Influences on Health	Responsible Personal Behavior	*relationships and interactions*
improvising	Interpersonal Communication	Responsible Social Behavior	*rules of citizens*
composing and arranging	Skills	Inclusion and Understanding	*civic life*
reading	Goal-Setting Skills	Understanding of Opportunities	*politics and political systems*
Theater: Demonstrates	Health Advocacy	Regular Participation in Activity	
script writing			
acting skills			
designing, producing, directing			
Visual Arts: Understands and Uses			
media, techniques, and processes			
structure and functions			
subject matter, symbols, and ideas			
merits of work			
Art Connections			

areas. These sources include Marzano and Kendall 1996 (the database is also available on the World Wide Web URL www.mcrel.org/standard.html); Struggling for Standards: A Special Series Available on Disk (1995); and Education Week, Special Reports on Disk, 4301 Connecticut Avenue, NW, Suite 250, Washington, DC, 20008. In lieu of accessing a more comprehensive resource, you may want to obtain copies of the individual standards documents listed in the appendix. Obviously, each document provides a more in-depth discussion of the content area standards in each discipline than that provided in either of the comprehensive resources.

What Cognitive Strategies Will Students Demonstrate through Performance?

In all content areas, there is a foundation of skills that learners use to process information; these fundamental cognitive strategies are represented throughout the standards documents and shape student thinking in a variety of disciplines. Since these "habits of mind" are the hallmarks of disciplined thinking, we believe that they should be included as an explicit component of student performance.

However, there are a variety of cognitive strategy frameworks that might be imbedded in any definition of student performance. Brain-based learning principles (Caine and Caine 1997), multiple intelligence theory (Gardner 1983; Armstrong 1994), and dimensions of learning (Marzano, Pickering, and McTighe 1993) are but a few of the cognitive frameworks that we have worked with effectively in developing assessment packages. By including a cognitive strategy component in our definition of student performance, we can integrate an aspect of teacher training that is often addressed in isolation.

Regardless of the framework used, thinking skills need to be explicitly connected to content area learning experiences. By adding this area to our definition of student performance, we are able to assess how students employ cognitive strategies in a variety of content area applications. In the matrix we are building to define student performance, we will be using the dimensions of learning model (Marzano, Pickering, and McTighe 1993). The dimensions of learning model explores several areas of learning by outlining attitudes and perceptions, habits of mind, skills of acquiring and integrating knowledge, skills of extending and refining knowledge, and skills of using knowledge meaningfully. Specifically, we've included the dimensions that relate to extending and refining knowledge and to using knowledge meaningfully because we feel that these dimensions are required in order for students to use knowledge to perform. The dimensions we've included are comparison, classification, induction, deduction, error analysis, constructing support, abstracting, analyzing perspectives, decision making, investigation, experimental inquiry, problem solving, and invention.

What Task Management Skills Will Students Demonstrate through Performance?

When students are asked to perform with knowledge, they must orchestrate their participation, manage the work involved in completing tasks, and integrate knowledge and skills in a specific context. These activities often require skills that heretofore students may not have needed in order to complete their work. For example, in the performance assessment tasks we've outlined in this volume, the student has responsibility for structuring the work, for completing work according to flexible schedules, and, often, for working with other students effectively to complete portions of the task. Based upon our observations of the management strategies required to complete these assessment packages successfully, we've outlined a group of task management skills and included these as an explicit component of student performance in the assessment matrix. They are analyzing the task, establishing time lines, staying productive, meeting

deadlines, accepting feedback, working cooperatively, making a contribution, respecting others, assessing resources, striving for accuracy, and striving for excellence. As with the other components of student performance, teachers can make modifications to the task management strategies in the matrix. Regardless of the specific skills listed in this section, it is important that some aspect of task management behavior be considered in any definition of student performance.

What Authentic Roles Will Students Adopt through Performance?

Perhaps more than any other single researcher or consultant, Grant Wiggins (1993) has challenged educators to develop more authentic assessments of student performance. Wiggins argues that, by placing student performance in a more authentic context, we ensure that students have the opportunity to integrate knowledge and skills in the context of "roles and situational challenges" that are "common to professional life" (222). Wiggins suggests that these "roles and situations might serve as possible templates for better test design" (222) by providing a direction for more purposeful learning experiences. If we are asking students to demonstrate the proficient use of content knowledge, content skills, cognitive strategies, and task management skills, we need to provide demanding and challenging tasks that require students to integrate these various components into a multidimensional performance.

These roles are included as a specific component in our student performance matrix. We find that considering an authentic role for students also helps us design effective performance assessment tasks and packages. Obviously, it is not always possible to provide actual engagement in these roles for students. That is, it is unlikely that they will always be involved in the physical development of an exhibit for a museum or the organization of a tour for actual tourists. However, it is possible to simulate situations that enable these kinds of performances and, whenever possible, ensure that there is an audience beyond the teacher (peers, other grades, other schools, the community) for the work produced by students. In short, when students ask why they are engaging in specific performances, there should be a reason that goes beyond the fact that the task has been assigned by a teacher. As you'll see in the assessment packages that follow, we've attempted to structure performance tasks so that students experience authentic roles and share their work with authentic audiences. The roles we've included were compiled by Grant Wiggins (1993) and are museum curator, reviewer, engineer/designer, representative, expert witness, character, ad agency director, tour operator, bank manager, psychologist/sociologist, archaeologist, philosopher, historian, writer/editor, teacher, job applicant, and speaker-listener. We have also left a blank for additional roles that you may develop.

In the assessment packages, we've established a context for student performance based upon these roles. As a result of reports such as *What Work Requires of Schools: A SCANS Report for America 2000* (Department of Labor 1991), many school districts are placing increasing emphasis on preparing students for roles in the working world. Teachers may want to adapt the assessment matrix to include specific "worker attributes" targeted by their school district.

What Assessment Products Will Students Generate through Performance?

When we think about the ways in which students can share evidence of their learning, we are adding another component to our definition of performance. Using the components already discussed, students can generate a variety of products in the context of an authentic role. We've grouped these into the following categories, which appear on the assessment matrix:

Portfolio

A collection of work generated over a period of time; the student and the teacher use the record of work to reflect upon development, progress, and performance. Although artifacts in the portfolio can take many different forms, they should facilitate comparison and make visible student growth over time. Examples include learning logs and writing portfolios.

Publication

Individually or in groups, students produce a written product that is meant to be shared with others; students work to ensure that the material has been edited and prepared appropriately for publication, which can include simply sharing with an audience. The publication can include text, charts, graphs, graphics, photographs, and other illustrations to explain to an audience. Examples include newspapers, poetry anthologies, and museum guides.

Demonstration

Students convey information about a topic and instruct others in a process through oral presentation. The presentation may include materials, visual aids, graphics, and the use of media or technology. Students should view the demonstration as a means of teaching the audience. Examples include laboratory experiments, cooking demonstrations, and design seminars.

Performance

Students present their learning through role play, drama, or other performing arts. There is an emphasis on the student's and the audience's interpretation of meaning. Examples include monologues, testimonials, plays, and scenario development.

Exhibition

An exhibition is a comprehensive forum through which students demonstrate their learning in a variety of ways; an exhibition may incorporate any or all of the categories listed previously. An exhibition is experienced collaboratively by the student and the audience; there are many opportunities for interaction and reflection. Examples include learning carousels, walking tours, interactive museum exhibits, multimedia presentations, and focus group discussions.

Throughout the assessment packages, these products will be combined in ways that reflect the content of the learning experience. This final component in the performance assessment matrix gives us a complete picture of the qualities we'll be looking for in student performance.

A Comprehensive Look at Performance

We can represent our definition through the completed assessment matrix; we also need to provide a strategy for keeping track of our observations. We need to include a format for evaluating student performance. Throughout these packages, we've used four different formats for evaluating student performance.

Student Checklist

The student checklist includes performance criteria that will be used to evaluate student work. Not all packages include a student checklist. Students are encouraged to self-assess their work by asking questions about the quality of their performance, by indicating whether or not they've addressed the criteria through their performance, and by indicating what they might do in order to improve in specific areas.

Teacher Checklist

A teacher checklist is the most common evaluation format that we've used. Keeping in mind that these assessment packages are used primarily by teachers to assess work in their classrooms, we feel that this informal assessment approach is ideal and represents the kinds of things teachers need to know in order to inform their instructional planning. The teacher checklist includes performance criteria that will be used to evaluate student work. Using the checklist, teachers indicate whether individual student performance is "excellent," "satisfactory," or "needs improvement" as compared to the stated performance criteria. In the classroom implementation guide that accompanies each package, performance criteria listed reference each portion of the task that will be assessed. In the teacher checklist, all criteria are clustered together in the checklist format.

Analytic Scoring Guide

An analytic scoring guide builds upon the teacher checklist by articulating specific performance criteria associated with all three levels of performance. You can build rubrics by taking the performance criteria listed in each package for the satisfactory level and using it as the center column of the rubric. When you are able to define the aspects of student performance that distinguish excellent performances from satisfactory level performances, you can describe these criteria in the left column of the rubric. In addition, when you are able to define the aspects of student performance that need improvement, you can use the right column of the rubric to describe them. An excellent example of this evaluation format is contained in the assessment package "Biomedical Ethics" (page 197). However, we have not used the rubric extensively throughout the assessment packages for several reasons. First of all, we find that, in most cases, the teacher checklist is sufficient for meeting evaluation needs in the classroom. Secondly, we find that a rubric is most easily developed in the context of examining student work samples. It becomes much easier to describe the qualities of student performance after teachers have had at least one opportunity to use the assessment package and analyze the student work. Therefore, we've included a rubric planning sheet (figure 1-4) as an option for teachers to use in constructing their own rubrics based upon the performance criteria for each package and their observations of student work.

Holistic Scoring Guide

Another option for evaluating student work is the holistic scoring guide. Many teachers like this option because it enables them to give students an overall evaluation for the package. Like the rubric, the holistic scoring guide builds upon the teacher checklist by combining all the performance criteria in one category and labeling it "satisfactory." In addition, we give a complete description for performance categories at the "excellent" and "needs improvement" levels. This evaluation format is easier to use with smaller packages involving a single product of student performance. Holistic scoring has a major shortcoming, however, that makes it a less desirable option than the teacher checklists. As students generate work for performance packages, they typically perform at different levels within each package. In other words, some aspects of their performance may be excellent, others satisfactory, and still others may need improvement. The holistic scoring guide makes it difficult to capture the nuances of student performance and to develop a profile of varying

Figure 1-4. Analytic Scoring Guide (Rubric)

Rubric Planning Sheet

Performance Criteria	Excellent	Satisfactory	Needs Improvement
Task 1:			
Task 2:			
Task 3:			
Task 4:			

levels of performance. On the other hand, by using the teacher checklist and addressing each performance criterion separately, student performance patterns are visually evident to the teacher and the student.

The Performance Assessment Matrix

When we include all aspects of student performance and our strategy list for keeping track of student performance, the completed matrix includes content knowledge, content skills, cognitive strategies, task management strategies, student role, assessment product, and evaluation format (see matrices in assessment packages). This matrix is the one we use throughout the assessment packages.

Obviously, this matrix can and should be modified to reflect the standards and curriculum used in individual school settings. The important first step, however, is to make sure that teachers, schools, and districts consider the questions we've outlined in this chapter.

Despite slight differences from school district to school district, we find tremendous similarities in the ways that educators are beginning to think about learning and performance. These similarities are captured and reflected throughout the assessment packages. As a result, you will find that you can easily adapt the matrix and use the assessment packages in your classrooms.

2
Designing Assessment Packages

By thoughtfully considering the question "What do we want students to know and to be able to do?" we've established a foundation that will support our bridge between learning, curriculum, and assessment. Using our comprehensive definition of performance, we have provided a focus for student learning and for the design of curriculum-based assessment packages.

In this chapter, we follow Derek Lowe, a high school English teacher, as he goes through the process of designing an assessment package for his classroom. He selects an instructional unit, uses the performance assessment matrix, generates a performance task, and develops a classroom implementation guide.

As we use this framework, think about the kind of assessment package you might design in your own classroom by engaging in the following activities:

- Select an instructional unit that you have used in the past; think about your objectives for student learning, the instructional experiences you designed, and the student work generated throughout the unit.
- Using the performance assessment matrix, target standards in the four areas (content knowledge, content skills, cognitive strategies, and management strategies) that are addressed within the instructional unit; in addition, investigate opportunities for addressing supplementary standards by designing a culminating project for the unit.
- Generate a performance task by identifying a student role, selecting an assessment product as a final project for the unit, and deciding upon an evaluation format that will allow you to assess how well the standards have been met.
- Develop a classroom implementation guide for the assessment package with a time line, a detailed description of assessment tasks, the performance criteria you will use, and curriculum notes.

Selecting an Instructional Unit

In Derek Lowe's English classroom, students engage in a variety of exciting learning experiences. Because he enjoys thematic teaching, Derek has developed a series of units that he uses throughout the year. One of the most interesting units he teaches is a unit called "The Heroine's Journey." When he teaches this unit, he uses a variety of materials to direct students through a critical examination of the role of women in traditional folk literature and mythology; as they interact with these materials, students come to understand how authors portray women in heroic roles, they learn to identify common text structures within this body of literature, and they compare and contrast female characters in folk literature from a variety of cultural traditions. Students view a Joseph Campbell and Bill Moyers video *The Power of Myth* (1988), and they read the accompanying book. In class, students pay special attention to Campbell's outline of the hero's adventure. They consider the implications for female characters portrayed in the same body of traditional literature as Campbell uses and examine the structure of texts to look for components of the heroic cycle. They read widely from anthologies that represent a variety of cultural traditions, analyze these texts, and write their own "Heroine's Journey" narratives. In addition, Derek arranges to have storytellers visit the classroom as guest speakers; these storytellers share the rich oral tradition of folk literature with Derek's students. Derek's class usually continues the exploration in two areas: they conduct an inquiry into the historical role of women using nonfiction materials and they examine other stereotypes and icons in literature.

When Derek thinks about the kind of culminating project he'd like students to do, he wants students to demonstrate a thorough understanding of the "Heroine's Journey" structure in text and the implications for plot and character development. He wants the students to exit the unit with the understanding that this approach to critical analysis is one they might employ to understand, interpret, and compare narrative texts.

Using the Assessment Matrix

In thinking about his instructional unit, Derek feels that it targets content knowledge in language arts and social studies. Specifically, drawing upon the national standards from each document, the unit addresses the following:

- "Standard 1: Students read a wide range of print and non-print texts to build an understanding of texts, of themselves, and of the cultures of the United States and the world . . . Among these texts are fiction, nonfiction, classic, and contemporary works" (International Reading Association and National Council of Teachers of English 1996, 3).
- "Standard 2: Students read a wide range of literature from many periods in many genres to build an understanding of the many dimensions . . . of human experience" (International Reading Association and National Council of Teachers of English 1996, 3).
- "Standard 3: Students apply a wide range of strategies to comprehend, interpret, evaluate and appreciate texts" (International Reading Association and National Council of Teachers of English 1996, 3).
- "Standard 6: Students apply knowledge of . . . genre to create, critique, and discuss print and non-print texts" (International Reading Association and National Council of Teachers of English 1996, 3).
- "Standard 7: Students conduct research on issues and interests by generating ideas and questions and by posing problems. They gather, evaluate, and synthesize data from a variety of sources . . . to communicate discoveries in ways that suit their purpose and audience" (International Reading Association and National Council of Teachers of English 1996, 3).
- "Standard 9: Students develop an understanding of and respect for diversity in language use,

patterns, and dialects across cultures, ethnic groups, geographic regions, and social roles" (International Reading Association and National Council of Teachers of English 1996, 3).
- "Standard 1: Culture (High School)—Apply an understanding of culture as an integrated whole that explains the functions and interactions of language, literature, the arts, traditions, beliefs and values, and behavior patterns" (National Council for the Social Studies 1994, 33).
- "Standard 4: Individual Development and Identity (High School)—Compare and evaluate the impact of stereotyping, conformity, acts of altruism, and other behaviors on individuals and groups" (National Council for the Social Studies 1994, 37).

Finally, Derek examines his state curriculum framework and discovers that the instructional unit addresses the standard in the content area of "Arts Analysis and Interpretation" (Minnesota's High Standards in the Profile of Learning, Minnesota Department of Children, Families, and Learning 1996):
- "interpret and evaluate complex works of . . . literature . . . applying specific criteria"
- "know a critical approach to interpreting and analyzing works of art"
- "understand the elements and structure of the art form and how it is used to create meaning"
- "know the . . . cultural background of selected artworks"

Students demonstrate content skills in literacy, social studies and history, and the visual arts through the work they generate for the unit. Notice that, although the primary focus of the unit is on language arts, the unit addresses content skills in other curriculum areas. In addition, students will be able to demonstrate four cognitive strategies by the time they reach the end of the unit—comparison, classification, constructing support, and investigation. Finally, as he thinks about the work he requires of students, Derek decides that they also need to analyze tasks, make a contribution, access resources, and strive for excellence; these are the task management strategies he emphasizes throughout the unit.

Generating a Performance Task

Derek considers several different possibilities for a final project. He wonders, "What would be the best way for students to demonstrate what they know and are able to do?" After weighing his options, he decides to have students adopt the role of museum curator and to have them create a museum exhibit as an assessment product. He's going to call the assessment package "The Heroine's Journey." As students analyze a wide range of texts, they will keep a portfolio and synthesize their learning in an exhibition. Finally, he decides to develop one evaluation format—a teacher checklist to record his observations about student performance.

When he has made these decisions, he records them on the assessment matrix. He indicates his choices by writing in the standards for content knowledge and making selections in the areas of content skills, cognitive strategies, task management skills, student roles, assessment products, and evaluation format (see figure 2-1).

Developing a Guide for Implementation

To implement this assessment package in his classroom, Derek knows that he'll need to plan the performance task in greater detail, specify performance criteria for the task, and make connections between the task and the curriculum. In this stage, Derek is going to develop a classroom implementation guide for his assessment package.

Describing the Task

In general, a performance task can take on a variety of forms. However, by centering the task around a specific student role and selecting a category for the assessment product, the task takes on a preliminary shape. Once this shape is determined, the task description needs to be written in greater detail so that students can implement the task successfully and so that other teachers can use the assessment package in their classrooms.

Derek has decided to engage students as museum curators and to have them contribute to an exhibition entitled "The Heroine's Journey." To encourage students to demonstrate what they've learned about the image of females in traditional literature, he has decided that each student will analyze ten examples of traditional literature from at least four different cultural traditions and synthesize their findings, interpretations, and impressions via a display board. As he describes each step in the task, he does the following:

- Writes the task description using language that will have meaning for the students
- Breaks the task down into a series of progressive steps leading to the development of a product or products that can be used to assess the performance of the individual student
- Specifies for students the important things to consider as they complete each step
- Builds in opportunities for progress checks, conferences with students, and peer interaction
- Provides examples and models to help students visualize the requirements of the task

Derek has outlined a task that he feels will enable his students to demonstrate what they have learned in the unit and enable him to assess their performance in the standard areas outlined on the performance assessment matrix (see figure 2-2 for one such task).

As Derek Lowe has done, we have written the task descriptions in each assessment package for the students by using language similar to that found in the performance tasks used as a component of standards-based testing programs in many states. Part of our goal is to help students develop the strategies necessary to read performance tasks, to independently manage the work required in the performance task, and to produce the appropriate final products. By developing these skills, students will be better prepared to perform well on statewide tests.

The task description pages are copyrighted, and you may photocopy them for use in your classroom (note that the copyright allows use only in one classroom). We have seen teachers use these descriptions in a variety of ways. Some teachers simply photocopy entire task descriptions, distribute them, and answer questions that individual students may have as they go through the process. Other teachers make overhead transparencies of the descriptions; as a class, the students ask questions as they complete the various steps in the task description. Still other teachers break down the task descriptions into steps that they distribute one at a time in sequence. You know what will be most effective for your class; we encourage you to experiment with a variety of possibilities.

Figure 2-1. Performance assessment matrix for "The Heroine's Journey"

Performance Assessment Matrix

Package Title: Heroine's Journey

Curriculum Area: Language Arts, Social Studies

Package: Grade 11, package 4

Student: _____

Content Knowledge

Language Arts: Standard 1 (Read a wide range of texts to build an understanding of texts, of themselves, and of culture.)
Standard 2 (literature from many periods and genres, and understanding human experience)
Standard 3 (Apply wide range of strategies to comprehend, interpret, and evaluate texts.)
Standard 6 (Apply knowledge of . . . genre to create, critique, and discuss print and nonprint text.)
Standard 7 (Conduct research; generate questions; gather data; communicate discoveries.)
Standard 9 (respect for diversity in language use, patterns, and dialects across cultures)

Social Studies: Standard 1 (culture as an integrated whole; functions and interactions of literature)
Standard 4 (Individual development and identity: compare and evaluate the impact of stereotyping, conformity, and other behaviors)

Content Skills

Literacy	Mathematics	Science	Social Studies	Visual Arts	
Reading	Problem solving	Defining questions	Acquiring information	Creating	
for aesthetic response	Communication	Forming hypotheses	*reading*	*conceptual skills*	
for information/understanding	Reasoning	Investigating	*study skills*	*production skills*	
for critical analysis/evaluation	Connecting	Observing	*reference skills*	*evaluation skills*	
Writing	Estimation	Monitoring	*technical skills*	*application*	
for response/expression	Numeration	Measuring	Organizing/Using information	Responding	
for social interaction	Computation	Keeping records	*thinking skills*	*descriptive skills*	
for information/understanding	Data analysis	Transforming records	*decision-making skills*	*analytical skills*	
for critical analysis/evaluation	Measurement	Collaborating	*metacognitive skills*	*valuing skills*	
Listening	Patterning/Relating	Interpreting information	Relationships	*application*	
for response/expression		Integrating information	*personal skills*		
for information/understanding			*group interaction*		
for critical analysis/evaluation			*social/political participation*		
Speaking			Historical thinking		
for response/expression			*chronological thinking*		
for social interaction			*historical comprehension*		
for information/understanding			*analysis and interpretation*		
for critical analysis/evaluation			*historical research*		
			issues and decisions		

Figure 2-1. Performance assessment matrix for "The Heroine's Journey"

Performance Assessment Matrix

Performance Skills

Cognitive Strategies	Task Management Strategies	Student Role	Assessment Products	Evaluation Format
Comparison	Analyzing the task	Museum curator	Portfolio	Student checklist (attached)
Classification	Establishing time lines	Reviewer	Publication	Teacher checklist (attached)
Induction	Staying productive	Engineer/Designer	Demonstration	Analytic scoring guide/ rubric (attached)
Deduction	Meeting deadlines	Representative	Performance	Holistic scoring guide (attached)
Error analysis	Accepting feedback	Expert witness	Exhibition	
Constructing support	Working cooperatively	Character		
Abstracting	Making a contribution	Ad agency director		
Analyzing perspectives	Respecting others	Tour organizer		
Decision making	Accessing resources	Bank manager		
Investigation	Striving for accuracy	Psychologist/Sociologist		
Experimental inquiry	Striving for excellence	Archaeologist		
Problem solving		Philosopher		
Invention		Historian		
		Writer/Editor		
		Teacher		
		Job applicant		
		Speaker/Listener		

Anecdotal Observations

19

Figure 2-2. Step 6 in a task description

The Heroine's Journey
Language Arts

Assessment Products: portfolio (vocabulary words, comparison grid, retelling); museum exhibit
Time: 2 weeks

Task Description	Performance Criteria	Curriculum Notes
6. Using a comparison grid (see example 3, page 187), record the events that correspond or conflict with stages in the heroine's journey. Evaluate each selection using the heroine's journey pattern.		

Writing Performance Criteria

Keeping the performance assessment matrix in mind, Derek's next step is to identify the specific performance criteria that he will use to evaluate the task. Derek writes performance criteria for several processes in the task. Next to each step in the task description that contains an opportunity for assessment, Derek lists the criteria that he will use to evaluate student performance. He does the following:

- References processes or products that can be observed and assessed for the individual student
- Includes in each statement a verb that describes what students should be able to do
- Includes a clear description of satisfactory level of performance for each aspect of the task
- Uses qualifiers that make interpretation clear (*accurately, completely, independently*)
- avoids using qualifiers that make interpretation difficult (*thoughtfully, conscientiously*)

In the following examples from the assessment package "Book Illustration" (Monson 1998a, 82), the verb and description of what students should be able to do is underlined and the observable description of satisfactory student performance is written in italics:

- <u>Generates</u> *questions that begin with "How do . . . ?" or "In what ways do . . . ?"*
- <u>Lists</u> *research questions* and <u>defines</u> *element on cover sheet of scrapbook.*

- <u>Uses chart to record</u> *information and observations for five selections.*
- <u>Answers</u> *research questions* or <u>identifies</u> *the need for additional investigation.*
- <u>Chooses, reproduces, and reflects upon</u> *sample illustrations (two for each artistic element).*
- <u>Explains reasoning</u> *using language learned and knowledge gathered throughout the inquiry.*

When used, qualifiers (in bold in the following list) facilitate interpretation of student work:

- <u>Records</u> *results* **accurately.**
- <u>Conducts</u> *polling* **accurately.**

Using these guidelines and examples as a guide, Derek writes performance criteria for his own task (see figure 2-3 for the performance criteria for the task in figure 2-2); he writes a criterion statement next to the portion of the task being assessed. In addition, he transfers these performance criteria to a teacher checklist (see figure 2-4). Since his students are in high school, he won't need to adapt this format for a student checklist; he gives students the same checklist for self-assessment that he will use for his evaluation of their performance. In addition to the performance assessment matrix he completes for this task, Derek uses the teacher checklist as a cover sheet for the work samples he will eventually collect from students.

Figure 2-3. The performance criteria for step 6

The Heroine's Journey
Language Arts

Assessment Products: portfolio (vocabulary words, comparison grid, retelling); museum exhibit
Time: 2 weeks

Task Description	Performance Criteria	Curriculum Notes
6. Using a comparison grid (see example 3, page 187), record the events that correspond or conflict with stages in the heroine's journey. Evaluate each selection using the heroine's journey pattern.	▪ Notes events that correspond or conflict with the heroine's journey pattern on a comparison grid for each selection ▪ Evaluates each selection using the heroine's journey pattern	

Figure 2-4. The performance criteria in a teacher checklist

Teacher Checklist for "The Heroine's Journey			
Performance Criteria	Excellent	Satisfactory	Needs Improvement
▪ Notes events that correspond or conflict with the heroine's journey pattern on a comparison grid for each selection	_____	_____	_____
▪ Evaluates each selection using the heroine's journey pattern	_____	_____	_____

Curriculum Notes

Derek's next step is to make curriculum notes. He keeps a record of the curriculum resources he will use to implement the package and he lists any special considerations that might be a factor in implementing the package. Because he wants other teachers in his grade level and his department to experiment with the package, Derek makes suggestions that will help them interpret the task in their own classrooms. When he's done, the classroom implementation guide includes a task description, performance criteria, and curriculum notes (see figure 2-5).

What's Next?

The performance assessment package Derek has just designed is classroom based, curriculum centered, and standards referenced. It will give Derek an opportunity to assess student performance in the context of his own classroom; it will also help other teachers in his school assess the juniors in their classrooms. As they do, these teachers will experience what it is like to learn from student performance. By examining the work that students do, these teachers will draw conclusions about how best to support learners in their classrooms.

Figure 2-5. The task description, performance criteria, and curriculum notes for step 6

The Heroine's Journey
Language Arts

Assessment Products: portfolio (vocabulary words, comparison grid, retelling); museum exhibit
Time: 2 weeks

Task Description	Performance Criteria	Curriculum Notes
6. Using a comparison grid (see example 3, page 187), record the events that correspond or conflict with stages in the heroine's journey. Evaluate each selection using the heroine's journey pattern.	■ Notes events that correspond or conflict with the heroine's journey pattern on a comparison grid for each selection ■ Evaluates each selection using the heroine's journey pattern	Johnson, T. D., and D. R. Louis (1990; *Bringing It All Together: A Program for Literacy*. Portsmouth, N.H.: Heinemann) explain and describe comparison grids.

3
Using Assessment Packages

In this chapter, we check in with Derek Lowe as he goes through the process of collecting and analyzing student work based upon the assessment package he designed in the previous chapter. He implements the assessment package in his classroom, develops a class profile of student performance, analyzes patterns of student performance for information to use in action planning, and collaborates with his colleagues to develop a program matrix. Using this example of our framework, think about the steps you would take to work through your own assessment packages in your classroom as you engage in the following activities:

- Implement the assessment package in your classroom and gather representative examples of student work; evaluate the efficacy of the assessment tasks and performance criteria; consider needed modifications.

- Develop a class profile of student performance, share your class profile with other teachers at your grade level, and aggregate results for your grade level; evaluate the efficacy of the assessment tasks and performance criteria; consider needed modifications.

- Based upon student performance patterns in your classroom and at your grade level, consider the implications for instruction and curriculum; develop an action plan for educational improvement.

- Using a program matrix, work collaboratively with teachers at your grade level, in your school, and within your district to ensure that the full range of performance standards are addressed through instructional units and assessed using packages throughout the K–12 curriculum.

Implementing Assessment Packages

As with all of the assessment packages included in this volume, "The Heroine's Journey" package is designed for use after students have engaged in a variety of learning experiences and have completed the regular classroom work associated with this instructional unit. In Derek's classroom, students have spent several weeks doing the activities he has always planned as part of his instructional program. Now, it is time for him to assess his students' performance.

Prior to implementing the assessment package, Derek shares the task description and checklist with his students so that his students understand what is required of them, how they will be asked to assess their own learning, and how Derek will evaluate their work when they have completed the package. When working on the tasks in the assessment package, students need to use task management strategies to negotiate their way through the package. Because Derek has built the opportunity for small group discussion and portfolio review into the package, students have an opportunity to share their plans and get feedback before completing their project. In designing the package, Derek estimated it would take students two weeks to complete the tasks in the package (see classroom implementation guide, page 178). His estimate is based on a schedule in which a daily class session of forty-five minutes is devoted to this project. Considering the other activities in which the students are engaged at the time he is implementing the package, Derek establishes an exact due date for completion of the final product. Before they turn in their work, he asks them to use the checklist to self-assess and modify their work as needed.

As students complete their work, Derek uses the performance assessment matrix and the teacher checklist to keep track of individual student performance. Whenever possible, he collects physical artifacts of their performance and attaches these to the cover sheets. In this example, Derek cannot collect all parts of the performance task; however, he may require that students document their work by showing evidence of progress and he may observe students as they work to complete the task. He can collect the products that each student generates—a portfolio that contains vocabulary words, comparison grids, and written retellings, and a display board. As he observes student work and collects student products, he completes the teacher checklist for each student.

Derek finds that three of his students read and completed a retelling of an African folktale "Unanana and the Elephant" (Phelps 1978; see figure 3-1 for Anna's work). As he thinks about their work and compares it to that of others in the class, Derek evaluates each student's performance using the teacher checklist. Keeping these retellings in mind, let's take a look at the way in which Derek has evaluated Anna's performance (see figure 3-2).

Although we have only one work sample, we can draw some conclusions about two aspects of her performance—the extent to which the student uses the heroine's journey framework to outline a retelling and the extent to which the written retelling includes character, setting, stages of the heroine's journey, the correct sequence of events, and appropriate details. Anna has completed a successful retelling on several levels. Using the heroine's journey as a framework, she includes character, setting, stages of the journey, the correct sequence of events, and an appropriate level of detail. However, she spends a great deal of time describing the beginning of the story and very little time describing the end. It is not clear from her retelling that the main character acted with agency in resolving the conflict of the story; the character's "heroism" is not made explicit. Derek scores her as "satisfactory" in using the framework to outline her retelling and as "needing improvement" in writing the complete retelling. Do you agree with Derek's evaluation of Anna's performance on the retelling?

As Derek proceeds to evaluate the work that students have produced for the package, he begins to collect representative examples of student work. Eventually, he'd like to be able to use these work samples to

- generate a detailed rubric to use in conjunction with this task
- provide students with models to which they can refer as they generate their own work for the package

- include in the assessment packages as exemplars of various performance levels to facilitate scoring

In addition, Derek also begins to think about the efficacy of the assessment package that he has designed. Using student performance as a guide, he asks himself a series of questions (see figure 3-3) about the task and the performance criteria. He concludes that the task works well as a measure of student performance, but he has some reservations about the wording of several of the performance criteria. He decides to bring this problem up with the other teachers in his department when they meet to discuss their implementation efforts.

Adapting Packages for Implementation

In our example, Derek designs a package that is based upon his own curriculum and an instructional unit that he has used in the past. We've attempted to discuss the process of package design and to provide strong models for use in classrooms. Most of these models are generic in the sense that they can be easily integrated into the curriculum; these include packages such as "HyperCard Stack" (grade 11, package 8), "Teaching Kit" (grade 11, package 5), and "Career Exploration" (grade 8, package 5). To illustrate many of the standards, however, we've designed packages to focus on specific areas in the curriculum. Many of these assessment packages will need to be adapted to your individual curriculum approaches, the grades you teach, and your students' abilities. We've found the following strategies useful for modifying performance assessment packages:

- **Changing the content of the package.** Many of the packages involve a specific topic that can be adapted easily while maintaining the integrity of the package as a whole. For example, "American Indian Perspectives" (grade 8, package 2) may be adapted to examine perspectives on other cultural groups; "Leonardo's Legacy" (grade 11, package 3) may be used to investigate the contributions of other artists and scientists; and "Biomedical Ethics" (grade 11, package 6) may be used to explore ethical considerations in other disciplines.

- **Varying the instructional materials used in the package.** In the curriculum notes section, we often make suggestions about specific resources

Figure 3-1. Student example

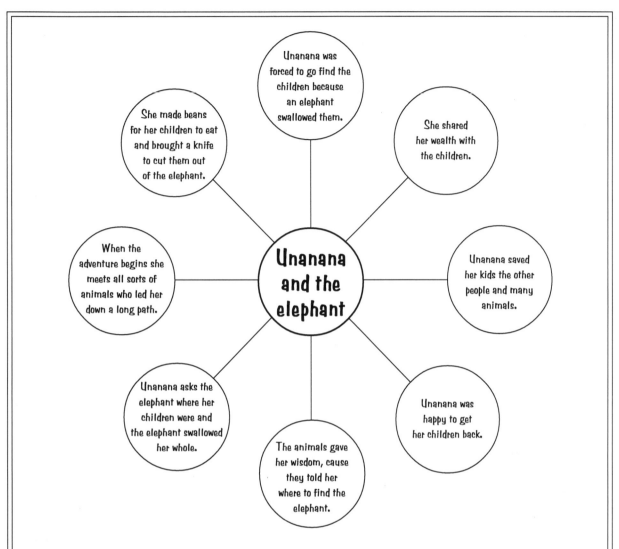

Circles around central "Unanana and the elephant":

- Unanana was forced to go find the children because an elephant swallowed them.
- She made beans for her children to eat and brought a knife to cut them out of the elephant.
- She shared her wealth with the children.
- When the adventure begins she meets all sorts of animals who led her down a long path.
- Unanana saved her kids the other people and many animals.
- Unanana asks the elephant where her children were and the elephant swallowed her whole.
- The animals gave her wisdom, cause they told her where to find the elephant.
- Unanana was happy to get her children back.

Unanana and the elephant

Unanana and the elephant is about a woman who had two beautiful children. One day Unanana went out to gather fire-wood and she left the two children with their cousin. While Unanana was gone three animals came up to the cousin and asked whose children they were, and each time the cousin would reply Unanana. The one special animal that came up to Unanana was a one-tusked elephant, and when the cousin replied Unanana to his question the elephant said, "Well, I shall take them with me" and he swallowed them whole. The cousin didn't know what to do about it so she waited until Unanana came home. As soon as Unanana came home the cousin told her what happened so Unanana packed some beans for her

children and a knife in case she needed it.

Unanana was on her way when she met three animals, and each animal told her she could find the elephant where there are high trees and white stones. So Unanana followed the path until she came to the elephant.

There she asked the elephant two times if he had eaten her children and both times he said no. And the third time Unanana said Where are my children, and the elephant got mad and swallowed up Unanana.

After a few days the elephant died and Unanana cut a hole through the elephant as a door and everyone inside was free.

Figure 3-2. Teacher evaluation of Anna's work

Teacher Checklist for "The Heroine's Journey"			
Performance Criteria	**Excellent**	**Satisfactory**	**Needs Improvement**
▪ Generates several questions prior to group discussion		X	
▪ Shares questions and participates in group discussion			X
▪ Selects at least ten selections that represent at least four cultural traditions	X		
▪ Reads, views, or listens to these selections independently	X		
▪ Develops a record of vocabulary words used to create an image of the female character in each selection	X		
▪ Uses a strategy to demonstrate understanding of the words	X		
▪ Notes events that correspond or conflict with the heroine's journey pattern on a comparison grid for each selection		X	
▪ Evaluates each selection using the heroine's journey pattern		X	
▪ Uses the heroine's journey framework to outline retelling		X	
▪ Includes character, setting, stages of heroine's journey, correct sequence of events, and appropriate details in written retelling		X	
▪ Completes and submits all activities related to ten reading, viewing, and listening selections		X	
▪ Draws conclusions about female image in traditional literature	X		
▪ Supports conclusions with critical examples from reading, viewing, or listening	X		
▪ Uses display board and interpretive guide to convey and support conclusions effectively	X		

that can be used in the package; when these are not available, you can substitute materials you have on hand.

▪ **Utilizing portions of the package.** Many of the packages include multiple tasks. You may want to adapt the package by selecting specific tasks to implement with your students and by eliminating others.

Obviously, you will need to modify the assessment matrix and evaluation formats to reflect these changes.

Developing a Class Profile

Using one of the teacher checklists as a guide (see figure 3-2), Derek creates a class profile by compiling aggregate scores for his entire class on each performance criterion. His colleagues, Kim Watson, Alexis Walker, and Ernest Cummings, do the same (see figure 3-4). In addition, they make a composite profile by including all scores for their junior classes (see figure 3-5). As the teachers meet to discuss their results, they notice several patterns. To guide their discussion, the teachers ask themselves a series of questions about the task design (see figure 3-6) and the performance criteria (see figure 3-7) in the package they have implemented.

In light of student performance, the teachers decide that the task allows students to apply knowledge and demonstrate skills that represent the key outcomes of the unit. The teachers don't feel that modifications to the task are necessary. However, they identify several performance criteria that they feel will require modification. They all had difficulty interpreting the statements "Generates several questions prior to group discussion" and "Uses the

Figure 3-3. Questions to consider after using the packages

Questions to Consider: Using the Packages

Focus on the Task

- What parts of the task worked well?

- What parts of the task would I revise in the future?

- As students completed the task, did I provide them with an opportunity to demonstrate the standards?

- Overall, how did students perform on the task? Is there anything I could do differently to improve student performance?

Focus on Performance Criteria

- What parts of the evaluation checklist worked well?

- What parts of the evaluation checklist would I revise in the future?

- Was I able to distinguish different levels of performance? Do I need to be more specific about what is required of my students?

- Were specific criteria difficult to interpret? Do these criteria need to be phrased differently or should I change them altogether?

heroine's journey framework to outline retelling." All of their students generated questions; however, these questions differed with respect to quantity and quality, and the teachers weren't sure how to distinguish the various levels of performance. They decided that the wording of this statement makes interpretation difficult. Alexis and Derek described students in their classes who had completed this portion of the task at the excellent level. These students asked a series of complex questions that related directly to the themes contained in the initial readings; they seemed to understand the concept, the implications, and the power of imagery. The teachers also discussed students whose portion of the task needed improvement. Although these students generated questions, they were limited in number, limited in scope, and tangential to the initial readings. In order to capture these qualities of performance more effectively, the teachers decide to rewrite the statement to read: "Generates a series of questions related to the themes and images contained in the initial readings." They also decide to improve the clarity of the performance criterion: "Uses the heroine's journey framework to

outline retelling." In thinking about their instruction and in evaluating student performance, the teachers realize that they want students to do more than "use" the framework to outline the retelling. Because they asked students to "use" the framework to outline, many of the students seemed to stop there. The teachers actually want students to use it as a way of expressing their understanding of the underlying structure of the story and to incorporate the framework into their retelling. Derek encourages the teachers to revise the checklist so that what they want is stated explicitly; an explicit statement will help students direct their performance and will help teachers evaluate performance. They revise the statement to read: "Demonstrates an understanding of story structure by using the heroine's journey framework to outline the sequence of events." They also add an additional statement: "Incorporates all stages of the heroine's journey framework into the written retelling." These changes are reflected in the performance assessment package included in this volume, "The Heroine's Journey" (grade 11, package 4).

Figure 3-4. Four teachers' class profiles for "The Heroine's Journey"

Class Profile for "The Heroine's Journey"
Teacher: *Alexis Walker (N=29)* Date:

Performance Criteria	Excellent	Satisfactory	Needs Improvement
Generates several questions prior to group discussion	2	24	3
Shares questions and participates in group discussion	20	6	3
Selects at least ten selections that represent at least four cultural traditions	14	10	5
Reads, views, or listens to these selections independently	0	24	5
Develops a record of vocabulary words used to create an image of the female character in each selection	20	5	4
Uses a strategy to demonstrate understanding of the words	18	9	2
Notes events that correspond or conflict with the heroine's journey pattern on a comparison grid for each selection	11	9	9
Evaluates each selection using the heroine's journey pattern	11	9	9
Uses the heroine's journey framework to outline retelling	0	28	1
Includes character, setting, stages of heroine's journey, correct sequence of events, and appropriate details in written retelling	4	5	20
Completes and submits all activities related to ten reading, viewing, and listening selections	10	17	2
Draws conclusions about female image in traditional literature	10	17	2
Supports conclusions with critical examples from reading, viewing, or listening	10	17	2
Uses display board and interpretive guide to convey and support conclusions effectively	14	10	5

Class Profile for "The Heroine's Journey"
Teacher: *Kim Watson (N=29)* Date:

Performance Criteria	Excellent	Satisfactory	Needs Improvement
Generates several questions prior to group discussion	0	29	0
Shares questions and participates in group discussion	20	4	5
Selects at least ten selections that represent at least four cultural traditions	27	1	1
Reads, views, or listens to these selections independently	29	0	0
Develops a record of vocabulary words used to create an image of the female character in each selection	21	7	1
Uses a strategy to demonstrate understanding of the words	21	7	1
Notes events that correspond or conflict with the heroine's journey pattern on a comparison grid for each selection	29	0	0
Evaluates each selection using the heroine's journey pattern	29	0	0
Uses the heroine's journey framework to outline retelling	0	25	4
Includes character, setting, stages of heroine's journey, correct sequence of events, and appropriate details in written retelling	3	15	11
Completes and submits all activities related to ten reading, viewing, and listening selections	29	0	0
Draws conclusions about female image in traditional literature	18	5	6
Supports conclusions with critical examples from reading, viewing, or listening	20	4	5
Uses display board and interpretive guide to convey and support conclusions effectively	11	9	9

Class Profile for "The Heroine's Journey"
Teacher: *Ernest Cummings (N=30)* Date:

Performance Criteria	Excellent	Satisfactory	Needs Improvement
Generates several questions prior to group discussion	0	30	0
Shares questions and participates in group discussion	2	25	3
Selects at least ten selections that represent at least four cultural traditions	11	15	4
Reads, views, or listens to these selections independently	0	22	8
Develops a record of vocabulary words used to create an image of the female character in each selection	20	7	3
Uses a strategy to demonstrate understanding of the words	14	8	8
Notes events that correspond or conflict with the heroine's journey pattern on a comparison grid for each selection	10	16	4
Evaluates each selection using the heroine's journey pattern	10	16	4
Uses the heroine's journey framework to outline retelling	0	30	0
Includes character, setting, stages of heroine's journey, correct sequence of events, and appropriate details in written retelling	7	7	16
Completes and submits all activities related to ten reading, viewing, and listening selections	5	20	5
Draws conclusions about female image in traditional literature	5	3	22
Supports conclusions with critical examples from reading, viewing, or listening	5	3	22
Uses display board and interpretive guide to convey and support conclusions effectively	3	12	15

Class Profile for "The Heroine's Journey"
Teacher: *Derek Lowe (N=28)* Date:

Performance Criteria	Excellent	Satisfactory	Needs Improvement
Generates several questions prior to group discussion	1	25	2
Shares questions and participates in group discussion	10	16	2
Selects at least ten selections that represent at least four cultural traditions	1	27	0
Reads, views, or listens to these selections independently	3	20	5
Develops a record of vocabulary words used to create an image of the female character in each selection	10	13	5
Uses a strategy to demonstrate understanding of the words	8	15	5
Notes events that correspond or conflict with the heroine's journey pattern on a comparison grid for each selection	12	12	4
Evaluates each selection using the heroine's journey pattern	12	12	4
Uses the heroine's journey framework to outline retelling	0	26	2
Includes character, setting, stages of heroine's journey, correct sequence of events, and appropriate details in written retelling	2	12	14
Completes and submits all activities related to ten reading, viewing, and listening selections	7	11	10
Draws conclusions about female image in traditional literature	7	6	15
Supports conclusions with critical examples from reading, viewing, or listening	7	6	15
Uses display board and interpretive guide to convey and support conclusions effectively	4	17	7

Figure 3-5. Composite profile of four classes for "Heroine's Journey"

Class Profile for "Heroine's Journey"			
Teacher: *Composite (Aggregated Data)* $N = 116$ Date:			
Performance Criteria	Excellent	Satisfactory	Needs Improvement
■ Generates several questions prior to group discussion	3	108	5
■ Shares questions and participates in group discussion	52	51	13
■ Selects at least ten selections that represent at least four cultural traditions	52	54	10
■ Reads, views, or listens to these selections independently	32	66	18
■ Develops a record of vocabulary words used to create an image of the female character in each selection	71	32	13
■ Uses a strategy to demonstrate understanding of the words	61	39	16
■ Notes events that correspond or conflict with the heroine's journey pattern on a comparison grid for each selection	62	37	17
■ Evaluates each selection using the heroine's journey pattern	62	37	17
■ Uses the heroine's journey framework to outline retelling	0	109	7
■ Includes character, setting, stages of heroine's journey, correct sequence of events, and appropriate details in written retelling	16	39	61
■ Completes and submits all activities related to ten reading, viewing, and listening selections	51	48	17
■ Draws conclusions about female image in traditional literature	40	31	45
■ Supports conclusions with critical examples from reading, viewing, or listening	42	30	44
■ Uses display board and interpretive guide to convey and support conclusions effectively	32	48	36

After piloting the assessment package, the teachers take time to evaluate the efficacy of the task they've designed and the performance criteria they've used to evaluate student performance. By doing so, the teachers hope to modify the package to improve it and to strengthen its connection to student learning and the curriculum in their school.

Analyzing Patterns of Student Performance

After discussing the task design and performance criteria, the teachers need to take an additional step. The most important aspect of using assessment packages is that doing so provides an opportunity to examine patterns of student performance. In fact, an assessment package is simply a strategy for revealing these patterns in ways that relate to the classroom learning experience.

As the teachers revisit their class profiles and think about the students in their classrooms, they focus on student performance by asking themselves a series of questions (see figure 3-8). As they review their class profiles, they look to see if the pattern of performance approximates a normal distribution; that is, the majority of students should perform at a satisfactory level with smaller percentages performing at excellent levels or levels that need improvement. If such is not the case, teachers should examine and discuss unusual peaks and valleys in the profile to see if they can be associated with specific parts of the task, with specific performance criteria,

Figure 3-6. Questions to consider about the task design

Questions to Consider: Implementation Guide

■ Does the task	■ Focus on Task Design
assess the standards?	Is there a match between the standards and the task? Is completing the package equivalent to meeting standards?
represent good measurement?	Do the tasks measure areas addressed in the standard? Will it enable students to demonstrate knowledge and skills?
challenge students to perform?	Will the tasks be sufficiently challenging to students? Is the package designed to yield a range of performance?
represent best practice?	Does the package reflect best practice in the content area? Is the task design aligned with national standards?
encourage an active student role?	Are students demonstrating what they know and can do? Are students making decisions throughout the package?
include authentic applications?	Will these products and skills be used in other settings? Is there a reason for doing the work in the package?
provide a comprehensive model?	Is there enough information for teachers to use the task? Are the package materials accessible to teachers?
work well in classrooms?	What challenges will teachers face when implementing the package? What resources will teachers need to be successful?
provide useful information?	What forms of data will be most useful? What support will be needed to manage the data?

Figure 3-7. Questions to consider about the teacher checklists

Questions to Consider: Teacher Checklists

■ Focus on Performance Criteria

- Does each statement relate to the standards listed on the performance assessment matrix for this package?

- Does each statement refer to a portion of the task described in the package?

- Does each statement refer to a process or product of individual student performance that can be observed and assessed?

- Does each statement include a verb that indicates what students should be able to do?

- Does each statement provide a clear statement of what constitutes a satisfactory performance?

- Are all important aspects of performance represented in the checklists, analytic scoring guide, or holistic scoring guide?

Figure 3-8. Questions to consider about class profiles

Questions to Consider: Class Profiles
■ **Focus on Patterns in Student Performance**
■ Does the pattern of student performance approximate a normal distribution?
■ Are there peaks and dips associated with parts of the task? With specific performance criteria?
■ Are there peaks and dips that indicate different approaches to classroom implementation?
■ Are there peaks and dips that indicate different approaches to interpretation?
■ What does the pattern of student performance reveal about student learning with respect to knowledge, skills, task management, and the need for instructional preparation?

with differences in how the teachers implemented the package in their classroom, and with different interpretations.

In our example, Kim Watson's classroom profile indicates that the majority of her students are performing at excellent levels. When she meets with the other teachers in her grade level, she examines the reasons for this level of performance. Through dialogue, she discovers that her intervention with students and their work in the package has been extensive; she is providing much more structure and support to students than are the other teachers in her grade level. The four teachers discuss appropriate levels of support and their expectations for student independence. After talking about these issues, Kim feels that she understands how to implement the assessment package in her classroom more effectively and how to allow students to demonstrate what they know and can do. After this initial discussion, the teachers examine some of the peaks and valleys revealed in their profiles. In discussing the criterion statement "Written retelling includes character, setting, all stages of the heroine's journey, the correct sequence of events, and appropriate details," the four teachers note the large numbers of students who performed at levels that need improvement. "Couldn't part of the problem be that we've lumped so many different things together in this statement?" asks Derek. "Yes, they may need improvement in one or more of those areas.

It would be more informative to the student and us if we knew exactly where they were having difficulty," says Kim. "Also, we resolved the issues of the stages of the heroine's journey by adding that additional statement earlier. Isn't it a bit redundant to include it here as well?" asks Ernest. "Let's break out the components of this statement and list each one on the checklist," suggests Alexis. This breakdown is reflected in the completed package, "The Heroine's Journey" (grade 11, package 4).

Next, the group moves on to consider the statement "Selects at least ten selections that represent at least four cultural traditions." Derek feels that students either make ten appropriate selections or don't. But Alexis and Ernest disagree with Derek's interpretation of student work. They feel that there are ways in which students could perform at a level they feel to be excellent. In describing their reasons, Alexis and Ernest recall students who identified several alternative selections, selected similar types of stories for comparative analysis, selected challenging reading material, or integrated the assignment with other course work by making foreign language selections. Alexis also described students whose work she felt needed improvement in this area. In these cases, students seemed reluctant to explore the body of literature as a whole; they made selections from one anthology rather than surveying a variety of options. Other students selected material written well below their grade level. As a result of their conversation about this statement and others on the checklist, all four teachers feel that they are better able to decide what work is excellent, satisfactory, or needs improvement.

Finally, the teachers also look to patterns of student performance to draw conclusions about student learning and to develop an action plan to support it. In our example, the teachers examine their class profiles to see what each reveals about student learning in their classrooms. In which areas—knowledge, skills, and task management—did students seem to perform effectively? In which areas did students seem to find it difficult to perform effectively? What do the patterns of student performance reveal about the need for instructional preparation? In our example, larger numbers of students did well in generating questions, participating in discussions, reading the selections, developing the portfolio work samples, and drawing conclusions. The support material in the package provides a great deal of concrete guidance in these areas. The portfolio work samples involve literal comprehension, comparison, and classification skills. In our example, the majority of students seem to have the greatest difficulty in two areas that require complex thinking and greater independence—specifically, the areas of using the display board to convey and support conclusions and supporting conclusions with critical examples. As they think about their curriculum, the teachers realize that they spent very little time teaching students how to convey information using a display board. Although they require students to find information and to display information on a regular basis, they feel they spend more time demonstrating how to design effective and communicative displays of information. They consider gathering some models the next time they implement the unit and the assessment package.

The teachers also consider the skill that students found challenging—supporting a conclusion with critical examples. The teachers begin to identify specific instructional strategies that support student learning in these areas. Ernest suggests that they provide students with a planner to complete prior to working on the museum display; students would use the planner to record their conclusions and identify examples from the reading that directly support these conclusions. Kim suggests doing a mind map

with the whole class prior to sending them off to work on the display. She envisions having the group generate the conclusions they have reached and share examples to support these conclusions; she feels that students could learn a great deal from hearing one another talk about these issues. Derek suggests building a conference into the assessment package. After the students turn in their portfolios, he would conference with them to get a sense of their preliminary conclusions, and they'd look together for critical examples within the portfolio. Finally, Alexis brings up another unit used by the four teachers. In this unit, students develop persuasive writing skills. "Couldn't we make a connection between this assignment and the five-paragraph essay assignment," she asks, "so that they understand the underlying processes are the same although the products are different?" All the suggestions are effective; if implemented, they could substantively improve student performance on this package and, more importantly, improve the general ability of students to support a conclusion with critical examples.

Using an action planning sheet (see figure 3-9), the teachers record their observations about student performance and identify a plan of action to support student learning. Although it is not necessary for teachers to complete these steps with every performance assessment package, it is an invaluable way to learn from student performance. Time engaged in this activity is time well spent; it has the potential to result in educational improvement.

Developing a Program Matrix

When we think about the wide range of standards that need to be addressed in classrooms, the challenges for individual teachers seem so complex and comprehensive that it is difficult to imagine any individual teacher being able to respond to them in ways that would have meaning for students. Because we believe that the national curriculum standards target important areas for student learning, we value efforts to prevent them from being addressed in a hit-or-miss fashion. By using a program matrix and working collaboratively with teachers at grade level, within a school, and across a district, teachers ensure that a full range of state and national performance standards are addressed. The question is, "How do we create such a matrix?"

Figure 3-9. Action planning work sheet

Action Planning Work Sheet **Teacher Response and Input** **Assessment Package:** Teacher:
What did you notice about the patterns of student performance for this assessment package? Attach class profile.
Choose a student who performed most of the task at the excellent level. How would you characterize her performance?
Choose a student who performed most of the task at the satisfactory level. How does his performance differ from that of a student who performed at the excellent level?
Choose a student who performed most of the task at the needs improvement level. What would the student need to do to perform at higher levels?
What instructional support would you need to provide to enable all students to perform at higher levels?

Excellent	Satisfactory	Needs Improvement

Figure 3-9. Action planning work sheet (continued)

Action Planning Work Sheet
Teacher Response and Input
Assessment Package:

Teacher:

How would you improve the design of the task(s) in this package?

How would you improve the checklist(s) used in this package?

What do the patterns of student performance reveal about the task and the performance criteria?

What do the patterns of student performance reveal about your implementation of this package?

What do the patterns of student performance reveal about your interpretation of student work on this package?

Guided by Performance, ©1998 Zephyr Press, Tucson, Arizona

Figure 3-9. Action planning work sheet (continued)

Action Planning Work Sheet
Teacher Response and Input
Assessment Package:

Teacher:

Think about student performance. In which areas do students need better instructional preparation to perform effectively?

Content Knowledge	Content Skills and Cognitive Skills	Task Management Strategies

What changes should be made to the curriculum that would address these areas?

What changes will you implement in your instructional approach to address these areas?

What would you need (strategies, resources, materials) to provide support through curriculum and instruction?

What kinds of professional development would enable you to provide this instructional support most effectively?

Through the examples in this book, we've provided assessment packages designed to assess middle school and high school standards in a variety of curriculum areas; in our first book, we provide assessment packages targeted at the primary and intermediate grade standards in these same areas. In the program matrix (see figure 3-10), we've taken these packages and demonstrated how they might be used to develop a comprehensive profile of student performance in all curriculum areas. Although we've built the matrix using sample assessment packages in this book, the matrix could be adapted to include packages developed by individual teachers. You'll see, for example, that the package developed by Derek Lowe is included in the matrix for reading. When we use this matrix with school districts, individual teachers take responsibility for implementing and gathering data on student performance through the use of at least one performance assessment package; taken together, the efforts of all the teachers provide a comprehensive picture of student learning in the school or district. This data can be used to evaluate the effectiveness of the educational program and to target specific areas for educational improvement.

In addition to the use of assessment packages at eighth- and eleventh-grade benchmarks, the instructional program needs to support the development of the content knowledge, content skills, cognitive skills, and task management strategies required for effective performance. Another use for the matrix is to make explicit connections between the instructional program, the curriculum, and the assessment packages. What kinds of instructional experiences do students encounter in kindergarten through grade 2 that prepare them for the kind of work required in the assessment packages targeted for grade 3? Similarly, how do the instructional experiences in grade 4 support performance in grade 5? In grades 6 and 7 for grade 8? In grades 9 and 10 for grade 11? The matrix requires us to be explicit about the instructional preparation that enables students to perform effectively on performance assessment packages; we can't take it for granted that connections between student learning, curriculum, and assessment exist. Teachers can identify additional opportunities to address standards within the curriculum and enter these into the matrix as instructional preparation units. By emphasizing the way that instructional units in these grades feed into student performance in the benchmark grades, we also emphasize that the responsibility for student performance is a shared responsibility across all grades and curriculum areas.

◆◆

Figure 3-10. Program matrix of assessment packages

Guided by Performance Program Matrix

Curriculum Area (Focus)	Instructional Preparation Units	Primary Assessment Packages	Instructional Preparation Units	Intermediate Assessment Packages	Instructional Preparation Units	Middle Level Assessment Packages	Instructional Preparation Units	High School Assessment Packages
Research/ Inquiry	K, 1, 2	1. Pioneer Living	4	1. Children and World War II	6, 7	2. American Indian Perspectives	9, 10, 11	1. Market Research
Reading	K, 1, 2	2. Wolves: Fact and Fiction	4	2. The Mystery of Mysteries	6, 7	2. American Indian Perspectives	9, 10, 11	4. The Heroine's Journey
Writing	K, 1, 2	3. A Day in the Life	4	3. Publication Portfolio	6, 7	3. First Amendment	9, 10, 11	2. Procedural Writing in the Lab
Listening/ Speaking	K, 1, 2	4. Author Study	4	4. Literature Circles	6, 7	5. Career Exploration	9, 10, 11	5. Teaching Kit
Visual and Performing Arts	K, 1, 2	5. Book Illustration	4	5. Method Improvising	6, 7	1. Harlem Renaissance	9, 10, 11	3. Leonardo's Legacy
History	K, 1, 2	6. Bioline	4	6. Meeting of Many Minds	6, 7	6. Coming to America	9, 10, 11	9. Decades Project
Social Studies	K, 1, 2	7. Fishbowl	4	7. Home: A Walking Tour	6, 7	4. That Was Then— This Is Now!	9, 10, 11	7. Grant Proposal
Mathematics	K, 1, 2	8. Softball Fields	4	8. Design a Bike Path	6, 7	12. Fractals	9, 10, 11	10. Fast Food Quality: A Statistics Problem
Life Sciences	K, 1, 2		4		6, 7	9. Human Genetics	9, 10, 11	3. Leonardo's Legacy
Earth Sciences	K, 1, 2		4	9. Mapping the Terrain	6, 7	7. Origins	9, 10, 11	3. Leonardo's Legacy
Physical Sciences	K, 1, 2	9. Shadow Caper	4		6, 7	8. Soil Sample	9, 10, 11	3. Leonardo's Legacy
Technology	K, 1, 2	10. Slide Show	4	10. Home Page	6, 7	10. Putting Math to Work	9, 10, 11	8. Hypercard Stack
Health/ Fitness	K, 1, 2	11. Board Game	4	11. Decision Trees	6, 7	11. Understanding HIV	9, 10, 11	6. Biomedical Ethics

4

Performance Assessment Packages for Grade 8

Harlem Renaissance
Classroom Implementation Guide

Curriculum Area: Visual Arts, Social Studies
Product

Scrapbook of artist's work, personal response, historical context, and comparative analysis

Time: 2 weeks
Curriculum Notes

Please read the student task sheets carefully. Note any materials you will need for each task. Performance criteria are listed in the teacher checklist.

This package was designed to encourage demonstrations in the areas of description, interpretation, and analysis. A rich cultural and historical period, the Harlem Renaissance could also be the focus of study in the areas of the performing and literary arts. A similar assessment package could be constructed around the work of other cultural groups, historical periods, schools or movements.

This study could include the works of Aaron Douglas, Richmond Barthe, Palmer Hayden, William H. Johnson, Augusta Savage, Malvin Gray Johnson, Jacob Lawrence, Joseph Delaney, Horace Pippin, and Harriet Powers. Students can access the artwork using CD-ROM, exhibition catalogs, or art books. Estes (1995) contains a bibliography that will be quite useful to teachers and students. You may also want to contact History through Art at ZCI, One Datran Center, 9100 S. Dadeland Blvd. Ste. 1500, Miami, FL 33156, for software. The Studio Museum in Harlem, New York, has an important collection of work that can be accessed through published catalogs.

In designing this assessment task, we referred to the National Art Education Association (1994) for useful information on standards for response in the visual arts.

Resource List

Estes, G. E. 1995. "The Harlem Renaissance and After." *Book Links* 4, 3: 17–24.

National Art Education Association Visual Arts Assessment and Exercise Specifications. 1994. Reston, Va.: NAEP.

Performance Assessment Matrix

Package Title: Harlem Renaissance

Curriculum Area: Visual Arts, Social Studies

Package: Grade 8

Student: _____

Content Knowledge

Arts (Art Connections): Standard 1 (Understands connections among art forms and other disciplines)

Arts (Visual Arts): Standard 3 (Knows a range of subject matter, symbols, and ideas in the visual arts)

Standard 4 (Understanding the visual arts in relation to history and cultures)

Social Studies: Standard 1, Culture (The arts . . . contribute to the development and transmission of culture.)

Content Skills

Literacy		Mathematics	Science		Social Studies		Visual Arts	
Reading		Problem solving	Defining questions		Acquiring information		Creating	
for aesthetic response		Communication	Forming hypotheses		reading		conceptual skills	
for information/understanding		Reasoning	Investigating		study skills		production skills	
for critical analysis/evaluation		Connecting	Observing		reference skills	▓	evaluation skills	
Writing		Estimation	Monitoring		technical skills		application	
for response/expression		Numeration	Measuring		Organizing/Using information		Responding	
for social interaction		Computation	Keeping records		thinking skills		descriptive skills	▓
for information/understanding		Data analysis	Transforming records		decision-making skills	▓	analytical skills	▓
for critical analysis/evaluation	▓	Measurement	Collaborating		metacognitive skills		valuing skills	
Listening		Patterning/Relating	Interpreting information		Relationships		application	▓
for response/expression			Integrating information		personal skills			
for information/understanding					group interaction			
for critical analysis/evaluation					social/political participation			
Speaking					Historical thinking			
for response/expression					chronological thinking			
for social interaction					historical comprehension			
for information/understanding					analysis and interpretation			
for critical analysis/evaluation					historical research			
					issues and decisions			

Guided by Performance, ©1998 Zephyr Press, Tucson, Arizona

Performance Assessment Matrix

Performance Skills

Cognitive Strategies	Task Management Strategies	Student Role	Assessment Products	Evaluation Format
Comparison	Analyzing the task	Museum curator	Portfolio	Student checklist (attached)
Classification	Establishing time lines	Reviewer	Publication	Teacher checklist (attached)
Induction	Staying productive	Engineer/Designer	Demonstration	Analytic scoring guide/ rubric (attached)
Deduction	Meeting deadlines	Representative	Performance	Holistic scoring guide (attached)
Error analysis	Accepting feedback	Expert witness	Exhibition	
Constructing support	Working cooperatively	Character		
Abstracting	Making a contribution	Ad agency director		
Analyzing perspectives	Respecting others	Tour organizer		
Decision making	Accessing resources	Bank manager		
Investigation	Striving for accuracy	Psychologist/Sociologist		
Experimental inquiry	Striving for excellence	Archaeologist		
Problem solving		Philosopher		
Invention		Historian		
		Writer/Editor		
		Teacher		
		Job applicant		
		Speaker/Listener		

Anecdotal Observations

Teacher Checklist for "Harlem Renaissance"

Performance Criteria	Excellent	Satisfactory	Needs Improvement
Step 1			
■ Accurately identifies artists associated with Harlem Renaissance	_____	_____	_____
■ Finds five representative pieces of artist's work and arranges them chronologically in scrapbook	_____	_____	_____
■ Formats scrapbook according to guidelines (see example 1, page 44)	_____	_____	_____
Step 2			
■ Crafts thoughtful response by demonstrating consideration of one or more of listed questions	_____	_____	_____
Step 3			
■ Identifies key historical events that might have influenced artist	_____	_____	_____
■ Substantiates potential influence of these events on artist's work	_____	_____	_____
Step 4			
■ Identifies three additional artists for comparative analysis	_____	_____	_____
■ Uses style, subject/theme, and medium as basis (or bases) of comparison	_____	_____	_____
■ Compares work of four artists by noting similarities and differences in work	_____	_____	_____
■ Supports comparative analysis with specific examples drawn from work	_____	_____	_____

Guided by Performance, ©1998 Zephyr Press, Tucson, Arizona

Harlem Renaissance
Student Guide

After World War I, African American artists made important and lasting contributions in the visual and performing arts. Art historians call this period the "Harlem Renaissance." Although many art historians set this period from 1917 to 1935, these dates are approximate and open to interpretation; many artists from this period are still working today. In this assessment package, you make connections between the visual art of the Harlem Renaissance and historical events that had an effect on their work. You respond to the artwork created by these artists. To begin, select an artist's body of work to explore in greater detail.

Task: Scrapbook

1. Arrange copies of the artist's work in the scrapbook in chronological order. You can photocopy the work in color and paste it on one side of a page, leaving room for historical notes and personal response on the facing page (see example 1, page 44). If it is not possible for you to photocopy the work, include a citation and description. Include at least five examples of the artist's work.

2. Record your personal response to the piece on the top of the facing page. You may respond to the artwork using words or images (see example 1, page 44). Following are some questions to think about as you respond:

   - What ideas is the artist exploring through the work?
   - What does the work make you think about?
   - What feelings do you have as you look at the work?
   - What patterns do you notice (style, subject/theme, medium) in the artist's work?
   - Do you like parts of the work? If so, which aspects of the work do you like?
   - Do you like the overall effect of the work? If so, why? If not, why not? Use specific examples to support your responses.

3. Research and record events that occurred during the period of time the work was created. Pay special attention to events that you think may have influenced the artist in some way (see example 1, page 44). At the bottom of the facing page in your scrapbook, list the events and the reasons you think they influenced the artist. In deciding which events to include, remember that you need to be clear about your reasoning. Although you do not need to include a large number of events, you must provide a strong reason to support your selections.

4. At the end of the scrapbook, include the work of three other artists that you feel are related in some way to the artist you have chosen (see example 2, page 45). The artists you select for comparison can be artists of the Harlem Renaissance or artists from other periods of time or cultural traditions. Compare at least three elements (style, subject/theme, and medium) of the work of the artists you select to the same elements in the work of your main artist. Identify the artists, the basis of comparison, your observations about similarities and differences in the work, and any questions you have. Support your analysis with specific examples from the artists' work.

Example 1: Sample Categories and Questions

Reproduced Work
Placed Here

The Migration Series
Panels 18 through 24
by Jacob Lawrence (1941–1942)

In Lawrence, J. 1993.
The Great Migration.
New York: HarperCollins

Personal Response

When you look at these panels, it seems like the artist wanted to be very dramatic. So he used big shapes and lots of bold colors. There are really no lines separating things. It is just the effect of having a dark color right next to a light color that gives things shape.

When I was looking at his art in a book, it said that he had a "primitive" style. I agree with this, because his paintings are very simple and there is not a lot of detail. But, I like the way he does this. You get the idea of what he is drawing. But he seems to spend more time trying to give you a sense of movement and feeling, instead of making you see every eyelash on the character's face. So, his work has a lot of energy and emotion. This was one of the most recent things he has painted.

Historical Events

1. The Great Migration (1900)—In the early twentieth century, black families left the rural South in large numbers. They were trying to find better jobs. They thought there were more opportunities for work in the North because there was more industrialization. At the beginning of the century, there was a big change in the population. Almost one fourth of the African-American population lived in urban areas. Many African-Americans were discriminated against when they came to the North. Other people (white workers and new immigrants) resented the fact that they were taking jobs from them. In his work, Jacob Lawrence tries to express the hope that the African-American people had when they came to the North. He also tries to express some of the disappointment or fear that was also part of what moving North involved for people. As you can see in these panels, he does this through color, facial expressions, and body arrangement.

Guided by Performance, ©1998 Zephyr Press, Tucson, Arizona

Example 2: Sample Categories and Questions

Grand Performance
by Jacob Lawrence

Still Life with Score
by Eric Satie

**Basis for Comparison:
STYLE**

These two artists are very similar in terms of style. They both use shapes and contrasting colors in simple ways. There are not a lot of details in the paintings. I don't think things are drawn to scale or are made to be realistic. The images are very strong and things stand out in bold ways. What is different about these two works of art is that the *Grand Performance* has a lot of movement, action, and energy. *Still Life with Score* is a good name, because it gives you a calm, still feeling when you look at it.

**Basis for Comparison:
SUBJECT/THEME**

I selected this piece of Satie's work because I thought it was connected to *Grand Performance.* Both artists are expressing something about music or performing art and they're using visual art to do that. But, Satie's painting has some of the things used by musicians and Lawrence's painting focuses on the people. That made me think about the fact that lots of Lawrence's paintings have people in them. But, since I haven't seen all of his work, I don't know if he has a lot of pieces with musicians in them. I do think he has a lot of pieces with historical figures in them. I wonder if Satie has done a lot of work using this subject or theme. I wonder if he does mostly still life painting or if some of his work includes people and activities.

American Indian Perspectives
Curriculum Implementation Guide

Curriculum Areas: Language Arts, History, Social Studies
Products

3 structural organizers to aid comprehension of complex ideas
Summary of information in conference with school professional

Time: 2 weeks
Curriculum Notes

Please read the student task sheets carefully. Note any materials you will need for each task. Performance criteria are listed in the teacher checklist.

Although this package focuses on American Indian perspectives, you could use it to look through the lenses of other cultures, sexes, or orientations. Provide some guidance in the selection of materials, but it would also be useful for students to conduct research by interviewing teachers or by exploring curriculum resource libraries.

For **step 4**, you may want to use Hyerle (1996), which includes examples of structural organizers to be used for various purposes and outlines other instructional resources in this area. The software program *Inspiration* is also helpful for this purpose (7412 SW Beaverton, Hillsdale Highway, Ste. 102, Portland, OR 97225-2167; (503) 297-3004; www.inspiration.com).

In **step 7**, students need a basis for identifying differences in the authors' points of view. We used Slapin and Seale (1992) to identify the dimensions listed in the structural organizer. In addition to providing guidance in creating the structural organizer, this resource contains essays on the historical and cultural portraiture of American Indians, reviews of trade books and instructional materials that students might also review to complete this assessment package, and bibliographies and resource lists that students can use for variety.

Resource List

Hyerle, D. 1996. *Visual Tools for Constructing Knowledge.* Alexandria, Va.: Association for Supervision and Curriculum Development (ASCD).
Slapin, B., and D. Seale. 1992. *Through Indian Eyes: The Native Experience in Books for Children.* Philadelphia: New Society.

Performance Assessment Matrix

Package Title: American Indian Perspectives

Curriculum Area: Language Arts, History, Social Studies

Package: Grade 8

Student: _____

Content Knowledge

Language Arts:	Standard 1 (Read print and nonprint texts to build an understanding of cultures) Standard 3 (Employ strategies to evaluate texts) Standard 7 (Conduct research; gather, evaluate, and synthesize data from a variety of sources)
Social Studies:	Standard I, Culture (B: Interpretation of information and experiences from diverse cultural perspectives)
History:	The standard addressed will depend upon the historical period the student selects for analysis.

Content Skills

Literacy		Mathematics	Science		Social Studies		Visual Arts	
Reading		Problem solving	Defining questions		Acquiring information		Creating	
for aesthetic response		Communication	Forming hypotheses		*reading*		*conceptual skills*	
for information/understanding		Reasoning	Investigating		*study skills*		*production skills*	
for critical analysis/evaluation		Connecting	Observing		*reference skills*		*evaluation skills*	
Writing		Estimation	Monitoring		*technical skills*		*application*	
for response/expression		Numeration	Measuring		Organizing/Using information		Responding	
for social interaction		Computation	Keeping records		*thinking skills*		*descriptive skills*	
for information/understanding		Data analysis	Transforming records		*decision-making skills*		*analytical skills*	
for critical analysis/evaluation		Measurement	Collaborating		*metacognitive skills*		*valuing skills*	
Listening		Patterning/Relating	Interpreting information		Relationships		*application*	
for response/expression			Integrating information		*personal skills*			
for information/understanding					*group interaction*			
for critical analysis/evaluation					*social/political participation*			
Speaking					Historical thinking			
for response/expression					*chronological thinking*			
for social interaction					*historical comprehension*			
for information/understanding					*analysis and interpretation*			
for critical analysis/evaluation					*historical research*			
					issues and decisions			

Guided by Performance, ©1998 Zephyr Press, Tucson, Arizona

Performance Assessment Matrix

Performance Skills

Cognitive Strategies	Task Management Strategies	Student Role	Assessment Products	Evaluation Format
Comparison ▪	Analyzing the task ▪	Museum curator	Portfolio	Student checklist (attached)
Classification	Establishing time lines	Reviewer	Publication ▪	Teacher checklist (attached) ▪
Induction	Staying productive	Engineer/Designer ▪	Demonstration	Analytic scoring guide/rubric (attached) ▪
Deduction	Meeting deadlines	Representative	Performance	Holistic scoring guide (attached)
Error analysis	Accepting feedback	Expert witness	Exhibition	
Constructing support ▪	Working cooperatively ▪	Character		
Abstracting	Making a contribution	Ad agency director		
Analyzing perspectives ▪	Respecting others ▪	Tour organizer		
Decision making	Accessing resources	Bank manager		
Investigation	Striving for accuracy	Psychologist/Sociologist		
Experimental inquiry	Striving for excellence	Archaeologist		
Problem solving		Philosopher		
Invention		Historian		
		Writer/Editor		
		Teacher		
		Job applicant		
		Speaker/Listener		

Anecdotal Observations

Guided by Performance, ©1998 Zephyr Press, Tucson, Arizona

Teacher Checklist for "American Indian Perspectives"

Performance Criteria	Excellent	Satisfactory	Needs Improvement
Step 1			
■ Selects ten sources of information that enable reading, viewing, and listening	_____	_____	_____
Step 2			
■ Targets time frame or historical period	_____	_____	_____
Step 3			
■ Surveys materials by reading, viewing, or listening for general impressions	_____	_____	_____
Step 4			
■ Uses structural organizer to identify main ideas and supporting details relevant to targeted period	_____	_____	_____
Step 5			
■ Highlights inconsistencies in main ideas or supporting details on structural organizer	_____	_____	_____
■ Notes inconsistent sources of information on structural organizer	_____	_____	_____
Step 6			
■ Uses structural organizer to compare and contrast information from at least one highlighted area and at least two inconsistent sources of information	_____	_____	_____
Step 7			
■ Uses structural organizer to identify differences in points of view of two authors in several areas	_____	_____	_____
Step 8			
■ Addresses structural organizers, findings, and conclusions during conference	_____	_____	_____
■ Demonstrates adequate comprehension of information through structural organizers and in summary of conference	_____	_____	_____

American Indian Perspectives
Student Guide

To complete this assessment package, you read, view, and listen to a variety of instructional materials. The materials you select may be those used in this middle school, in the high schools, or in the elementary schools in your school district. As you read, view, and listen, conduct an analysis of the ways in which American Indian histories and First Nation cultures are portrayed. To demonstrate this standard, review the materials and share conclusions based upon your comprehension of the ideas presented.

Task: Structural Organizer

1. Identify the instructional materials you will be evaluating. Look for materials that are used to teach American history. Gather at least ten sources of information, which must include at least one of the following: social studies textbook; film, video, or other media selection; nonfiction trade book; software program; musical recording; teaching chart, display, or bulletin board graphic; essay or editorial; newspaper article.

2. Target a particular time or historical period in American history to examine in greater depth. You may choose from the following periods, but you are not limited to them:

   Columbus's voyages to the Americas
   European colonization of the Americas
   the Pilgrims
   exploration of the western United States
   French and Indian Wars
   westward expansion
   dispossession and reservations
   the continuity of sovereign peoples

3. Paying special attention to the ways in which American Indian peoples are portrayed, read, view, or listen to the instructional materials you have selected. This is your first survey of these materials; your goal is to get an overall or general impression of the portrayal of American Indians during the historical period.

4. Develop a structural organizer or visual tool for identifying the main ideas and supporting details relevant to the material you have read. Read, view, or listen to the materials again in order to ensure accuracy.

5. As you add main ideas and supporting details to your organizer, you are likely to find inconsistencies in the information presented in the various sources. Highlight any inconsistencies on the organizer and make note of the sources in which the inconsistencies occur.

6. Develop a structural organizer or visual tool for comparing and contrasting information in at least one of the highlighted areas. Compare and contrast at least two of the inconsistent sources of information for each highlighted area.

7. You have been able to examine these materials several times. Of the ten sources you have been using, choose two that you perceive to be written from very different points of view. Read, view, or listen to these two sources for the purpose of identifying differences in the points of view of the authors and how their points of view are reflected in their portrayals. Using a double-entry structural organizer (see record sheet 1, page 52), read these materials and list differences in the areas listed. I also have resources that give many varied examples of double-entry organizers.

8. When you have completed this process, review the structural organizers you have used in your reading, viewing, and listening. What conclusions can you draw about the ways in which American Indian peoples are portrayed in these instructional materials? What have you learned from your comparison and contrast of the main ideas and supporting details contained in these selections? What have you learned from your analysis of differences in the points of view of the authors of two of these selections? Arrange a conference with me, with a teacher who is using these materials, or with other educational professionals (principal, counselor, curriculum specialist) at the school who are using these materials. Referring to your structural organizers during the conference, summarize your findings and conclusions. Submit your structural organizers and a tape of your conference to me for final review.

Record Sheet 1: Structural Organizer (Differences in Points of View)

Look ⬇	Author: _____ Title: _____ Publication Date: _____ City: _____ Publisher: _____ Pages: _____	Author: _____ Title: _____ Publication Date: _____ City: _____ Publisher: _____ Pages: _____
at the pictures		
for stereotypes		
for loaded words		
for tokenism		
for distortions of history		
at lifestyles		
at the dialogue		
for standards of success		
at the role of women		
at the role of elders		
for effects on self-esteem		
at the author's background		
for specific facts		
for statements of opinion		
How would you summarize this author's point of view?		

Guided by Performance, ©1998 Zephyr Press, Tucson, Arizona

First Amendment
Classroom Implementation Guide

Curriculum Areas: Language Arts, Social Studies, Civics

Products

Story
Persuasive speech

Time: 2 weeks

Curriculum Notes

Please read the student task sheets carefully. Note any materials you will need for each task. Performance criteria are listed in the teacher checklist.

For the purposes of providing a model, resources, and concrete examples, we have selected one topic for both products that students produce. In adapting the package for classroom use, you may vary the topic or encourage students to select from a wide range of potential topics. You might elect to have students explore writing in each genre separately; here the two are presented simultaneously.

The resource list contains novels that are appropriate for students in the middle grades and would provide good examples of narrative writing. The resource list also includes nonfiction resources that are appropriate for students in the middle grades, present issues related to the topic, and contain good examples of persuasive writing on this topic.

The assumption behind any assessment package is that students have received instruction prior to being asked to demonstrate the standard. However, while implementing this assessment package, you may find it useful to provide minilessons related to writing in the narrative and persuasive genre. The instructional resources in the resource list are useful sources of strategies and examples.

Resource List

Fiction

Christian, P. 1995. *The Bookstore Mouse.* New York: Harcourt.
Diaz, J. 1993. *The Rebellious Alphabet.* New York: Holt.
Facklam, M. 1989. *The Trouble with Mothers.* New York: Clarion.
Hentoff, N. 1983. *The Day They Came to Arrest the Book.* New York: Dell.
Krensky, S. 1995. *The Printer's Apprentice.* New York: Delacorte.
Lasky, K. 1994. *Memoirs of a Bookbat.* New York: Harcourt.
Meyer, C. 1995. *Drummers of Jericho.* New York: Harcourt.
Miles, B. 1980. *Maudie and Me and the Dirty Book.* New York: Knopf.
Peck, R. 1995. *The Last Safe Place on Earth.* New York: Delacorte.
Thompson, J. 1995. *The Trials of Molly Sheldon.* New York: Holt.
Tolan, S. 1993. *Save Halloween!* New York: Morrow.

Nonfiction

Faber, D., and H. Faber. 1987. *We the People: The Story of the United States Constitution since 1787.* New York: Scribner.

Gold, J. C. 1994. *Board of Education vs. Pico.* New York: Twenty-First Century.

Greenberg, K. 1995. *Adolescent Rights: Are Young People Equal under the Law?* New York: Holt.

Herda, D. 1994. New York Times v. *United States: National Security and Censorship.* Hillside, N.J.: Enslow.

Kronenwetter, M. 1993. *Under 18: Knowing Your Rights.* Hillside, N.J.: Enslow.

Meltzer, M. 1990. *The Bill of Rights: How We Got It and What It Means.* New York: HarperCollins.

Monroe, J. 1990. *Censorship.* New York: Crestwood House.

Pascoe, E. 1992. *Freedom of Expression: The Right to Speak Out in America.* New York: Millbrook.

Rappaport, D. 1993. *Tinker vs. Des Moines: Student Rights on Trial.* New York: HarperCollins.

Steele, P. 1992. *Censorship.* New York: New Discovery.

Steins, R. 1995. *Censorship: How Does It Conflict with Freedom?* New York: Holt.

Zeinert, K. 1995. *Free Speech: From Newspapers to Music Lyrics.* Hillside, N.J.: Enslow.

Teacher Resources

Brown, J. 1994. *Preserving Intellectual Freedom: Fighting Censorship in Our Schools.* Urbana, Ill.: National Council of Teachers of English.

Heins, M. 1993. *Sex, Sin, and Blasphemy: A Guide to America's Censorship Wars.* New York: New Press.

Hentoff, N. 1992. *Free Speech for Me—But Not for Thee: How the American Left and Right Relentlessly Censor Each Other.* New York: HarperCollins.

Intellectual Freedom Manual. 1992. Chicago: American Library Association.

Johnson, C. 1994. *Stifled Laughter: One Woman's Fight against Censorship.* New York: Fulcrum.

Lehr, S., ed. 1995. *Battling Dragons: Issues and Controversy in Children's Literature.* Portsmouth, N.H.: Heinemann.

McWhirter, D. 1994. *Freedom of Speech, Press, and Assembly.* Phoenix, Ariz.: Oryx Press.

Reichman, H. F. 1993. *Censorship and Selection: Issues and Answers for Schools.* Chicago: American Library Association.

Organizations

American Library Association, Office for Intellectual Freedom, 50 E. Huron Street, Chicago, IL 60611.

First Amendment Congress, University of Colorado at Denver, Graduate School of Public Affairs, 1445 Market Street, Suite 320, Denver, CO 80202

Performance Assessment Matrix

Package Title: First Amendment

Curriculum Area: Language Arts, Social Studies, Civics

Package: Grade 8

Student: _____

Content Knowledge

Language Arts: Standard 3 (Range of strategies to comprehend, interpret, and evaluate texts [textual features])
Standard 4 (Adjust use of written language for audience and purpose)
Standard 5 (Range of strategies to write for a variety of audiences and purposes)

Social Studies: Standard VI (Power, authority and governance [a. rights, roles, and status of individual; c. mechanisms])

Civics: Standard V (Roles of citizens in democracy [rights of citizens])

Content Skills

Literacy		Mathematics	Science		Social Studies		Visual Arts	
Reading		Problem solving	Defining questions		Acquiring information		Creating	
for aesthetic response		Communication	Forming hypotheses		reading		conceptual skills	
for information/understanding		Reasoning	Investigating		study skills		production skills	
for critical analysis/evaluation		Connecting	Observing		reference skills		evaluation skills	
Writing		Estimation	Monitoring		technical skills		application	
for response/expression		Numeration	Measuring		Organizing/Using information		Responding	
for social interaction		Computation	Keeping records		thinking skills		descriptive skills	
for information/understanding		Data analysis	Transforming records		decision-making skills		analytical skills	
for critical analysis/evaluation		Measurement	Collaborating		metacognitive skills		valuing skills	
Listening		Patterning/Relating	Interpreting information		Relationships		application	
for response/expression			Integrating information		personal skills			
for information/understanding					group interaction			
for critical analysis/evaluation					social/political participation			
Speaking					Historical thinking			
for response/expression					chronological thinking			
for social interaction					historical comprehension			
for information/understanding					analysis and interpretation			
for critical analysis/evaluation					historical research			
					issues and decisions			

Performance Assessment Matrix

Performance Skills

Cognitive Strategies		Task Management Strategies		Student Role		Assessment Products		Evaluation Format	
Comparison		Analyzing the task	▓	Museum curator		Portfolio		Student checklist (attached)	
Classification		Establishing time lines		Reviewer		Publication	▓	Teacher checklist (attached)	▓
Induction		Staying productive		Engineer/Designer		Demonstration		Analytic scoring guide/ rubric (attached)	
Deduction		Meeting deadlines		Representative		Performance		Holistic scoring guide (attached)	
Error analysis		Accepting feedback		Expert witness		Exhibition			
Constructing support		Working cooperatively		Character					
Abstracting		Making a contribution		Ad agency director					
Analyzing perspectives		Respecting others		Tour organizer					
Decision making		Accessing resources	▓	Bank manager					
Investigation		Striving for accuracy		Psychologist/Sociologist					
Experimental inquiry	▓	Striving for excellence		Archaeologist					
Problem solving				Philosopher					
Invention				Historian					
				Essayist/Writer/Editor	▓				
				Teacher					
				Job applicant					
				Speaker/Listener					

Anecdotal Observations

Guided by Performance, ©1998 Zephyr Press, Tucson, Arizona

Teacher Checklist for "First Amendment"

Performance Criteria	Excellent	Satisfactory	Needs Improvement
Step 1			
■ Develops a conceptual map as evidence of brainstorming and reading on the topic	_____	_____	_____
Step 2			
■ Prepares for conference by identifying a potential focus for writing in the narrative and persuasive forms	_____	_____	_____
Step 3			
■ Completes a graphic organizer for the narrative and persuasive pieces	_____	_____	_____
■ Actively participates in a peer response group	_____	_____	_____
■ Records feedback from peers on graphic organizer	_____	_____	_____
■ Meets deadlines for submitting graphic organizers for feedback	_____	_____	_____
Step 5			
■ Provides evidence of having made substantive revisions to improve content in both drafts	_____	_____	_____
Step 6			
■ Provides evidence of having made substantive revisions to improve form in both drafts	_____	_____	_____
Step 7			
■ Provides evidence of having made substantive revisions to improve mechanics in both drafts	_____	_____	_____
Step 8			
■ Actively participates in individual conference with teacher and in peer response group	_____	_____	_____
■ Records feedback from conference and response group	_____	_____	_____
Step 9			
■ Integrates revisions into final copies	_____	_____	_____
Step 10			
■ Uses appropriate strategies to edit for correct spelling and mechanics	_____	_____	_____
Step 11			
■ Completes a self-assessment of each piece of writing	_____	_____	_____
Step 12			
Includes the following in final narrative			
■ description of events from direct experience or observation that relate to a First Amendment issue	_____	_____	_____
■ details and language relevant to the issue	_____	_____	_____
■ figurative language to create an image of setting, characters, and events	_____	_____	_____
■ sequence of events that lead to a logical conclusion	_____	_____	_____
■ vivid and realistic dialogue between characters	_____	_____	_____
■ correct spelling and mechanics	_____	_____	_____
Includes following in final persuasive piece			
■ clear statement of opinion accompanied by a strong rationale	_____	_____	_____
■ evidence to support opinion	_____	_____	_____
■ correct spelling and mechanics	_____	_____	_____
■ Meets deadlines for submitting all working drafts, two finished products, and self-assessments	_____	_____	_____

First Amendment
Student Guide

F or this assessment package, you develop two pieces of writing (one narrative and the other persuasive). Although both pieces of writing are on the First Amendment, you experiment with two different genres. As you work on improving the quality of your writing in each of these pieces, document all stages of the writing process.

Task: Story

1. **Brainstorm and explore.** Examine the topic from various angles, look for issues associated with the topic, and read examples of published writing on this topic. Look for examples of writing in the narrative and persuasive form. As you read, create a conceptual map that illustrates the issues you associate with your topic.

2. **Focus your writing.** Select an issue that really interests you. Think about how you might write about that issue in a narrative and in a persuasive form. How might you write a story or an essay about one of these issues? Sign up for a conference to discuss what direction you think you would like to pursue. Be prepared to share your conceptual map.

3. **Plan your writing.** Complete a graphic organizer (see record sheets 1 and 2, pages 60 and 61) for each of the writing pieces you intend to develop. For the narrative piece, develop a story about a First Amendment issue. Drawing upon events from your own experience or observation, create a setting, characters, a problem, and events leading to a logical conclusion. Your story must include details, figurative language, and dialogue between characters. For the persuasive piece, develop an essay, argument, editorial, or speech on a First Amendment issue. In your writing, state an opinion, provide a rationale, and use evidence to support your ideas. After you have prepared your graphic organizer, I will arrange for you to share your plans in peer response groups of three to four students. Make enough copies of your graphic organizers for each student in your group. Present your plans. Peers give one another feedback by
   - indicating areas of the writing that seem effective
   - asking questions about areas of the writing that are unclear
   - providing information from their own reading that might prove helpful

   Record peer feedback on self-stick notes and attach them to the appropriate graphic organizer. Submit your graphic organizers with self-stick notes for additional feedback.

4. **Prepare a draft of your writing in each genre.** As you write your drafts, keep in mind the characteristics of each form listed in step 3. As you edit the draft, look for the characteristics listed.

5. **Revise your writing to improve content.** As you examine your drafts for the first time, find places where you wish to add details and facts that are related to the First Amendment issue. Use a specific vocabulary that demonstrates your knowledge of the topic. You might want to revisit some of the resources you examined in step 1 to develop your ideas. Using a red pen, make changes to your draft.

6. **Revise your writing to improve form.** As you examine your working drafts for the second time, make substantive changes to strengthen it as an example of writing from the particular genre. I might suggest resources that highlight the characteristics of the narrative or persuasive genre. Using a green pen, make changes to your draft.

7. **Revise your writing to improve mechanics.** As you examine your drafts for the third time, write to improve paragraphing, sentence structure, punctuation, and spelling. Use a blue or black pen to make changes to your draft.

8. **Schedule conferences.** Meet with me some time during step 5, 6, or 7 to discuss your progress. I will also provide an opportunity for you to meet with a peer response group. During the conference and your meeting with the peer response group, record feedback on self-stick notes and attach them to your draft.

9. At this point, you have made three levels of revision to each piece of writing. In addition, you have received feedback from me and feedback from your peers. As you prepare a final draft of each piece, keep all of these revisions, suggestions, and questions in mind. Read through your draft and your self-stick notes to make sure that these revisions are reflected in your final copy.

10. **Proofread your writing for correct spelling and mechanics.** You may wish to have another reader examine the writing to highlight spelling and mechanical errors. Before submitting a finished product, make sure that you have made all necessary corrections to your final copy so that it represents your best work.

11. **Self-assess your writing.** If you wish to include any additional changes as a result of your self-assessment, do so before submitting the final products. Attach the self-assessment to the final product.

12. When you are satisfied with the quality of your writing in the narrative and persuasive form, submit all drafts, each finished product, and your self-assessment.

Record Sheet 1: Graphic Organizer (Narrative)

Setting

Characters

Problem or goal

Events	

Conclusion

Guided by Performance, ©1998 Zephyr Press, Tucson, Arizona

Record Sheet 2: Graphic Organizer (Persuasive)

State your opinion and provide a rationale

_____
_____
_____
_____
_____
_____
_____
_____

THREE REASONS

Support your opinion and give evidence

_____
_____
_____
_____
_____

Support your opinion and give evidence

_____
_____
_____
_____
_____
_____

Support your opinion and give evidence

_____
_____
_____
_____
_____

Summarize, restate, and conclude

_____
_____
_____
_____
_____

That Was Then . . . This Is Now
Classroom Implementation Guide

Curriculum Areas: History, Social Studies, Language Arts
Products

Audiovisual documentary

Time: 3 weeks
Curriculum Notes

Please read the student task sheets carefully. Note any materials you will need for each task. Performance criteria are listed in the teacher checklist.

Ideally, students study their own community or a neighboring community. Although several students may select the same community, each student will select a different area of the community (a street, neighborhood, or landmark within the community). Students make their selections after they have acquired some general background information on the community. Background information may be found in a series of bibliographies published by Oryx Press. For example, see Latrobe (1994). Other geographic regions are also represented in this series.

Obviously, site selections and historical periods will vary from the example used in this package. Like many historical organizations, the Minnesota Historical Society provides excellent resources for use in this package. For students conducting research on Minneapolis and St. Paul, for example, Millett (1996) is helpful. For those conducting research on other communities, the book provides an excellent model. We have also found similar volumes published on various cities in the United States.

For **step 3**, prepare the materials for the student and provide them as a resource; doing so might require you to prepare or to cooperate with a local historical association. For research on areas in the Twin Cities, *Twin Cities: Then and Now* will provide the necessary information. For research on areas in other communities, contact the state historical society for suggested local resources and for a catalog of publications (such as the Minnesota Historical Society at 345 Kellogg Blvd W., St. Paul, MN 55102, 1-800-657-3773, www.mnhs.org). In cases where photographs or drawings are unavailable, students may need to rely upon firsthand narrative descriptions of the area.

Students' choice of format in **step 7** will depend upon available resources. All students in class may use the same format and present their areas of the community in sequence, which will result in one publication, exhibition, slide show, videotape, or stack. For models and ideas on how to format presentation, students can refer to Millett (1993, 1996), Lorenz (1996), Microsoft's *Encarta 96,* the Timelines series by Franklin Watts, and The Vanishing Cultures series by Harcourt Brace.

In **step 8,** to the greatest extent possible, help students present to an audience that includes members of the community who may have participated in, contributed to, or been influenced by the changes in the community that are being examined. Such an audience will enhance student understanding of historical events and change from these points of view. When students have created a single documentary, they may solicit audience feedback on the entire presentation or by individual area.

Resource List

Encarta 96 Encyclopedia. 1996. Microsoft.

Latrobe, K. H. 1994. *Exploring the Great Lakes States through Literature*. Phoenix, Ariz.: Oryx Press.

Lorenz, A. 1996. *Metropolis: Ten Cities, Ten Centuries*. New York: Abrams.

Millet, L. 1993. *Lost Twin Cities*. St. Paul, Minnesota: Minnesota Historical Society Press.

———. 1996. *Twin Cities: Then and Now*. St. Paul, Minn.: Minnesota Historical Society Press.

Timelines. Series. New York: Franklin Watts.

Vanishing Cultures. Series. San Diego, Calif.: Harcourt Brace.

Performance Assessment Matrix

Package Title: That Was Then . . . This Is Now

Curriculum Area: History, Social Studies, Language Arts

Package: Grade 8

Student: _____

Content Knowledge

History:
Social Studies: Specific standards will vary depending upon locations selected and historical eras studied.
Standard II (Time, continuity, and change [c. patterns of change; d. reconstructing the past])
Standard III (People, places, and environments [a. mental maps; g. people create places; h. local settings])
Standard X (Civic ideals and practices [c. local issues and multiple points of view])

Language Arts: Standard 4 (Adjust language use for audience and purpose)
Standard 7 (Conducting research, generating questions, gathering data, communicating discoveries)

Content Skills

Literacy		Mathematics	Science		Social Studies		Visual Arts	
Reading		Problem solving	Defining questions		Acquiring information		Creating	
for aesthetic response		Communication	Forming hypotheses		reading		conceptual skills	
for information/understanding		Reasoning	Investigating		study skills		production skills	
for critical analysis/evaluation		Connecting	Observing		reference skills		evaluation skills	
Writing		Estimation	Monitoring		technical skills		application	
for response/expression		Numeration	Measuring		Organizing/Using information		Responding	
for social interaction		Computation	Keeping records		thinking skills		descriptive skills	
for information/understanding		Data analysis	Transforming records		decision-making skills		analytical skills	
for critical analysis/evaluation		Measurement	Collaborating		metacognitive skills		valuing skills	
Listening		Patterning/Relating	Interpreting information		Relationships		application	
for response/expression			Integrating information		personal skills			
for information/understanding					group interaction			
for critical analysis/evaluation					social/political participation			
Speaking					Historical thinking			
for response/expression					chronological thinking			
for social interaction					historical comprehension			
for information/understanding					analysis and interpretation			
for critical analysis/evaluation					historical research			
					issues and decisions			

Guided by Performance, ©1998 Zephyr Press, Tucson, Arizona

Performance Assessment Matrix

Performance Skills

Cognitive Strategies		Task Management Strategies		Student Role		Assessment Products		Evaluation Format	
Comparison	▓	Analyzing the task		Museum curator		Portfolio		Student checklist (attached)	
Classification		Establishing time lines		Reviewer		Publication		Teacher checklist (attached)	▓
Induction		Staying productive		Engineer/Designer		Demonstration		Analytic scoring guide/ rubric (attached)	
Deduction		Meeting deadlines		Representative		Performance	▓	Holistic scoring guide (attached)	
Error analysis		Accepting feedback	▓	Expert witness		Exhibition			
Constructing support		Working cooperatively		Character					
Abstracting		Making a contribution		Ad agency director					
Analyzing perspectives	▓	Respecting others	▓	Tour organizer					
Decision making		Accessing resources	▓	Bank manager					
Investigation	▓	Striving for accuracy		Psychologist/Sociologist					
Experimental inquiry		Striving for excellence		Archaeologist					
Problem solving				Philosopher					
Invention				Historian					
				Writer/Editor	▓				
				Teacher					
				Job applicant					
				Speaker/Listener	▓				

Anecdotal Observations

Teacher Checklist for "That Was Then . . . This Is Now"

Performance Criteria	Excellent	Satisfactory	Needs Improvement
Step 1			
▪ Selects two decades and an area of the local community as a focus for research	_____	_____	_____
Step 2			
▪ Makes a comparison by accessing appropriate resources from the historical period and by making appropriate observations for the contemporary period	_____	_____	_____
▪ Records visible evidence of observed changes in an area of the community	_____	_____	_____
▪ Identifies accurately one or two major changes in an area of the community for further investigation	_____	_____	_____
▪ Generates a list of questions related to the historical events and individuals that may have influenced changes in an area of the community	_____	_____	_____
▪ Prepares for a progress conference	_____	_____	_____
Step 3			
▪ Accesses appropriate documents in order to find information on the historical events that influenced changes in an area of the community	_____	_____	_____
▪ Records accurate information related to the influence of historical events on changes in this area of the community	_____	_____	_____
Step 4			
▪ Conducts interviews with at least three individuals to gather information on their involvement with changes in an area of the community	_____	_____	_____
▪ Ensures that the interviews represent several points of view (participant, observer, positive impact, negative impact)	_____	_____	_____
Step 5			
▪ Prepares for a progress conference	_____	_____	_____
Step 6			
▪ Constructs an accurate visual representation of an area of the community from the historical period; labels changes that will be discussed	_____	_____	_____
▪ Constructs an accurate visual representation of an area of the community from the contemporary period; labels changes that will be discussed	_____	_____	_____
▪ Constructs an accurate time line of the historical events that influenced changes in an area of the community	_____	_____	_____
▪ Provides an audio description that reflects an understanding of ways in which historical events influenced changes in an area of the community, ways in which individuals contributed to and participated in these changes, and variety of points of view individuals have with respect to these changes	_____	_____	_____

Guided by Performance, ©1998 Zephyr Press, Tucson, Arizona

Teacher Checklist for "That Was Then . . . This Is Now"

Performance Criteria	Excellent	Satisfactory	Needs Improvement
■ Provides an audio summary that draws logical conclusions about changes in the community that can be substantiated by information gathered through document analysis and interviews	_____	_____	_____
■ Prepares a final presentation containing all components and using an approved format	_____	_____	_____
Step 7			
■ Presents documentary to community members	_____	_____	_____
■ Solicits written and oral feedback on the presentation; uses a written response sheet or records responses on tape	_____	_____	_____
Step 8			
■ Meets established deadline for submitting final products	_____	_____	_____

That Was Then . . . This Is Now
Student Guide

F or this assessment package, you demonstrate an understanding of the ways in which individuals and historical events influence change on a local community. To do so, conduct research on an area of the community, collect information from documents, collect information through interviews, and present your findings through an audiovisual documentary that you present to a panel of community members.

Task: Audiovisual Documentary

1. I will help you focus your work in this assessment package by outlining potential sites for community research. Choose two time periods and one area of the community you select for your research. When selecting time periods, choose one ten-year period from earlier this century and the ten-year period leading up to the present day. Then, select a street, land-mark, or neighborhood that you believe has experienced change during these time periods. For example, if you select 1900–1910 and 1987–1997, you might select Sixth Street North (near the Target Center) in Minneapolis or the Upper Levee Flats in St. Paul.

2. Identify the changes that have occurred in the selected area during these periods of time. To do so, find photographs or drawings of your area from the earlier time period and compare these to your own observations of the area during the contemporary time period. Keep track of visible evidence of change—buildings, structures, names of streets, signs, and different uses of the space. For further investigation, select one or two of the major changes that you observed. List questions that you have about these changes (see example 1, page 70); remember that your goal is to find out about the historical events and individuals that may have influenced those changes, so your questions focus on these goals. Sign up for a progress conference with me when you have finished your comparison, identified one or two major changes, and listed questions about the historical events and individuals that may have influenced each change.

3. Find information on the ways in which historical events and individuals have influenced these changes. You have two approaches to take to gather information: analyzing documents and interviewing individuals. You must use both. For document analysis, find published literature, community archives and records, and newspaper articles. You may find these materials using the Internet, the local library, the school library, local government offices, and your local historical society. Record the source and information about the historical events that resulted in the changes you have observed in your area of the community (see example 2, page 71).

Guided by Performance, ©1998 Zephyr Press, Tucson, Arizona

4. As you record this information, you will probably find the names of individuals who might have been involved in the changes you have observed. Keep track of any specific names that are mentioned. To gather a variety of points of view, conduct at least three interviews, if possible, with individuals who contributed to changes in your community. Interview someone who contributed to change in your area, someone who feels the change(s) were positive, and someone who feels the changes were negative. To make sure that each of these points of view is represented, you may need to do more than three interviews. Although I will help you identify appropriate interview sources, the interview subjects might also be able to suggest other people. Use an interview guide for each interview; also, ask for permission to tape record your interview.

5. After you have gathered sufficient information, sign up for a progress conference with me to present your findings. When I feel you have enough information to proceed, begin to prepare your audiovisual documentary.

6. Your documentary must have the following components:
   - a visual representation (drawings, photographs, or models) of your area of the community from each time period (historical and contemporary), with changes you are explaining and describing labeled
   - a visual time line that lists the historical events that influenced the changes
   - an audio description of ways in which the historical events influenced changes (possibly written down before you tape)
   - an audio description of ways in which individuals contributed to these changes and individuals' different points of view about the changes, quoted or paraphrased (possibly written down before you tape)
   - an audio summary of your conclusions about changes in your area of the community, the historical events that may have influenced those changes, and the points of view shared by individuals within the community (possibly written down before you tape)

Although your documentary must have several components, you might choose several different formats for your presentation:
   - Prepare a booklet with the visual components and an audiotape to accompany it.
   - Prepare a model with the visual components and an audiotape to accompany it.
   - Prepare a slide show by photographing or scanning your visual components and an audiotape to accompany it.
   - Prepare a video of the visual components and your presentation of the audio components.
   - Prepare an audiovisual presentation using computer software (for example, create a HyperCard stack).

7. When your documentary is prepared and formatted, present it to a panel of community members. Include community response to your documentary in the last section. You might include a blank written response sheet at the end of the publication that allows community members to write down their comments about your presentation, or you might include a tape of feedback.

8. Submit your documentary and community response for final evaluation.

Example 1: Comparison of Area in Two Time Periods

THEN

Sixth Street North near First Avenue
Minneapolis, Minn.
1902

Photograph or drawing
would show
Central Market buildings,
stalls, horses/carriages,
and warehouse.

NOW

Sixth Street North near First Avenue
Minneapolis, Minn.
1997

Photograph or drawing
would show
Target Center,
parking lots, and
Butler Brothers warehouse.

Visible Evidence of Change

- Central Market buildings are all gone.
- All old warehouses have been eliminated.
- There is still one warehouse on the site; not part of original Market Building, but it doesn't look as new as Target Center.
- Target Center is on the site of the Central Market buildings.
- Parking lot needed for Target Center events.

Major Change

- Central Market replaced by Target Center.
- Older warehouses replaced by one warehouse.

Questions about Events and People

- Has the Central Market been relocated? Where is it now? Why was it moved to a new location? Who made the decision to move it? When was Target Center built? Why was it built? Who was responsible for building it? Who paid for the construction?
- What are the warehouses being used for? When was the new warehouse built? Why was a new warehouse needed? Who uses the warehouse?

Guided by Performance, ©1998 Zephyr Press, Tucson, Arizona

Example 2: Recording Information

Central Market replaced by Target Center	Older warehouses replaced by one warehouse
Has the Central Market been relocated? Where is it now? Why was it moved to a new location? Who made the decision to move it? When was Target Center built? Why was it built? Who was responsible for building it? Who paid for the construction?	What are the warehouses being used for? When was the new warehouse built? Why was a new warehouse needed? Who uses the warehouse?

Source	**Source**
Historical Events	**Historical Events**
On May 21, 1934, on this site, there was a confrontation between striking teamsters and a special group of deputies hired by Minneapolis businessmen. There were many injuries. Were there any deaths? The city (who?) decided to move the market shortly after this.	The new warehouse was built in 1907. The builder (or architect) was Harry Jones. People have praised the design of the new warehouse. Has it won awards? It is called the Butler Brothers warehouse. Who are they?
Names of People Involved	**Names of People Involved**
	Harry Jones, Butler Brothers

Source	**Source**
Historical Events	**Historical Events**
Names of People Involved	**Names of People Involved**

Source	**Source**
Historical Events	**Historical Events**
Names of People Involved	**Names of People Involved**

Career Exploration
Classroom Implementation Guide

Curriculum Area: Language Arts

Products

Two career option portfolios
Presentation of one portfolio in career development fair

Time: 3 weeks

Curriculum Notes

Please read the student task sheets carefully. Note any materials you will need for each task. Performance criteria are listed in the teacher checklist.

The resource list contains assessment tools (inventories and questionnaires) and other information (picture files, job descriptions, interviews with representatives from various career fields) that will help students make choices based upon their interests and abilities. You may want to schedule periodic progress conferences throughout this process.

You might enlarge the record sheets or reproduce them as overhead transparencies so you can do examples for students.

As you structure the career development fair in **step 4**, establish the full range of careers that students have selected. Once these options are established, form small groups that are representative of various career categories (that is, careers in medicine, careers in agriculture, careers in the arts, careers in business, careers in social services). To the greatest extent possible, invite representatives from each of these fields to participate in the career development fair. Using summary sheets as a guide, students present their portfolio to peers who have selected careers in the field and to practitioners in that field. Follow each presentation with discussion. If time and resources allow, you can modify this package so that students present both portfolios.

Resource List

Organizations

American Vocational Association, 1410 King Street, Alexandria, VA 22314

College Placement Council, 62 Highland Avenue, Bethlehem, PA 18017; (800) 544-5272

Educational Testing Service (ETS), Princeton, NJ 08541; (609) 734-5689

Minnesota Career Information System, 932 Capitol Square Building, 550 Cedar Street, St. Paul, MN 55101; (800) 599-6247

National Occupational Information Coordinating Committee, 2100 M Street NW, Ste. 156, Washington, DC 20037; (202) 653-5665

Wisconsin Career Information System, 1078 Educational Sciences Unit 1, 1025 Johnson Street, Madison, WI 53706; (608) 263-2725

Books

Barkley, N. 1995. *The Crystal-Barkley Guide to Taking Charge of Your Career.* New York: Workman.

Brustein, M., and M. Mahler. 1994. *AVA Guide to the School-to-Work Opportunities Act.* Alexandria, Va.: American Vocational Association.

Ettinger, J. M., ed. 1996. *Improved Career Decision Making in a Changing World: Participant's Resource Guide.* Garrett Park, Md.: Garrett Park Press.

Feichtner, S. H. 1990. *Janus Employability Skills Program: Teacher's Guide and Resource.* Hayward, Calif.: Janus.

Jew, W. 1987. *Job Planner: A Guide to Career Planning.* Hayward, Calif.: Janus.

———. 1989. *Janus Job Interviewing Practicepack.* Hayward Calif.: Janus.

Mitchell, J. S., ed. *The College Board Guide to Jobs and Career Planning.* New York: The College Board.

Seligman, L. 1994. *Developmental Career Counseling and Assessment.* Thousand Oaks, Calif.: Sage.

Tieger, P. D., and B. Barron-Tieger. 1995. *Do What You Are: Discover the Perfect Career for You through the Secrets of Personality Type.* Boston: Little Brown.

Websites

CareerMosaic's JOBS—http://www.careermosaic.com

CareerWeb—http://www.cweb.com

Performance Assessment Matrix

Package Title: Career Exploration

Curriculum Area: Language Arts

Package: Grade 8

Student: _____

Content Knowledge

Language Arts: Standard 4 (Adjust use of spoken language for a variety of audiences and purposes)

Standard 8 (Use a variety of technological and information resources to gather and synthesize information)

Standard 12 (Use spoken language to accomplish own purposes)

Content Skills

Literacy		Mathematics		Science		Social Studies		Visual Arts	
Reading		Problem solving		Defining questions		Acquiring information		Creating	
for aesthetic response		Communication		Forming hypotheses		reading		conceptual skills	
for information/understanding		Reasoning		Investigating		study skills		production skills	
for critical analysis/evaluation		Connecting		Observing		reference skills		evaluation skills	
Writing		Estimation		Monitoring		technical skills		application	
for response/expression		Numeration		Measuring		Organizing/Using information		Responding	
for social interaction		Computation		Keeping records		thinking skills		descriptive skills	
for information/understanding		Data analysis		Transforming records		decision-making skills		analytical skills	
for critical analysis/evaluation		Measurement		Collaborating		metacognitive skills		valuing skills	
Listening		Patterning/Relating		Interpreting information		Relationships		application	
for response/expression				Integrating information		personal skills			
for information/understanding						group interaction			
for critical analysis/evaluation						social/political participation			
Speaking						Historical thinking			
for response/expression						chronological thinking			
for social interaction						historical comprehension			
for information/understanding						analysis and interpretation			
for critical analysis/evaluation						historical research			
						issues and decisions			

Guided by Performance, ©1998 Zephyr Press, Tucson, Arizona

Performance Assessment Matrix

Performance Skills

Cognitive Strategies	Task Management Strategies	Student Role	Assessment Products	Evaluation Format
Comparison	Analyzing the task	Museum curator	Portfolio	Student checklist (attached)
Classification	Establishing time lines	Reviewer	Publication	Teacher checklist (attached)
Induction	Staying productive	Engineer/Designer	Demonstration	Analytic scoring guide/ rubric (attached)
Deduction	Meeting deadlines	Representative	Performance	Holistic scoring guide (attached)
Error analysis	Accepting feedback	Expert witness	Exhibition	
Constructing support	Working cooperatively	Character		
Abstracting	Making a contribution	Ad agency director		
Analyzing perspectives	Respecting others	Tour organizer		
Decision making	Accessing resources	Bank manager		
Investigation	Striving for accuracy	Psychologist/Sociologist		
Experimental inquiry	Striving for excellence	Archaeologist		
Problem solving		Philosopher		
Invention		Historian		
		Writer/Editor		
		Teacher		
		Job applicant		
		Speaker/Listener		

Anecdotal Observations

Teacher Checklist for "Career Exploration"

Performance Criteria	Excellent	Satisfactory	Needs Improvement
Step 1			
■ Uses assessment tool and other sources of information to select two career options	_____	_____	_____
■ Writes an entry for each job application portfolio that includes the selected career option, a rationale for selection, and questions for exploration	_____	_____	_____
Step 2			
■ Uses available resources effectively to gather information on two career options (preparation, work activities, and effects on personal, family, and community life)	_____	_____	_____
■ Consults at least three different sources of information; includes a maximum of two print sources and a minimum of one nonprint source	_____	_____	_____
■ Records information accurately on data sheet (preparation, work activities, and effects on personal, family, and community life)	_____	_____	_____
Step 3			
■ Describes effectively and accurately a relationship between career options and potential effects on personal, family, and community life	_____	_____	_____
Step 4			
■ Selects one career option to present during the career development fair	_____	_____	_____
Summarizes and demonstrates age-appropriate understanding of			
• the preparation required and the work activities associated with the career	_____	_____	_____
• the personal importance of that career	_____	_____	_____
• the relationship between being successful in the career and interests and abilities	_____	_____	_____
• the potential effects of the career choice on personal, family, and community life	_____	_____	_____
■ Prepares and presents one portfolio during career development fair	_____	_____	_____
Step 5			
■ Records feedback from portfolio presentation	_____	_____	_____
■ Reflects upon portfolio presentation	_____	_____	_____
Step 6			
■ Submits completed portfolios (one containing three entries and one containing five entries) by deadline	_____	_____	_____

Guided by Performance, ©1998 Zephyr Press, Tucson, Arizona

Career Exploration
Student Guide

In this assessment package, you select two careers that reflect your personal interests and abilities. After gathering information about each of these options, you prepare two career portfolios. Each portfolio summarizes the information you gathered during your research and includes information on the relationship between these career choices and your personal, family, and community life. You present your portfolio to a small group of people during a career development fair.

Task: Career Portfolio

1. I will provide you with an assessment that will help you determine your areas of interest and ability. The assessment will provide you with information that you may use to select two careers you would like to explore in greater depth. I might also provide you with additional information to use in selecting two careers. After you have surveyed a variety of careers, select two for further exploration. Develop a portfolio on each career. Include in the first entry in each portfolio the career you have selected, reasons for your selection, and questions you have (see record sheet 1, page 79).

2. Gather information from at least three sources on the preparation, work activities, and effects associated with each career you have selected (no more than two of your sources may be print sources; at least one source must involve observation, interview, simulation, media, or mentor). As you gather your information, return to sources you use earlier to get a more in-depth perspective. Many professional organizations, such as the American Medical Association, the United Auto Workers Association, and the National Science Teachers Association, can provide you with information on specific careers. I have information on some of these organizations. I might set up classroom role-play simulations for various careers (such as those in the *Janus Job Interview Practicepack*). You can also get information from people who actually do the work. You might choose to observe people in the role you've identified (computer technician at 3M, lawyers in district court, football coach at the high school, or a local small business operator) or contact them to request an interview. I might request that you set up more formal, long-term mentoring opportunities with some individuals. For anything involving out-of-school experiences (observation, interview, or mentor), I will help link you with appropriate resources and will facilitate the process. As you gather information, use a data sheet to keep track of your sources and the information you are gathering (see record sheet 2, page 80). Once completed, the data sheet will be the second entry in your portfolio; attach all materials you have gathered to the data sheet.

3. Evaluate the careers you have chosen by describing how each might affect your personal, family, and community life. The career option reflection sheet (see record sheet 3, page 81) will help you describe the potential effects. The reflection sheet is the third entry in your career portfolios.

4. Based upon what you have learned, select the career that you find most desirable. Prepare a presentation of one of your portfolios for the career development fair. Summarize what you have learned about the career, why that career is important to you, how your interests and abilities would help you succeed in that career, and how the career might affect your personal, family, and community life. Prepare a job application summary (see record sheet 4, page 82) that outlines each of these points. The summary will be the fourth entry in the career portfolio you have chosen to present; the portfolio for the other career will not contain a fourth entry.

5. After you have presented your portfolio, get feedback from at least one other person who heard your presentation and complete the self-evaluation (see record sheet 5, page 83). The evaluation is the fifth entry in the career portfolio you have chosen to present; the portfolio for the other career will not contain this entry.

6. Submit both portfolios for final review.

Guided by Performance, ©1998 Zephyr Press, Tucson, Arizona

Record Sheet 1: Career Selection and Rationale

Complete one for each career portfolio.

What sources of information did you use to research your careers?	Which career have you selected to explore in greater depth?	Give at least three reasons for choosing to research this option.
1. _____ _____ _____ 2. _____ _____ _____ 3. _____ _____ _____ Others _____ _____ _____ _____		1. _____ _____ _____ 2. _____ _____ _____ 3. _____ _____ _____ Others _____ _____ _____

Explaining Your Reasons

Which source of information did you find most valuable in helping you make this selection? What did you learn from this source that helped you select this career?	What do you know about your skills and abilities that makes this an interesting career for you?	Do you know anyone who does this kind of work? Did that person influence your decision? Can that person help you find out more about this career?

Questions

What questions do you have about *preparation* for this career?	What questions do you have about the *work* associated with this career?	What questions do you have about ways in which the work might *affect* your personal, family, or community life?

Record Sheet 2: Career Option Data Sheet

Complete three for each career portfolio.

Career Option

Information Source	_____ Print
	_____ Observation
	_____ Interview
	_____ Simulation
	_____ Media
	_____ Mentor

What have you learned about preparation for this career?

What have you learned about the work associated with this career?

Effects on Personal Life	Effects on Family Life	Effects on Community Life

New Questions

Guided by Performance, ©1998 Zephyr Press, Tucson, Arizona

Record Sheet 3: Career Reflection Sheet

Complete one for each career portfolio.

Career Option		
Questions for Reflection	**What benefits do you see?**	**What challenges do you see?**
If you chose to pursue this career, what would you need to do in order to prepare for it?		
If you chose to pursue this career, what kind of work activities would you expect to be doing?		
If you chose to pursue this career, what effect might it have on your personal life?		
If you chose to pursue this career, what effect might it have on your family life?		
If you chose to pursue this career, what effect might it have on your community life?		
Would you be likely to choose to pursue this career? Why or why not?		

Record Sheet 4: Summary

Complete one sheet for the career portfolio you will present.

Career

If you were applying for a job in this field, what points would you want to make in an interview?
Summarize what you have learned about this career and about yourself.

While exploring this career, I have learned a lot about the preparation required and the activities associated with the career. The most important things I've learned are

_____

_____

_____

A career in this field is important to me because

_____

_____

_____

Given what I know about the preparation required and the activities associated with this career, I think I have the following interests and abilities that will help me succeed:

_____

_____

_____

I believe that this career would affect my personal life in the following ways:

_____

_____

_____

I believe that this career would affect my family life in the following ways:

_____

_____

_____

I believe that this career would affect my community life in the following ways:

_____

_____

_____

Guided by Performance, ©1998 Zephyr Press, Tucson, Arizona

Record Sheet 5: Feedback and Self-evaluation

Complete one sheet for the career portfolio you will present.

Feedback from Others	Self-Evaluation
Name of Observer	What career did you do your presentation on?
What do you think the student has learned about this career?	What are the most important things you've learned about this career?
Based upon your experience in or research of this career, do you think the student is developing an appropriate understanding of the career in terms of the preparation, activities, and effects on personal, family, and community life associated with the career?	Do you think you were able to effectively summarize what you've learned during your presentation? What aspects of your presentation did you feel were effective? What aspects of your presentation would you like to improve?
Are there other things that the student should know, resources the student should consult, or additional questions that the student should investigate?	What additional questions do you have about this career as a result of your discussion with the group?

Coming to America
Classroom Implementation Guide

Curriculum Areas: History, Language Arts
Products

Visual organizer
Resource list
Multimedia presentation
Newspaper editorial pages

Time: 4 weeks

Curriculum Notes

Please read the student task sheets carefully. Note any materials you will need for each task. Performance criteria are listed in the teacher checklist.

Task 1: Visual Organizer, Resource List, Multimedia Presentation

The films in **step 1** are representative examples of the films and videos that could be viewed for this purpose. The visual organizer lists representative examples of immigrant groups; actual student work should include a greater number of groups. Other visual organizer possibilities include charts, geographical maps, and tables.

The issues included in **step 3** include volume 3, number 12 (December 1982) and volume 4, number 1 (January 1983). In addition, the magazine has devoted a number of issues to particular immigrant groups. A publication list and information on ordering back issues is available from Cobblestone Publishing, Inc., 7 School Street, Peterborough, NH 03458 (1-800-821-0115).

Task 2: Newspaper Editorial Pages

Although many nonfiction materials in the resource list could be used in this task, Knight (1993) would be an appropriate choice for reading out loud. Effective selections for **step 2** include Dudley (1990) and Szumski (1990). Series books on immigration (available from Chelsea House and Lerner Publishers) outline the controversial issues surrounding the arrival of various cultural groups; these resources present information in textual and visual form. The number of selections required to gather sufficient information will vary depending upon the period, cultural groups, and resources used.

Resource List
Fiction

Anzaldua, G. 1993. *Friends from the Other Side/Amigos del Otro Lado*. Chicago: Childrens Book Press.
Banks, L. R. 1973. *One More River*. New York: Avon.

Bartone, E. 1993. *Peppe the Lamplighter*. New York: Lothrop, Lee, and Shepard.

Beatty, P. 1981. *Lupita Manana*. New York: Morrow.

Berry, J. 1992. *Aheemah and His Sons*. New York: HarperCollins.

Branson, K. 1981. *Streets of Gold*. New York: Putnam.

Bulla, C. R. 1983. *Charlie's House*. New York: Knopf.

Cech, J. 1991. *My Grandmother's Journey*. New York: Bradbury.

Clapp, P. 1968. *Constance*. New York: Morrow.

Coerr, E. 1988. *Chang's Paper Pony*. New York: Harper and Row.

Cohen, B. 1982. *Gooseberries to Oranges*. New York: Lothrop, Lee, and Shepard.

————. 1983. *Molly's Pilgrim*. New York: Lothrop, Lee, and Shepard.

————. 1985. *Molly's Pilgrim* (video). Phoenix, Ariz.: Phoenix Film and Video.

Cohn, A., ed. 1993. *From Sea to Shining Sea: A Treasury of American Folklore and Folk Song*. New York: Scholastic.

Conlon-McKenna, M. 1992. *The Wildflower Girl*. New York: Holiday.

Crew, L. 1989. *Children of the River*. New York: Dell.

Cummings, B. 1979. *Now, Ameriky*. New York: Atheneum.

Fahrmann, W. 1985. *The Long Journey of Lucas*. New York: Bradbury.

Field, R. 1931. *Calico Bush*. New York: Macmillan.

Fisher, L. E. 1975. *Across the Sea from Galway*. New York: Four Winds.

Friedman, I. 1984. *How My Parents Learned to Eat*. Boston: Houghton Mifflin.

Garland, S. 1993. *The Lotus Seed*. New York: Harcourt.

Gilson, J. 1985. *Hello, My Name Is Scrambled Eggs*. New York: Lothrop, Lee, and Shepard.

Gross, V. 1990. *It's Only Good-bye*. New York: Viking.

Hesse, K. 1992. *Letters from Rifka*. New York: Holt.

Kroll, S. 1991. *Mary McLean and the St. Patrick's Day Parade*. New York: Scholastic.

Lasky, K. 1981. *The Night Journey*. New York: Viking-Penguin.

Leighton, M. 1992. *An Ellis Island Christmas*. New York: Viking.

Levine, E. 1989. *I Hate English!* New York: Scholastic.

Levitin, S. 1970. *Journey to America*. New York: Scholastic.

————. 1989. *Silver Days*. New York: Scholastic.

Levoy, M. 1972. *The Witch of Fourth Street and Other Stories*. New York: Harper and Row.

Lord, B. B. 1984. *In the Year of the Boar and Jackie Robinson*. New York: Harper and Row.

Lowry, L. 1989. *Number the Stars*. New York: Dell.

Madison, W. 1977. *Call Me Danica*. New York: Four Winds.

Maxwell-Worthington, J. 1982. "A Crossing Dark and Dangerous." *Cobblestone*. 3, 12:24–28.

McCunn, R. L. 1983. *Pie-biter*. San Francisco: Design Enterprises of San Francisco.

Meyerson, E. 1990. *The Cat Who Escaped from Steerage*. New York: Scribner.

Nhuong, H. Q. 1982. *The Land I Lost*. New York: Harper and Row.

Nixon, J. L. 1993. *Land of Promise*. New York: Bantam.

Paterson, K. 1988. *Park's Quest*. New York: Lodestar.

Perrera, H. 1992. *Kiki: A Cuban Boy's Adventures in America*. Miami: Pickering Press.

Polacco, P. 1988. *The Keeping Quilt*. New York: Simon and Schuster.

Reiff, T. 1989a. *Boat People*. Belmont, Calif.: David S. Lake.

————. 1989b. *A Different Home*. Belmont, Calif.: David S. Lake.

————. 1989c. *The Family from Vietnam*. Belmont, Calif.: David S. Lake.

————. 1989d. *For Gold and Blood*. Belmont, Calif.: David S. Lake.

————. 1989e. *Little Italy*. Belmont, Calif.: David S. Lake.

————. 1989f. *Old Ways, New Ways*. Belmont, Calif.: David S. Lake.

————. 1989g. *O Little Town.* Belmont, Calif.: David S. Lake.

————. 1989h. *Push to the West.* Belmont, Calif.: David S. Lake.

Sandin, J. 1981a. *The Long Way to a New Land.* New York: HarperCollins.

————. 1981b. *The Long Way Westward.* New York: HarperCollins.

Say, A. 1993. *Grandfather's Journey.* New York: Scholastic.

Shiefman, V. 1993. *Good-bye to the Trees.* New York: Atheneum.

Surat, M. 1983. *Angel Child, Dragon Child.* New York: Carnival.

Talbot, C. 1979. *An Orphan for Nebraska.* New York: Atheneum.

Tran-Khanh-Tuyet. 1987. *The Little Weaver of Thai-Yen Village.* San Francisco: Childrens Book Press.

Winter, J. 1992. *Kiara's New World.* New York: Knopf.

Yep, L. 1975. *Dragon Wings.* New York: Harper and Row.

————. 1993. *Dragon's Gate.* New York: Harper and Row.

Nonficton

Anderson, J. 1989. *Spanish Pioneers of the Southwest.* New York: Lodestar.

Ashabranner, B. 1991. *An Ancient Heritage: The Arab-American Minority.* New York: HarperCollins.

Ashabranner, B., and M. Ashabranner. 1987. *Into a Strange Land: Unaccompanied Refugee Youth in America.* New York: Putnam.

Benton, B. 1985. *Ellis Island: A Pictorial History.* New York: Facts on File.

Berstein, J. 1981. *A Young Soviet Immigrant.* Boston: Houghton Mifflin.

Bresnick-Pery, R. 1992. *Leaving for America.* Chicago: Children's Book Press.

Dudley, W. 1990. *Immigration: Opposing Viewpoints.* San Diego: Greenhaven Press.

Eiseman, A. 1970. *From Many Lands.* New York: Atheneum.

Fisher, L. E. 1977. *Letters from Italy.* New York: Four Winds Press.

————. 1986. *Ellis Island: Gateway to the New World.* New York: Holiday House.

Freedman, R. 1980. *Immigrant Kids.* New York: Dutton.

Girard, L. W. 1989. *We Adopted You, Benjamin Koo.* New York: Whitman.

Goldfarb, N. 1993. *Fighters, Refugees, Immigrants: Story of the Hmong.* Minneapolis: Carolrhoda.

Graff, N. 1993. *Where the River Runs.* New York: Little Brown.

Handin, O. 1971. *Statue of Liberty.* New York: Newsweek Book Division.

Heaps, W. 1967. *The Story of Ellis Island.* New York: Seabury Press.

Hewett, J. 1990. *Hector Lives in the United States Now: The Story of a Mexican-American Child.* New York: HarperCollins.

Hoobler, Dorothy, and Thomas Hoobler. *The American Family Albums.* New York: Oxford University Press.

Jacobs, W. 1990. *Ellis Island: New Hope in a New Land.* New York: Charles Scribner's Sons.

Katz, W. 1993. *The Great Migrations—1880s–1912: History of Multicultural America.* New York: Raintree.

Knight, M. 1993. *Who Belongs Here? An American Story.* Tilbury House.

Kukin, S. 1992. *How My Family Lives in America.* New York: Bradbury.

Langone, J. 1993. *Spreading Poison: A Book about Racism and Prejudice.* New York: Little Brown.

Levine, E. 1993. *If Your Name Was Changed at Ellis Island.* New York: Scholastic.

Reeves, P. 1991. *Ellis Island: Gateway to the American Dream.* New York: Crescent.

Rosenberg, M. 1986. *Making of a New Home in America.* New York: Lothrop, Lee, and Shepard.

Schefelman, J. 1992. *A Peddler's Dream.* Boston: Houghton Mifflin.

Siegel, B. 1985. *Sam Ellis's Island.* New York: Macmillan.

Sims, G. 1992. *Immigration: Literature-based Activities for Thematic Teaching.* Cypress, Calif.: Creative Teaching.

Stanek, M. 1985. *We Came from Vietnam.* New York: Whitman.

Stein, R. C. 1978. *The Story of the Golden Spike.* Chicago: Children's Book Press.

Szumski, B. 1990. *Immigration: Identifying Propoganda Techniques.* San Diego: Greenhaven Press.

Guided by Performance, ©1998 Zephyr Press, Tucson, Arizona

Performance Assessment Matrix

Package Title: Coming to America

Curriculum Area: History, Language Arts

Package: Grade 8

Student: _____

Content Knowledge

History:
Era 6: Standard 2 (immigration)
Era 10: Standard 2 (New immigration and demographic shifts)

Language Arts:
Standard 1 (Read and explore a wide range of print and nonprint texts to build an understanding of cultures)
Standard 2 (Read literature from many periods and genres to build understanding of human experiences)
Standard 4 (Adjust use of spoken, written, and visual language for audience and purpose)
Standard 7 (Conduct research by generating questions; gather, evaluate, and synthesize data; communicate results)

Content Skills

Literacy	Mathematics	Science	Social Studies	Visual Arts
Reading	Problem solving	Defining questions	Acquiring information	Creating
for aesthetic response	Communication	Forming hypotheses	reading	conceptual skills
for information/understanding	Reasoning	Investigating	study skills	production skills
for critical analysis/evaluation	Connecting	Observing	reference skills	evaluation skills
Writing	Estimation	Monitoring	technical skills	application
for response/expression	Numeration	Measuring	Organizing/Using information	Responding
for social interaction	Computation	Keeping records	thinking skills	descriptive skills
for information/understanding	Data analysis	Transforming records	decision-making skills	analytical skills
for critical analysis/evaluation	Measurement	Collaborating	metacognitive skills	valuing skills
Listening	Patterning/Relating	Interpreting information	Relationships	application
for response/expression		Integrating information	personal skills	
for information/understanding			group interaction	
for critical analysis/evaluation			social/political participation	
Speaking			Historical thinking	
for response/expression			chronological thinking	
for social interaction			historical comprehension	
for information/understanding			analysis and interpretation	
for critical analysis/evaluation			historical research	
			issues and decisions	

Performance Assessment Matrix

Performance Skills

Cognitive Strategies	Task Management Strategies	Student Role	Assessment Products	Evaluation Format
Comparison	Analyzing the task	Museum curator	Portfolio	Student checklist (attached)
Classification	Establishing time lines	Reviewer	Publication	Teacher checklist (attached)
Induction	Staying productive	Engineer/Designer	Demonstration	Analytic scoring guide/ rubric (attached)
Deduction	Meeting deadlines	Representative	Performance	Holistic scoring guide (attached)
Error analysis	Accepting feedback	Expert witness	Exhibition	
Constructing support	Working cooperatively	Character		
Abstracting	Making a contribution	Ad agency director		
Analyzing perspectives	Respecting others	Tour organizer		
Decision making	Accessing resources	Bank manager		
Investigation	Striving for accuracy	Psychologist/Sociologist		
Experimental inquiry	Striving for excellence	Archaeologist		
Problem solving		Philosopher		
Invention		Historian		
		Writer/Editor		
		Teacher		
		Job applicant		
		Speaker/Listener		

Anecdotal Observations

Guided by Performance, ©1998 Zephyr Press, Tucson, Arizona

Teacher Checklist for "Coming to America"

Performance Criteria	Excellent	Satisfactory	Needs Improvement
Preparation			
■ Identifies main ideas (groups and time periods) in film or video	_____	_____	_____
■ Identifies supporting details (reasons for emigration, immigration experience, contributions)	_____	_____	_____
■ Selects a logical and readable format for organizing information	_____	_____	_____
■ Includes the correct number of resources in each category	_____	_____	_____
■ Uses an approved format for bibliographic citations	_____	_____	_____
Presentation			
■ Presents data on immigration patterns effectively and accurately	_____	_____	_____
■ Uses information to make and support a logical prediction about future immigration	_____	_____	_____
■ Identifies, defines, and alphabetizes appropriate words in dictionary	_____	_____	_____
■ Draws upon reading to represent the experience of immigrant character before, during, and after immigration in triptych format	_____	_____	_____
■ Compares and contrasts settings (before, during, and after immigration)	_____	_____	_____
■ Uses figurative language to describe experiences and settings	_____	_____	_____
■ Identifies appropriate craft or food item from immigrant group for use as cultural artifact	_____	_____	_____
■ Follows directions to create craft or make food item	_____	_____	_____
■ Posts directions and displays results	_____	_____	_____
■ Includes all components in final display	_____	_____	_____
Editorial			
■ Associates appropriate immigrant groups with the identified period of immigration	_____	_____	_____
■ Uses double-entry journal to record facts and opinions on each immigrant group	_____	_____	_____
■ Represents various points of view through letters to the editor and editorial cartoons	_____	_____	_____
■ Develops own point of view in editorial	_____	_____	_____
■ Integrates facts and opinions in editorial	_____	_____	_____
■ Distinguishes between facts and opinions in editorial	_____	_____	_____

Coming to America
Student Guide

We have been learning about immigration to the United States during various periods in our history. In doing so, you have encountered real life and fictional characters that journeyed from their homelands to begin a new life in the United States. In this assessment, you pull together information from a variety of sources to develop a multimedia presentation on a fictional character of your choosing.

Task 1: Visual Organizer and Resource List

1. View the film *Our Immigrant Heritage* (Indiana University) or the videos *The Golden Door: Our Nation of Immigrants* (Knowledge Unlimited), *Ellis Island* (The History Channel), and *Coming to America* (Public Media Video). While viewing, take notes on the following questions:
   - What countries did the immigrants in the film come from?
   - During what period of time did this immigration occur?
   - What were some of the possible reasons for their emigration from these various countries?
   - What was the immigration experience like for these different groups?
   - What contributions have these groups made to the culture and economy of the United States?

   Summarize these ideas using a visual organizer.

2. Target a country of origin you are interested in, identify a character from that country whose experiences you would like to document, and gather at least two appropriate fiction texts (I have a resource list you may choose from). For example, if you choose Ireland, you might choose to document the experiences of a character from Maxwell-Worthington's *A Crossing Dark and Dangerous,* Conlon-McKenna's *The Wildflower Girl,* Cummings's *Now, Ameriky,* or Branson's *Streets of Gold.* List your selections on your reading list for this assessment.

3. Find five appropriate nonfiction selections to add to your reading list. For the example used in step 2, you might choose Bales's *Tales of the Elders: A Memory Book of Men and Women Who Came to America as Immigrants,* Condon-Johnston's *Minnesota's Irish,* Freedman's *Immigrant Kids,* or Levine's *If Your Name Was Changed at Ellis Island.* You might also find good informational articles in issues of *Cobblestone* magazine that are devoted to the topic of immigration.

4. Supplement your reading list by including at least one listening or viewing selection. For example, you might use *Listen to the Land* (SRI Selection Research), a series of cassettes that contain stories and songs by people who immigrated to this country from 1860 to 1990.

5. Finally, make sure that you have one source on your resource list that contains data on immigration patterns and on immigrants from the country of origin you have selected. This information may be contained in one of the nonfiction selections, your social studies textbook, or electronic and print encyclopedias. In addition, you can obtain extensive data through the United States Department of Justice/Immigration and Naturalization Service, Records Verification Center, 1441-21 Edwin Miller Boulevard, Martinsburg, WV 25401, and the National Archives and Records Service, Reference Services Branch, Washington, DC 20408. List the source of the information on your resource list. Your finalized list includes at least two fiction selections, at least five nonfiction selections, one or more listening/viewing selections, and a source of data on immigration patterns. Make sure you use the correct bibliographic citation format for listing each selection.

6. In order to complete your multimedia presentation, draw upon the information you have read, heard, or viewed. Focusing on the experience of the fictional character construct a presentation that includes the following components:

- **Background Data.** Using a graph or table, provide information on the number of immigrants that arrived from your target country and the years during which this immigration occurred. At the bottom of the graph or table, write a brief statement indicating what you learned about immigration patterns from your target country. Based upon what you have learned, make a prediction about future immigration from this country. Should we expect large numbers of immigrants from your target country? Why or why not?

- **Cultural Dictionary.** Throughout your reading, viewing, and listening, keep track of words or phrases that are new to you or are important in the experience of your immigrant character. Create a dictionary of these words by listing them in alphabetical order and defining them using words or pictures. For example, the following words might be words you would include in a cultural dictionary of words important to the experience of Irish immigrants—*famine, steerage, drisheen, salt herring, soda bread, buttonhook, trachoma, matron, quarantine, contract labor laws,* and *registry.*

- **Character Triptych.** Fold a large sheet of butcher paper into three sections. Through words and pictures, retell the story of your character before immigration in the leftmost section, during immigration in the center section, and after immigration in the rightmost section. Take on the role of your character and write this narrative in the first person; that is, retell the story through the eyes of your character. Include information on the country of origin, reasons for emigrating, the time period during which your character immigrated to the United States, experiences journeying to the new country, experiences upon arriving in the new country, and life in the United States. It is important that the reader/viewer get a clear picture of setting in the character's story. Compare and contrast the country of origin (before), the setting of the immigration journey (during), and arrival in the new country (after). Finally, use examples of figurative language to describe these experiences and settings. Some of these examples may come from the words and thoughts of your character—look for these as you read so that you can use them on your triptych. You may also create your own examples of figurative language in order to help the reader/viewer get a vivid picture of the setting and events in your character's story.

■ **Cultural Artifact.** Identify a craft or food, such as "fate cakes" for fortune-telling or Irish soda bread, that is associated with your character's immigrant group. Find instructions for making the craft or a recipe for making the food. Create an example of the craft project or a sample of the food for your display. Post your instructions and display your craft of food.

8. Once you have assembled the components of your presentation, display it in the designated area.

Task 2: Newspaper Editorial Pages

1. Immigration issues have often sparked controversy and debate in this country, and many different perspectives on cultural assimilation exist. At various points throughout U.S. history, immigrant groups have experienced acceptance and discrimination. Listen as I read about the experiences of a Cambodian refugee. As you listen, pay attention to the points of view represented in this selection.

2. Choose a period of immigration and read to identify the controversial issues of the time. Keep a double-entry journal in which you record information about the cultural groups discussed in your reading. For each cultural group, record facts and opinions that are presented in your readings.

3. Create an editorial page for a newspaper from the immigration period you've studied; write letters to the editor and/or draw editorial cartoons that represent various points of view on the immigration and assimilation of your cultural group. Each of these letters or cartoons reflects a point of view that you encountered in your reading. Summarize what you've learned in an editorial that develops your own point of view on the issues. Although you integrate both facts and opinions from your reading into your editorial, be sure to use language that distinguishes facts from your opinions.

4. Follow all steps of the writing process, then submit a final draft of your editorial for publication.

Guided by Performance, ©1998 Zephyr Press, Tucson, Arizona

Origins
Classroom Implementation Guide

Curriculum Areas: Earth Science, Language Arts, History

Products

Interactive museum display

Time: 4 weeks

Curriculum Notes

Please read the student task sheets carefully. Note any materials you will need for each task. Performance criteria are listed in the teacher checklist.

You can select a broad range of topics and themes for this package. A list of resources that focus on origins is included in this package. If you want to use this package and expand the range of earth science themes, you will need to expand the resource list accordingly.

Resource List

Folktale Collections

Doria, C., and L. Harris. 1976. *Origins: Creating Texts from the Ancient Mediterranean.* New York: Anchor, Doubleday.

Eliade, M. 1974. *Gods, Goddesses, and Myths of Creation.* New York: Harper and Row.

Hamilton, V. 1988. *In the Beginning: Creation Stories from around the World.* San Diego: Harcourt, Brace, Jovanovich.

Leach, M. 1956. *The Beginning: Creation Myths around the World.* New York: Funk and Wagnalls.

O'Brien, J., and W. Major. 1982. *In the Beginning: Creation Myths from Ancient Mesopotamia, Israel, and Greece.* Chicago: The American Academy of Religion, Scholars Press.

Sproul, B. C. 1979. *Primal Myths: Creating the World.*

Historical Resources

Asimov, I. 1989. *Asimov's Chronology of Science and Discovery.* New York: Harper and Row.

Blohm, H., S. Beer, and D. Suzuki. 1986. *Pebbles to Computers: The Thread.* New York: Oxford University Press.

Boorstin, D. J. 1991. *The Discoverers.* New York: Abrams.

Burke, J. 1985. *The Day the Universe Changed.* Boston: Little, Brown.

Cohen, I. B. 1985. *Revolution in Science.* Cambridge, Mass.: Harvard University Press.

Goldstein, T. 1980. *Dawn of Modern Science: From the Arabs to Leonardo da Vinci.* Boston: Houghton Mifflin.

Harre, R. 1983. *Great Scientific Experiments: Twenty Experiments That Changed Our View of the World.* New York: Oxford University Press.

Hellemans, A. 1988. *The Timetables of Science.* New York: Simon and Schuster.

Hoyle, F. 1972. *From Stonehenge to Modern Cosmology.* New York: W. H. Freeman.

Porter, R., ed. 1987. *Man Masters Nature: Twenty-five Centuries of Science.* New York: Braziller.

Ronan, C. A. 1982. *Science: Its History and Development among the World's Cultures.* New York: Facts on File.

Spangenburg, R., and D. K. Moser. 1993. *The History of Science from the Ancient Greeks to the Scientific Revolution.* New York: Facts on File.

Tomas, A. 1971. *We Are Not the First: Riddles of Ancient Science.*

Current Scientific Resources

Asimov, I. 1987. *Beginnings: The Story of Origins—of Mankind, Life, the Earth, the Universe.* New York: Walker.

Barrow, J. D. 1992. *Theories of Everything.* New York: Ballantine.

———. 1994. *The Origin of the Universe.* New York: Basic.

Barrow, J. D., and J. Silk. 1993. *The Left Hand of Creation.* Oxford: Oxford University Press.

Bartuski, M. 1993. *Through a Universe Darkly.* New York: HarperCollins.

Davies, P. 1988. *The Cosmic Blueprint: New Discoveries in Nature's Creative Ability to Order the Universe.* New York: Simon and Schuster.

———. 1992. *The Mind of God.* New York: Simon and Schuster.

Davies, P., and J. Brown. 1992. *Superstrings: A Theory of Everything?* Cambridge, Mass.: Cambridge University Press.

Drees, W. 1990. *Beyond the Big Bang: Quantum Cosmology and God.* La Salle, La.: Open Court.

Ellis, G. 1993. *Before the Beginning: Cosmology Explained.* New York: Boyars, Bowerdean.

Ferris, T. 1988. *Coming of Age in the Milky Way.* New York: Morrow.

Gribbin, J. 1986. *In Search of the Big Bang.* New York: Bantam.

———. 1993. *In the Beginning.* Boston: Little Brown.

Guth, A. H. 1997. *The Inflationary Universe.* Reading, Mass.: Addison-Wesley, Helix.

Hartmann, W. K. 1991. *The History of Earth: An Illustrated Chronicle of Our Planet.* New York: Workman.

Hawking, S. W. 1988. *A Brief History of Time.* New York: Bantam.

Henbest, N. 1992. *The Planets: A Guided Tour of the Solar System through the Eyes of America's Space Probes.* New York: Viking.

Lauber, P. 1993. *Journey to the Planets.* New York: Crown.

Lightman, A. 1991. *Ancient Light.* Cambridge, Mass.: Harvard University Press.

Longair, M. 1990. *The Origins of the Universe.* Cambridge, Mass.: Cambridge University Press.

Miller, R., and W. K. Hartmann. 1993. *The Grand Tour: A Traveler's Guide to the Solar System.* New York: Workman.

Peebles, P. 1993. *Principles of Physical Cosmology.* Princeton, N.J.: Princeton University Press.

Peters, T. 1989. *Cosmos as Creation.* Nashville, Tenn.: Abingdon Press.

Redfern, R. 1983. *The Making of a Continent.* New York: Times.

Riordan, M., and D. Schramm. 1991. *The Shadows of Creation.* New York: W. H. Freeman.

Sheffield, C. 1981. *Earth Watch.* New York: Macmillan.

Silk, J. 1994a. *Cosmic Enigmas.* New York: American Institute of Physics.

———. 1994b. *A Short History of the Universe.* New York: Scientific American Library.

Taylor, J. G. 1994. *When the Clock Struck Zero: Science's Ultimate Limits.* New York: St. Martin's Press.

Trefil, J. S. 1985. *Space, Time, Infinity: The Smithsonian Views of the Universe.* New York: Pantheon.

Weinberg, S. 1977. *The First Three Minutes.* New York: Basic.

Weiner, J. 1986. *Planet Earth.* New York: Bantam.

Performance Assessment Matrix

Package Title: Origins

Curriculum Area: Earth Science, Language Arts, History

Package: Grade 8

Student: _____

Content Knowledge

Science: Standard D (Structure of the Earth system; Earth's history; Earth in the solar system)
Standard G (Science as a human endeavor; nature of science; history of science)

Language Arts: Standard 1 (Read a wide range of texts; build understanding of cultures and the world; acquire new information)
Standard 7 (Students conduct research on issues by generating questions; gather, evaluate, and synthesize data from a variety of sources; communicate discoveries to an audience)

Content Skills

Literacy		Mathematics		Science		Social Studies		Visual Arts	
Reading		Problem solving		Defining questions		Acquiring information		Creating	
for aesthetic response		Communication		Forming hypotheses		reading		conceptual skills	
for information/understanding		Reasoning		Investigating		study skills		production skills	
for critical analysis/evaluation		Connecting		Observing		reference skills		evaluation skills	
Writing		Estimation		Monitoring		technical skills		application	
for response/expression		Numeration		Measuring		Organizing/Using information		Responding	
for social interaction		Computation		Keeping records		thinking skills		descriptive skills	
for information/understanding		Data analysis		Transforming records		decision-making skills		analytical skills	
for critical analysis/evaluation		Measurement		Collaborating		metacognitive skills		valuing skills	
Listening		Patterning/Relating		Interpreting information		Relationships		application	
for response/expression				Integrating information		personal skills			
for information/understanding						group interaction			
for critical analysis/evaluation						social/political participation			
Speaking						Historical thinking			
for response/expression						chronological thinking			
for social interaction						historical comprehension			
for information/understanding						analysis and interpretation			
for critical analysis/evaluation						historical research			
						issues and decisions			

Performance Assessment Matrix

Performance Skills

Cognitive Strategies		Task Management Strategies		Student Role		Assessment Products		Evaluation Format	
Comparison	▪	Analyzing the task	▪	Museum curator		Portfolio		Student checklist (attached)	
Classification		Establishing time lines		Reviewer		Publication		Teacher checklist (attached)	▪
Induction		Staying productive	▪	Engineer/Designer		Demonstration		Analytic scoring guide/ rubric (attached)	
Deduction		Meeting deadlines		Representative		Performance		Holistic scoring guide (attached)	
Error analysis		Accepting feedback		Expert witness		Exhibition	▪		
Constructing support	▪	Working cooperatively		Character					
Abstracting		Making a contribution		Ad agency director					
Analyzing perspectives	▪	Respecting others		Tour organizer					
Decision making		Accessing resources	▪	Bank manager					
Investigation	▪	Striving for accuracy		Psychologist/Sociologist					
Experimental inquiry		Striving for excellence	▪	Archaeologist					
Problem solving				Philosopher					
Invention				Historian	▪				
				Writer/Editor					
				Teacher					
				Job applicant					
				Speaker/Listener					

Anecdotal Observations

Guided by Performance, ©1998 Zephyr Press, Tucson, Arizona

Teacher Checklist for "Origins"

Performance Criteria	Excellent	Satisfactory	Needs Improvement
Step 1			
■ Makes appropriate selection from a list of acceptable topics	___	___	___
Step 2			
■ Identifies two stories from different cultural traditions that illustrate earth science themes	___	___	___
■ Accurately records the systems and processes that are begins explained and how they are explained in these stories	___	___	___
Step 3			
■ Conducts a thorough search of the historical and current literature; selects and reads appropriate sources	___	___	___
■ Outlines the evolution of thinking in this area based upon historical information	___	___	___
■ Outlines modern theories in this area based upon current scientific research	___	___	___
■ Demonstrates an understanding of earth science processes and systems as they relate to this stage of the investigation	___	___	___
Step 4			
■ Effectively shares data about the variety of explanations	___	___	___
Step 5			
■ Conducts an experiment that accurately re-creates or represents historical findings or conducts an experiment that accurately illustrates current research in the field	___	___	___
■ Prepares a lab report that includes			
• research question and hypothesis	___	___	___
• data collection methods	___	___	___
• appropriate measurement and data analysis techniques	___	___	___
• data records	___	___	___
• findings	___	___	___
• conclusions	___	___	___
■ Demonstrates an understanding of earth science processes and systems as they relate to this stage of the investigation	___	___	___

Origins
Student Guide

In this assessment package, you investigate the origins of the universe, planets, and Earth systems using folkloric, historic, and scientific sources. Your goal is to examine, compare, contrast, and explain the variety of ways in which complex cosmological, geophysical, and geochemical processes are explained. You demonstrate what you have learned by setting up an interactive museum display.

Task: Interactive Museum Display

1. I will help you identify the systems and processes you want to investigate based on some of the topics we covered in class. You may decide to explore any of the following: history of the universe, solar history, planetary history, motion in the solar system, planets, stars, moons, gravity, seasons, weather and climate, geosphere (crust, mantle, and core), hydrosphere, atmosphere, plate tectonics, land forms, soil composition, rock cycles, and water cycles. I might suggest additional topics or limit the list based upon class requirements.

2. Identify at least two stories (from two different cultural traditions) that address earth science themes and relate to the systems or processes that you want to investigate. You might want to investigate folklore collections from specific cultures or cross-cultural collections on earth science themes. Find ways in which various cultures have used stories to explain these systems or processes. Read the stories and analyze them carefully for the explanations they contain. In a double-entry journal, keep track of what is being explained and how it is being explained. For example, you might use "God Ra the Creator," an Egyptian tale, and "Mawu-Lisa the Creators," a tale from the Republic of Benin (Hamilton 1988) to see how they explained planetary history. Record how each of the myths describes the origins of the earth and begin to look carefully for connections to scientific explanations.

3. Conduct research on current scientific explanations for these processes or systems. Search for alternative explanations in historic and scientific resources. Find information on how humankind's understanding of these processes or systems has changed over time and familiarize yourself as much as possible with the most recent explanations. Record your findings.

4. When you think you have collected enough information, sign up for a conference. Beginning with the folklore, present the explanations for the processes or systems you've investigated. I might feel that you have gathered sufficient data, or I might suggest that you conduct additional investigations. Be sure you have my approval before proceeding to the next step.

5. Once you have a clear sense of the variety of explanations for your topic, conduct an experiment in which you represent or re-create historical findings or an experiment in which you

illustrate current research. Write a lab report that outlines the following (see record sheet 1, page 100):

- the research question you are investigating
- the hypothesis you are testing
- the methods of collecting data
- appropriate measurement or data analysis techniques
- data records
- findings
- your own conclusions

Given the nature of earth science themes, you might need to conduct your experiment using data generated by researchers who have more sophisticated technological resources. If so, access the variety of online sources that monitor cosmological, geophysical, and geochemical research projects and that offer up-to-date information on your topic. Although these sites are too numerous to list here, examples include NASA's K–12 Internet Initiative for the Quest Projects at http://quest.arc.nasa.gov or the Public Use of Remote Sensing Data website at http://rsd.gsfc.nasa.gov. Always record your sources.

6. Plan how you will create an interactive museum display that shows what you have learned. Your display must have several components:

- an overview and explanation of your investigation
- a presentation of the folktales you used
- a historical or conceptual time line that outlines the evolution of humankind's understanding of the processes or systems
- an explanation of current theories in this area
- a report on experimentation in which you represent historical findings or illustrate current thinking

At least one of these components must engage the viewer in some form of interaction with the information, such as question-and-answer cards, flip-up information panels, simulations, slides, web site access, or formats of your own design. Once you have a plan, sign up for a conference.

7. Once you have completed your display, I will help you set it up in a location and will ask you to make a final presentation. Before you present it to me, share your display with a peer to get feedback. In the final presentation, I will ask you to describe your display and I will review the display. Be prepared to answer questions about your work.

Record Sheet 1: Experiment Format

Experiment Title	
❑ Historical Re-creation ❑ Current Scientific Research	
Research question	
Hypothesis	
Data collection methods	
Measurement and data analysis (attach)	
Data records (attach)	
Findings	
Conclusions	

Guided by Performance, ©1998 Zephyr Press, Tucson, Arizona

Soil Sample
Classroom Implementation Guide

Curriculum Area: Physical Science
Products

Laboratory notebook
Journal
Research question
Research design
Laboratory report

Time: 2 weeks

Curriculum Notes

Please read the student task sheets carefully. Note any materials you will need for each task. Performance criteria are listed in the teacher checklist.

This assessment package presents students with a problem to solve using deductive reasoning. Given a sample of soil, they determine its components through a series of laboratory tests. Students are expected to establish a research question, design a laboratory investigation, conduct the tests, draw conclusions, and write a report stating the findings.

Resource List

Beisenherz, Paul, and M. Dantonio. 1996. *Using the Learning Cycle to Teach Physical Science.* Portsmouth, N.H.: Heinemann.

Brady, James, and A. Humiston. 1984. *General Chemistry: Principles and Structure.* 4th ed. New York: Wiley.

McGraw-Hill Dictionary of Chemical Terms. 1985. New York: McGraw-Hill.

Performance Assessment Matrix

Package Title: Soil Sample

Curriculum Area: Physical Science

Package: Grade 8

Student: _____

Content Knowledge

Science: Understands the structure and properties of matter
Identifies questions that can be answered through scientific investigation
Uses appropriate tools and techniques to gather, analyze, and interpret data
Designs and conducts scientific investigations

Content Skills

Literacy	Mathematics	Science	Social Studies	Visual Arts
Reading	Problem solving	Defining questions	Acquiring information	Creating
for aesthetic response	Communication	Forming hypotheses	reading	conceptual skills
for information/understanding	Reasoning	Investigating	study skills	production skills
for critical analysis/evaluation	Connecting	Observing	reference skills	evaluation skills
Writing	Estimation	Monitoring	technical skills	application
for response/expression	Numeration	Measuring	Organizing/Using information	Responding
for social interaction	Computation	Keeping records	thinking skills	descriptive skills
for information/understanding	Data analysis	Transforming records	decision-making skills	analytical skills
for critical analysis/evaluation	Measurement	Collaborating	metacognitive skills	valuing skills
Listening	Patterning/Relating	Interpreting information	Relationships	application
for response/expression		Integrating information	personal skills	
for information/understanding			group interaction	
for critical analysis/evaluation			social/political participation	
Speaking			Historical thinking	
for response/expression			chronological thinking	
for social interaction			historical comprehension	
for information/understanding			analysis and interpretation	
for critical analysis/evaluation			historical research	
			issues and decisions	

Guided by Performance, ©1998 Zephyr Press, Tucson, Arizona

Performance Assessment Matrix

Performance Skills

Cognitive Strategies	Task Management Strategies	Student Role	Assessment Products	Evaluation Format
Comparison	Analyzing the task	Museum curator	Portfolio	Student checklist (attached)
Classification	Establishing time lines	Reviewer	Publication	Teacher checklist (attached)
Induction	Staying productive	Engineer/Designer	Demonstration	Analytic scoring guide/ rubric (attached)
Deduction	Meeting deadlines	Representative	Performance	Holistic scoring guide (attached)
Error analysis	Accepting feedback	Expert witness	Exhibition	
Constructing support	Working cooperatively	Character		
Abstracting	Making a contribution	Ad agency director		
Analyzing perspectives	Respecting others	Tour organizer		
Decision making	Accessing resources	Bank manager		
Investigation	Striving for accuracy	Psychologist/Sociologist		
Experimental inquiry	Striving for excellence	Archaeologist		
Problem solving		Philosopher		
Invention		Historian		
		Writer/Editor		
		Teacher		
		Job applicant		
		Speaker/Listener		
		Scientist		

Anecdotal Observations

Teacher Checklist for "Soil Sample"

Performance Criteria	Excellent	Satisfactory	Needs Improvement
Task 1			
▪ Distinguishes properties of solids	_____	_____	_____
▪ Classifies and separates components of solids	_____	_____	_____
▪ Labels component properties of solids	_____	_____	_____
Task 2			
▪ Distinguishes five stages of soil formation	_____	_____	_____
▪ Identifies questions and concepts that guide scientific investigation	_____	_____	_____
▪ Designs and conducts scientific investigation	_____	_____	_____
Task 3			
▪ Finds mass of substance	_____	_____	_____
▪ Finds volume of substance	_____	_____	_____
▪ Calculates density of substance	_____	_____	_____
▪ Analyzes data and makes generalizations	_____	_____	_____
▪ Uses mathematics to improve investigations	_____	_____	_____
▪ Identifies components of soil samples using periodic chart of elements	_____	_____	_____
▪ Understands that a substance has characteristic properties such as density, boiling point, and solubility, none of which are affected by size of sample	_____	_____	_____
▪ Understands that chemical elements do not break down during normal laboratory reactions	_____	_____	_____
▪ Formulates new questions based on investigations	_____	_____	_____
Task 4			
▪ Uses technology to improve communication	_____	_____	_____
▪ Formulates and revises scientific explanations using logic and evidence	_____	_____	_____
▪ Recognizes and analyzes alternative explanations	_____	_____	_____
▪ Communicates and defends scientific conclusion	_____	_____	_____

Guided by Performance, ©1998 Zephyr Press, Tucson, Arizona

Soil Sample
Student Guide

Task 1: Preparatory Analysis

1. I will give each of you a 100 ml beaker that contains soil obtained from a local construction site. Conduct a preliminary analysis of the soil to determine the presence of organic and inorganic substances. Recall the five components of soil, draw five boxes on a sheet of paper, and label each box with one component. Look closely at your soil sample and separate out the components you see, placing each in the appropriate box.

2. Next to each component you have a sample for, draw a picture of the particles. Once separated, they will be easier to identify according to their characteristics. Note these characteristics in the boxes.

3. Write below the box your guess about what soil component it is. These characteristics, drawings, and guesses will guide your inquiry later.

Task 2: Establishing a Research Question and a Research Design

1. In your laboratory notebook, write your answers to the following questions.
    -   How many solids were you able to separate from the sample?
    -   What steps did you take to separate these solids?
    -   What stage of soil formation does this sample appear to indicate?

2. Write a research question that captures the outcome of your soil analysis. Your research question reflects the type of soil you believe you were given.

3. Design a process to deduce the type of soil (called the "research design"). Recall the property tests that were described in class and in your textbook. Your research design will indicate which property tests you will employ to analyze your sample.

4. Write a description of the process you use in the laboratory to determine the answer to your research question.

Task 3: Soil Analysis

This stage of the process may take up to four class periods.

1. In your laboratory notebook, write each of the following questions and complete them during the laboratory analysis:
    -   What component am I analyzing today?
    -   What mathematical calculations did I make?

- What were my findings?
- What conclusion was I able to make?

2. Weigh each component using a consistent unit of measure to determine the volume. Refer to the periodic chart of the elements discussed in class. Find the mass of the sample, then calculate the density using your figures for volume and mass. In your laboratory notebook, show how you arrived at each of these findings.

3. Draw from the list of analytic strategies discussed in class to determine what elements from the periodic chart are present in the soil sample. Note these results in your daily laboratory journal. Recall that scientific inquiry is a recursive process. Review your initial research question. Have any of your findings caused you to revise this question? If so, what led you to the new conclusion? Will a new research question require you to reanalyze any of the soil samples?

4. Turn in your laboratory notebooks.

Task 4: Conclusions and Summary Findings

1. Stand back from the data collected, examine it carefully in light of the research question you created earlier, summarize the data collected, and draw conclusions. Take notes for each in your laboratory notebook.

2. Write a formal report of your research. Your research report must include the following components:
   - *title page*
   - *abstract (state the research question and principal findings)*
   - *background section*
   - *research question and research design*
   - *summary of evidence gathered and findings, conclusions, and discussion of what you learned from this analysis*
   - *references*

      Guided by Performance, ©1998 Zephyr Press, Tucson, Arizona

Human Genetics
Classroom Implementation Guide

Curriculum Areas: Life Science, Language Arts

Products

Family tree
Written report
Essay or oral debate

Time: 1 week

Curriculum Notes

Please read the student task sheets carefully. Note any materials you will need for each task. Performance criteria are listed in the teacher checklist.

Why do some people seem to inherit certain physical characteristics and others do not? This is a question middle school students often ask as they watch their own bodies change rapidly in a short period of time. This assessment package requires students to answer this question by observing and recording traits that can be traced through generations. In addition, it extends their understanding of genetics through awareness of the roles that inheritance and environment play in shaping traits. Finally, it asks students to consider the ethical implications of scientific knowledge.

Resource List

The government's Human Genome Project has hundreds of research papers, articles, books, and multimedia resources to assist students in gathering recent information on genetics. The home page for the Project on the World Wide Web is http://www.oml.gov/TechResources/HumanGenome/

For task 1, note that designs for family trees vary widely. Most public libraries and school libraries have books on genealogies that will have models of family trees.

Performance Assessment Matrix

Package Title: Human Genetics

Curriculum Area: Life Science and Language Arts

Package: Grade 8

Student: _____

Content Knowledge

Science: Standard C (Life Science)

Language Arts: Standard 7 (Students conduct research on issues; gather, evaluate, and synthesize data from a variety of sources.)

Content Skills

Literacy		Mathematics		Science		Social Studies		Visual Arts	
Reading		Problem solving		Defining questions		Acquiring information		Creating	
for aesthetic response		Communication		Forming hypotheses		*reading*		*conceptual skills*	
for information/understanding		Reasoning		Investigating		*study skills*		*production skills*	
for critical analysis/evaluation		Connecting		Observing		*reference skills*		*evaluation skills*	
Writing		Estimation		Monitoring		*technical skills*		*application*	
for response/expression		Numeration		Measuring		Organizing/Using information		Responding	
for social interaction		Computation		Keeping records		*thinking skills*		*descriptive skills*	
for information/understanding		Data analysis		Transforming records		*decision-making skills*		*analytical skills*	
for critical analysis/evaluation		Measurement		Collaborating		*metacognitive skills*		*valuing skills*	
Listening		Patterning/Relating		Interpreting information		Relationships		*application*	
for response/expression				Integrating information		*personal skills*			
for information/understanding						*group interaction*			
for critical analysis/evaluation						*social/political participation*			
Speaking						Historical thinking			
for response/expression						*chronological thinking*			
for social interaction						*historical comprehension*			
for information/understanding						*analysis and interpretation*			
for critical analysis/evaluation						*historical research*			
						issues and decisions			

Guided by Performance, ©1998 Zephyr Press, Tucson, Arizona

Performance Assessment Matrix

Performance Skills

Cognitive Strategies	Task Management Strategies	Student Role	Assessment Products	Evaluation Format
Comparison	Analyzing the task	Museum curator	Portfolio	Student checklist (attached)
Classification	Establishing time lines	Reviewer	Publication	Teacher checklist (attached)
Induction	Staying productive	Engineer/Designer	Demonstration	Analytic scoring guide/ rubric (attached)
Deduction	Meeting deadlines	Representative	Performance	Holistic scoring guide (attached)
Error analysis	Accepting feedback	Expert witness	Exhibition	
Constructing support	Working cooperatively	Character		
Abstracting	Making a contribution	Ad agency director		
Analyzing perspectives	Respecting others	Tour organizer		
Decision making	Accessing resources	Bank manager		
Investigation	Striving for accuracy	Psychologist/Sociologist		
Experimental inquiry	Striving for excellence	Archaeologist		
Problem solving		Philosopher		
Invention		Historian		
		Writer/Editor		
		Teacher		
		Job applicant		
		Speaker/Listener		

Anecdotal Observations

Teacher Checklist for "Human Genetics"

Performance Criteria	Excellent	Satisfactory	Needs Improvement
Task 1			
■ Understands that every organism requires a set of instructions that specifies its traits	_____	_____	_____
■ Understands that heredity is the passage of these instructions from one generation to another	_____	_____	_____
Task 2			
■ Uses electronic technology to access relevant data	_____	_____	_____
■ Uses a variety of sources to answer questions and support a position	_____	_____	_____
■ Uses note taking to summarize main ideas and credits sources	_____	_____	_____
■ Explains that a gene carries a single unit of information	_____	_____	_____
■ Concludes that an inherited trait of an individual can be determined by one or by many genes and that a single gene can influence one trait	_____	_____	_____
■ Identifies main ideas and supporting details	_____	_____	_____
■ Compares and contrasts information on the same topic from various types of resources	_____	_____	_____
Task 3			
■ Comprehends, interprets, and evaluates information from a variety of nonfiction sources by reading and listening	_____	_____	_____
■ Writes a rationale that is supported by reasons	_____	_____	_____
■ Produces finished writing that has correct spelling and mechanics	_____	_____	_____
■ Communicates effectively in a small group of familiar people	_____	_____	_____

Guided by Performance, ©1998 Zephyr Press, Tucson, Arizona

Human Genetics
Student Guide

Task 1: My Family Pedigree

Have you often wondered why you have some of the same characteristics as your parents or grand-parents? What causes this passing down of characteristics? Why do some relatives have these characteristics and others not? These are important questions that scientists called *geneticists* try to answer.

1. To find out what traits have been passed on from one generation to the next, interview relatives from various generations to find out what characteristics they have in common. Secondary sex characteristics (such as male baldness, color blindness, and hemophilia) or other traits (such as left-handedness) represent observable characteristics that are more easily determined.

2. Make a chart or pedigree of your family (see example 1, page 113). Start with your own siblings and parents and work backward one generation at a time—your grandparents, great-grandparents, and so on. Don't forget to chart your mother's and your father's ancestors. Note on your chart who exhibits the specific characteristics.

3. Look for patterns. For example, do certain members of the family have baldness? Is it every generation or some generations and not others?

Task 2: Nature or Nurture?

How are these characteristics passed from one generation to the next? Scientists have tried to answer this question through observation for centuries. Are these characteristics inherited (in other words, by nature) or, have they been acquired through the environment (are they nurtured)? In the past twenty years much has been written about the most likely answers to these questions.

1. Using a computer that has a browser that will enable you to search the World Wide Web, use a search engine such as Yahoo, Lycos, or Gopher to locate articles that deal with possible answers to these questions. A good key phrase to start a search is "human genetics" or just "genetics." Hyperlinks will be embedded in the lists of articles or organizations that have dealt with these questions. Use these links to find the specific articles that reference these questions.

2. Read at least three articles. Take notes on each article on a separate note card, paying specific attention to the conclusion of each article. Note the bibliographic information on each note card.

3. Draw conclusions about how scientists have answered these questions and summarize these in writing, making sure you mention each of the studies and the names of the researchers. End your report by stating what you have learned.

Task 3: The Ethical Use of Scientific Knowledge

In your reading of the articles about whether traits are transmitted by nature (inherited) or through the environment (nurtured), did you notice that some of these traits can make life difficult or even tragic? Examples include Down syndrome, hemophilia, and alcohol dependence. Scientists know much more than they did even twenty years ago about the causes of these disorders.

1. Respond in writing (agree or disagree with) to the following question: Society and individual people would be better off if scientists would breed undesirable traits out of people. In explaining your response, describe the values you have that support your opinion. In other words, state why this would be good or bad for the individual or for society. Should scientific knowledge be used to change nature? Explain why or why not.

2. Share your opinions with the rest of the class.

3. As an alternative to a written analysis, you may wish to plan an oral debate with other classmates or students from another class.

Guided by Performance, ©1998 Zephyr Press, Tucson, Arizona

Example 1: Family Pedigree Chart

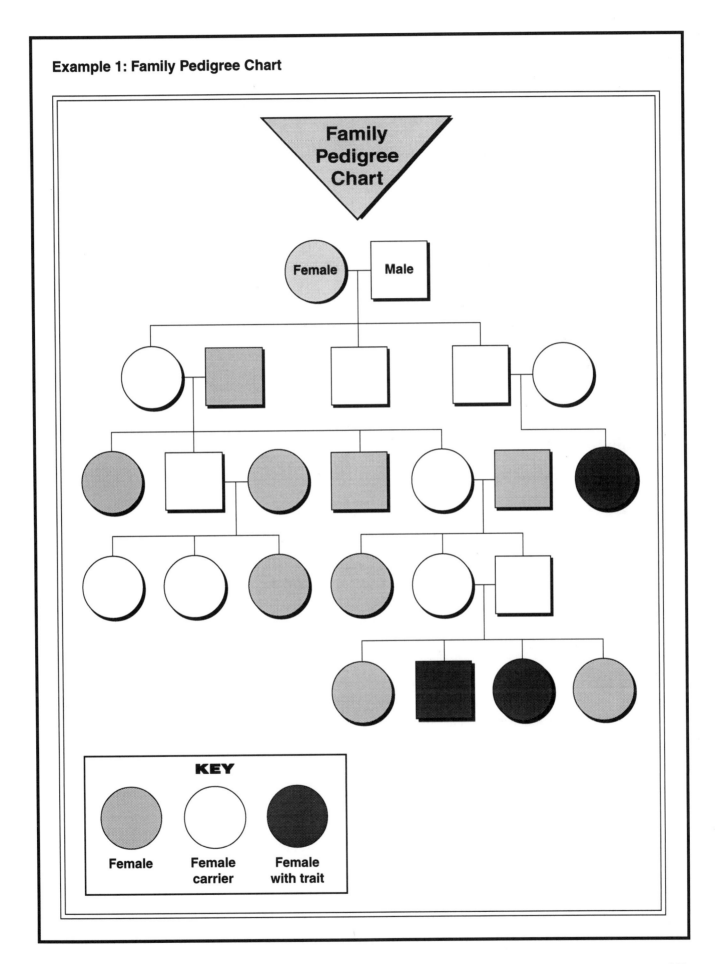

Putting Math to Work
Classroom Implementation Guide

Curriculum Areas: Mathematics, Technology
Products

Chart of math concepts
Four mathematical problems
Feedback form
Database spreadsheet

Time: 1 to 2 weeks

Curriculum Notes

Please read the student task sheets carefully. Note any materials you will need for each task. Performance criteria are listed in the teacher checklist.

This assessment package requires each student in an eighth grade math class to generate four problems that other students can solve. The four problems will each deal with one of the following: number and operation concepts, geometry and measurement concepts, functions and algebra concepts, and statistics and probability concepts. This project is ideally suited to an end-of-year project so students can demonstrate their understanding of these mathematical concepts by designing problems for next year's students to solve.

Resource List

Burns, Marilyn. 1990. *A Collection of Math Lessons from Grades 6 through 8*. White Plains, N.Y.: Math Solutions.

Kulm, Gerald. 1994. *Mathematics Assessment: What Works in the Classroom*. San Francisco: Jossey-Bass.

Moon, Jean, and Linda Shulman. 1995. *Finding Connections: Linking Assessment, Instruction, and Curriculum in Elementary Mathematics*. Portsmouth, N.H.: Heinemann.

Performance Assessment Matrix

Package Title: Putting Math to Work

Curriculum Area: Mathematics, Technology

Package: Grade 8

Student: _____

Content Knowledge

Mathematics: Explores problems and describes results using graphical, numerical, physical, algebraic, and verbal mathematical models

Uses problem solving approaches to investigate and understand mathematical content

Technology: Employs effectively a word processing or database management program to produce a product

Content Skills

Literacy	Mathematics		Science	Social Studies		Visual Arts	
Reading	Problem solving		Defining questions	Acquiring information		Creating	
for aesthetic response	Communication		Forming hypotheses	*reading*		*conceptual skills*	
for information/understanding	Reasoning		Investigating	*study skills*		*production skills*	
for critical analysis/evaluation	Connecting		Observing	*reference skills*		*evaluation skills*	
Writing	Estimation		Monitoring	*technical skills*		*application*	
for response/expression	Numeration		Measuring	Organizing/Using information		Responding	
for social interaction	Computation		Keeping records	*thinking skills*		*descriptive skills*	
for information/understanding	Data analysis		Transforming records	*decision-making skills*		*analytical skills*	
for critical analysis/evaluation	Measurement		Collaborating	*metacognitive skills*		*valuing skills*	
Listening	Patterning/Relating		Interpreting information	Relationships		*application*	
for response/expression			Integrating information	*personal skills*			
for information/understanding				*group interaction*			
for critical analysis/evaluation				*social/political participation*			
Speaking				Historical thinking			
for response/expression				*chronological thinking*			
for social interaction				*historical comprehension*			
for information/understanding				*analysis and interpretation*			
for critical analysis/evaluation				*historical research*			
				issues and decisions			

Performance Assessment Matrix

Performance Skills

Cognitive Strategies		Task Management Strategies		Student Role		Assessment Products		Evaluation Format	
Comparison		Analyzing the task		Museum curator		Portfolio		Student checklist (attached)	
Classification		Establishing time lines		Reviewer		Publication		Teacher checklist (attached)	▓
Induction	▓	Staying productive		Engineer/Designer		Demonstration		Analytic scoring guide/ rubric (attached)	
Deduction		Meeting deadlines		Representative		Performance		Holistic scoring guide (attached)	
Error analysis		Accepting feedback		Expert witness		Exhibition			
Constructing support	▓	Working cooperatively		Character					
Abstracting		Making a contribution	▓	Ad agency director					
Analyzing perspectives		Respecting others		Tour organizer					
Decision making		Accessing resources		Bank manager					
Investigation		Striving for accuracy		Psychologist/Sociologist					
Experimental inquiry		Striving for excellence		Archaeologist					
Problem solving	▓			Philosopher					
Invention	▓			Historian					
				Writer/Editor					
				Teacher	▓				
				Job applicant					
				Speaker/Listener					

Anecdotal Observations

Guided by Performance, ©1998 Zephyr Press, Tucson, Arizona

Teacher Checklist for "Putting Math to Work"

Performance Criteria	Excellent	Satisfactory	Needs Improvement
Task 1			
▪ Develops number sense for whole numbers, fractions, decimals, integers, and rational numbers	____	____	____
▪ Identifies similar and congruent shapes	____	____	____
▪ Represents relationships with tables, graphs in the coordinate plane, and verbal or symbolic rules	____	____	____
▪ Collects and organizes data and displays data with appropriate charts and graphs	____	____	____
Task 2			
▪ Identifies math expectations in each of the four content areas in a clear and concise way	____	____	____
▪ States the problem in a real situation and poses a question for the solver to complete	____	____	____
▪ States a strategy in clear and logical steps that will correctly solve the sample problem	____	____	____
▪ Writes a rationale that demonstrates an in-depth and clear understanding of the mathematics concepts being used to solve the problem	____	____	____
Task 3			
▪ Constructs feedback form that outlines clear expectations for areas of written feedback	____	____	____
Task 4			
▪ Constructs a database to record scores received on math problems	____	____	____
▪ Employs effectively a word processing or database management program to produce the product	____	____	____

Putting Math to Work
Student Guide

Task 1: Identifying Key Concepts

1. Review the contents of the math textbook you have used this past year.

2. On a piece of paper, draw four columns and at the top of each column write "numbers and operation concepts," "geometry and measurement concepts," "function and algebra concepts," and "statistics and probability concepts." Scan the chapters in your text to identify the key concepts in each of these four areas and list these on the paper in the appropriate columns. This sheet of paper will be your guide in constructing four problems.

Task 2: Creating Four Problems

1. Create problems that enable other students to use the concepts. Create problems that middle school students can relate to; in other words, the problems should reflect real-life situations (see example 1, page 120).

2. Create a handout (see record sheet 1, page 121) with the following components to enable the problem solver to solve the problem more effectively (see example 1, page 120).
    - The expectations or outcomes—Statements of math knowledge or math skill that the solver will be expected to demonstrate in solving the problem
    - Statement of problem—Description of the conditions that have created the problem, with enough detail to create the sense of realism described above; includes specific information needed to solve the problem and ends with a question that directs the solver's next step
    - Strategy for problem solving—Series of steps that will lead to the correct solution; also area where solver's work is shown
    - Solution and rationale—Space for solver to provide answer and explain how it was arrived at

Task 3: Field Testing Problems

1. Test your problems with peers to determine if the problems are clear enough for others to work them. Select four of your classmates (either from within the same math class or from others at the same level), each to work one of the problems and give you feedback. Decide how much time you expect them to take to work the problems and be sure they know your expectation.

Guided by Performance, ©1998 Zephyr Press, Tucson, Arizona

2. Design a feedback form for each solver that lists things you would like to know about your problems.

Task 4: Compiling Results

1. Review the comments and edit your problems to correct or make clearer those components that need extra work. Use a computer that has a word processing or database program. Construct a system for me to use to record results of next year's students attempts at solving your problems. Build and store the file on a floppy diskette so you can work on it at several different locations. The record-keeping system must allow me to record each student's name and class, the title of the math problem, and the score the students received on the problem. I will give additional credit if your database enables me to record scores for each component of the problem (that is, strategy and solution-rationale).

2. Turn in your record-keeping system on a diskette.

Example 1: Sample Problem

Putting Math to Work: Solving Everyday Problems
Math Content Area: Number and operations concepts

Name: *Sally Jones*   **Class Period:** *4th*

Expectations

The student will:
- compute with whole numbers
- develop, analyze, and explain methods for computations
- use computation, estimation, and proportions to solve problems

Statement of the Problem

Sally and Mike accompanied their parents to a major league baseball game. At the end of the fifth inning, the public address announcer invited all the fans to guess today's attendance and the fan with the guess closest to the actual attendance would receive an autographed baseball. The program booklet listed the stadium capacity as 65,000, in 250 sections on two decks that completely surround the field. Sally and Mike count 25 seats in a row. As they look across the stadium, they can see that it is more than half filled and all the outfield sections are closed off to spectators. How would you advise Sally and Mike to find the closest estimate to the actual attendance?

Strategy for Solving the Problem

The facts as I know them are: the stadium holds 65,000; there are 25 seats in a row and 250 sections in the stadium. Sections 220–250 in the upper deck outfield and section 189–219 in the lower deck are closed. 61 sections are closed meaning 15,250 seats cannot be occupied, leaving 49,750 seats if every seat was filled, which they aren't.

Select five sections at random from the lower deck and five sections at random from the upper deck and count how many people are sitting in each section (we can see there are more people in the lower deck than in the upper deck). Calculate the average number of seats filled in the five lower and 5 upper deck sections. Multiply this average by the total number of sections in lower deck and the total number of sections in the upper deck, add the two to arrive at the estimated attendance.

Solution and Rationale

Since I had no way of knowing what the actual attendance was that day (it wasn't given in the Statement of the Problem), I thought that the real problem was to find the process for solving the problem rather than the actual correct answer.

I assumed that all sections had the same number of seats (250). I checked the listed capacity of 65,000 and divided that number by the number of sections. I then subtracted the number of sections in the outfield that were closed that then gave me a remaining number of seats if all seats were filled, which I was told they were not.

Since I couldn't actually count the number of seats filled, the shorter way was to find a average number of seats filled in a section, realizing that the lower deck usually fills first and fewer people choose to sit in the upper deck. Therefore, a sample of sections would be a manageable count. After finding the upper and lower averages, I multiplied those two numbers of the remaining number of sections after I earlier subtracted those sections closed off.

This process gave me an estimate that I could enter in the contest. I hope I won!

Guided by Performance, ©1998 Zephyr Press, Tucson, Arizona

Record Sheet 1: Feedback Form

Name:

Name of Problem:

Expectations: Were they . . . (list criteria here)

Statement of the problem: Was it . . . (list criteria here)

Strategy for solving the problem: Was it . . . (list criteria here)

Solution and rationale: Was it . . . (list criteria here)

Understanding HIV and AIDS
Classroom Implementation Guide

Curriculum Areas: Health, Mathematics, Language Arts
Products

Public awareness advertising campaign (television and radio spots, billboards, pamphlets and other print)

Time: 6 weeks
Curriculum Notes

Please read the student task sheets carefully. Note any materials you will need for each task. Performance criteria are listed in the teacher checklist.

An excellent resource for **step 1** is Madaras (1988). You will want to review and evaluate resources before making them available to students.

In **step 6**, students do not need to produce actual television and radio spots; they should, however, be able to draft the text and produce graphics for the spots.

Resource List

Records and Statistics

AIDS Action Council, 2033 M. St. NW, Ste. 802, Washington, DC 20036; (202) 986-1300

AIDS Resource Center of Wisconsin, P.O. Box 92505, Milwaukee, WI 53202; (414) 273-1991

American Indian Health Care Association, 245 E. Sixth St., Ste. 499, St. Paul, MN 55101; (612) 293-0233

American Red Cross, Office of HIV/AIDS Education, 1709 New York Ave., Ste. 208, Washington, DC 20006; (202) 434-4074

Hispanic AIDS Forum, 121 Avenue of the Americas, Room 505, New York, NY 10013; (212) 966-6662

Multicultural Training Resource Center, 1540 Market St., Ste. 320, San Francisco, CA 94102; (415) 861-2142

National AIDS Network, 2033 M. St. NW, Ste. 800, Washington, DC 20036.

National Black Women's Health Project, 1217 Gordon St. SW, Washington, DC 20036; (202) 232-3600

National Minority AIDS Council, 200 First St. NE, 4th Floor, Washington, DC 20002; (202) 544-1076

US Public Health Service, Public Affairs Office, Room 717-H, 200 Independence Ave. NW, Washington, DC 20201; (202) 690-6867

Nonfiction Materials

Blake, J. 1996. *Risky Times: How to Be AIDS-Smart and Stay Healthy—A Guide for Teenagers.* New York: Workman.

Fiedler, J., and H. Fiedler. 1990. *Be Smart about Sex: Facts for Young People.* Hillside, N.J.: Enslow.

Ford, M. T. 1992. *100 Questions and Answers about AIDS: A Guide for Young People.* New York: Macmillan.

Hein, K., and T. DiGeronimo. 1989. *AIDS: A Guide for Young People.* New York: Macmillan.

Madaras, L. 1988. *Linda Madaras Talks to Teens about AIDS: An Essential Guide for Parents, Teachers, and Young People.* New York: Newmarket Press.

Newton, D. 1992. *AIDS Issues: A Handbook.* Hillside, N.J.: Enslow.

Nourse, A. E. 1990. *Teen Guide to AIDS Prevention.* New York: Franklin Watts.

Starkman, N. 1988. *Your Decisions.* Seattle: Comprehensive Health Education Foundation.

Udin, S. 1988. *Rappin', Teens, Sex, and AIDS.* San Francisco: Multicultural Training Resource Center.

Firsthand Accounts

Durant, P. R. 1992. *When Heroes Die.* New York: Atheneum.

Girard, L. 1991. *Alex, the Kid with AIDS.* New York: Albert Whitman.

Greenberg, K. 1992. *Magic Johnson: Champion with a Cause.* Minneapolis: Lerner.

Koertge, R. 1988. *The Arizona Kid.* New York: Little Brown.

Kuklin, S. 1989. *Fighting Back: What Some People Are Doing about AIDS.* New York: Putnam.

Schilling, S., and J. Swain. 1989. *My Name Is Jonathan and I Have AIDS.* Denver, Colo.: Prickly Pear.

Starkman, N. 1988. *Z's Gift.* Seattle, Wash.: Comprehensive Health Education Foundation.

White, R., and A. M. Cunningham. 1991. *Ryan White: My Own Story.* New York: Signet.

Performance Assessment Matrix

Package Title: Understanding HIV and AIDS

Curriculum Area: Health, Mathematics, Language Arts

Package: Grade 8

Student: _____

Content Knowledge

Health:	Standard 1 (knows the availability and effective use of health services, products, and information)
	Standard 7 (knows how to maintain and promote personal health)
	Standard 8 (knows essential concepts about the prevention and control of disease)
Mathematics:	Standard 2: Mathematics as communication (use the skills of reading and listening)
	Standard 10: Statistics (systematically collect, organize, and describe data; construct, read, and interpret tables, charts, and graphs; make inferences and convincing arguments that are based on data analysis)
Language Arts:	Standard 1 (read a wide range of print and nonprint text to acquire new information)
	Standard 4 (adjust use of spoken, written, and visual language to communicate effectively with a variety of audiences and for different purposes)
	Standard 8 (use a variety of technical and information resources to gather and synthesize information and to create and communicate knowledge)

Content Skills

Literacy		Mathematics		Science		Social Studies		Visual Arts	
Reading		Problem solving		Defining questions		Acquiring information		Creating	
for aesthetic response		Communication	▓	Forming hypotheses		*reading*		*conceptual skills*	
for information/understanding	▓	Reasoning		Investigating		*study skills*		*production skills*	▓
for critical analysis/evaluation		Connecting		Observing		*reference skills*		*evaluation skills*	
Writing		Estimation		Monitoring		*technical skills*		*application*	▓
for response/expression		Numeration		Measuring		Organizing/Using information		Responding	
for social interaction		Computation		Keeping records		*thinking skills*		*descriptive skills*	
for information/understanding	▓	Data analysis	▓	Transforming records		*decision-making skills*		*analytical skills*	
for critical analysis/evaluation		Measurement		Collaborating		*metacognitive skills*		*valuing skills*	
Listening		Patterning/Relating		Interpreting information	▓	Relationships		*application*	
for response/expression				Integrating information		*personal skills*			
for information/understanding	▓					*group interaction*			
for critical analysis/evaluation						*social/political participation*			
Speaking						Historical thinking			
for response/expression						*chronological thinking*			
for social interaction						*historical comprehension*			
for information/understanding	▓					*analysis and interpretation*			
for critical analysis/evaluation						*historical research*			
						issues and decisions			

Guided by Performance, ©1998 Zephyr Press, Tucson, Arizona

Performance Assessment Matrix

Performance Skills

Cognitive Strategies	Task Management Strategies	Student Role	Assessment Products	Evaluation Format
Comparison	Analyzing the task	Museum curator	Portfolio	Student checklist (attached)
Classification	Establishing time lines	Reviewer	Publication	Teacher checklist (attached)
Induction	Staying productive	Engineer/Designer	Demonstration	Analytic scoring guide/ rubric (attached)
Deduction	Meeting deadlines	Representative	Performance	Holistic scoring guide (attached)
Error analysis	Accepting feedback	Expert witness	Exhibition	
Constructing support	Working cooperatively	Character		
Abstracting	Making a contribution	Ad agency director		
Analyzing perspectives	Respecting others	Tour organizer		
Decision making	Accessing resources	Bank manager		
Investigation	Striving for accuracy	Psychologist/Sociologist		
Experimental inquiry	Striving for excellence	Archaeologist		
Problem solving		Philosopher		
Invention		Historian		
		Writer/Editor		
		Teacher		
		Job applicant		
		Speaker/Listener		

Anecdotal Observations

Teacher Checklist for "Understanding HIV and AIDS"

Performance Criteria	Excellent	Satisfactory	Needs Improvement
Step 1			
■ Selects an appropriate focus for a public awareness campaign on HIV and AIDS	____	____	____
■ Shares selection and provides rationale at conference	____	____	____
Step 2			
■ Conducts a thorough literature search	____	____	____
■ Conducts a thorough Internet search	____	____	____
■ Accesses resources and collects two sources from three categories of data			
• records and statistics	____	____	____
• nonfiction materials	____	____	____
• firsthand accounts	____	____	____
■ Develops a complete data gathering plan by recording these sources	____	____	____
■ Provides evidence of preparation when presenting data-gathering plan	____	____	____
Step 3			
■ Gathers information for use in public awareness campaign	____	____	____
■ Designs an effective strategy for recording facts, impressions, and resources	____	____	____
Step 4			
■ Gathers models to use in the process of designing own campaign	____	____	____
Step 5			
■ Takes comprehensive notes on the strategies other advertisers use to get attention, present facts, appeal to emotions, convey impressions, and inform the audience	____	____	____
■ Discusses how what has been learned from the models will be integrated into public awareness campaign	____	____	____
Step 6			
■ Develops a working draft of the following			
• television spot	____	____	____
• radio spot	____	____	____
• print advertisement	____	____	____
• billboard	____	____	____
• informational pamphlet	____	____	____
■ Includes accurate factual information about the focus in each element of the campaign	____	____	____
■ Conveys appropriate impression about focus in each element of campaign	____	____	____

Guided by Performance, ©1998 Zephyr Press, Tucson, Arizona

Teacher Checklist for "Understanding HIV and AIDS"

Performance Criteria	Excellent	Satisfactory	Needs Improvement
■ Provides accurate and complete information on resources that pertain to focus in each element of the campaign	_____	_____	_____
■ Integrates information from all three categories of data into the presentation	_____	_____	_____
■ Uses data in ways that demonstrate a solid understanding of the facts and issues associated with HIV and AIDS	_____	_____	_____
Step 7			
■ Self-assesses work before final review	_____	_____	_____
■ Solicits feedback from peers before final review	_____	_____	_____
■ Effectively presents campaign during agency meeting	_____	_____	_____
■ Answers questions about research and final products during agency meeting	_____	_____	_____
■ Demonstrates accurate and complete understanding of focus in every element of campaign	_____	_____	_____

Understanding HIV and AIDS
Student Guide

I n this assessment package, you demonstrate your understanding of the issues that surround HIV and AIDS. You present your understanding in a public awareness advertising campaign. The campaign includes television spots, radio spots, print advertisements, billboards, and informational pamphlets to distribute to health clinics.

Task: Public Awareness Advertising Campaign

1. Many issues surround HIV and AIDS. Select a particular issue or a set of related issues that you would like to address through a public awareness campaign. For example, you might focus on pediatric HIV and AIDS, on risk factors and exposure categories, on adolescents, on AIDS occurrences in various races and ethnic groups, on care givers and care-giving institutions, or on advocacy and research. Access general references on the topic. Sign up for a conference with me once you have settled on a focus. Be prepared to share your selection and the rationale behind selecting it.

2. Begin collecting data to support your campaign. Conduct a literature search and an internet search. Collect three categories of data: records and statistics on the disease; nonfiction materials; and diaries, letters, narratives, testimonials, and firsthand accounts of people who have been affected by the disease. Find at least two sources in each category. Complete a data-gathering plan. Once you have gathered enough materials, sign up for a conference and present your data-gathering plan.

3. Read, listen to, or view the materials to gather data. Keep track of specific facts you want to convey through your campaign, impressions you want to convey, and resources you want to highlight. Establish a balance in these three areas. Design your strategy for keeping track of the information (note cards, data sheet, computer file, and so on).

4. Before you design the elements of your campaign, gather models of television spots, radio spots, print advertisements, billboards, and informational pamphlets used in other public awareness efforts. Find at least one model for each element of your campaign.

5. Observe and take notes on the strategies advertising professionals use. Answer the following questions:
   - How does the advertiser get the attention of the audience?
   - How does the advertiser present facts?
   - In what ways does the advertiser appeal to the emotions of the audience?
   - How does the advertiser convey certain impressions?
   - How does the advertiser inform the audience about available resources?

Guided by Performance, ©1998 Zephyr Press, Tucson, Arizona

Use the same strategy for keeping track of this information that you designed in step 3. When you think your investigation of theses models has yielded you enough information, sign up for a conference to discuss how you will integrate this information into your campaign.

6. Develop a working draft or mock-up for each element of your campaign. As you work on each, make sure that you include factual information about your focus area, that you convey an impression, and that you provide information on resources. In addition, make sure you have integrated information from all three categories of data. Make sure that you understand this information and use it accurately to convey impressions and relay information. Incorporate information from your data sources if they are in the public domain (see example 1, pages 130–131). Always cite appropriate references.

7. Use the student checklist (see record sheet 1, page 132) to self-assess your work. Get feedback from your peers using the same criteria. When you are satisfied, I will conduct a simulated agency meeting in which small groups of students present their campaigns. During this presentation, I will give your work a final review. Be prepared to answer questions about your research and final products.

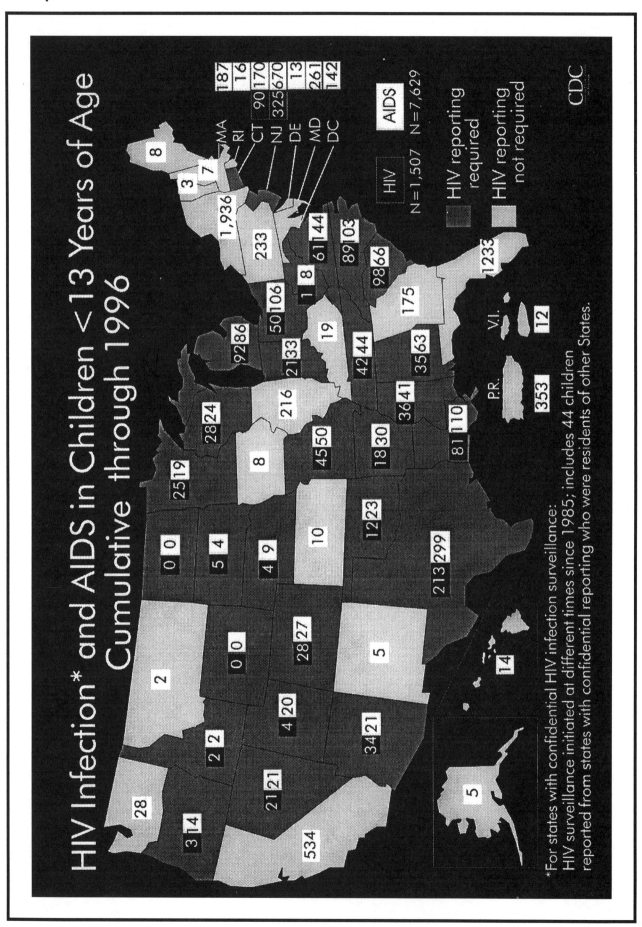

HIV Infection* and AIDS in Children <13 Years of Age
Cumulative through 1996

MA	187	90
RI	16	
CT	170	325
NJ	670	
DE	13	
MD	261	
DC	142	

HIV
N=1,507

AIDS
N=7,629

HIV reporting required

HIV reporting not required

CDC

*For states with confidential HIV infection surveillance:
HIV surveillance initiated at different times since 1985; includes 44 children
reported from states with confidential reporting who were residents of other States.

Guided by Performance, ©1998 Zephyr Press, Tucson, Arizona

AIDS in Children <13 Years of Age by Exposure Category, Reported in 1996 and Cumulative, United States

Exposure Category	1996		Cumulative 1982-1996	
	Number	%	Number	%
Perinatally acquired	606	89	6891	90
Transfusion-associated	9	1	373	5
Hemophilia	5	1	231	3
Risk not Reported	58	9	134	2
Total	678	100	7629	100

AIDS Cases in 13- to 19-Year Olds Reported in 1996 and 1996 Population Estimate of Adolescents by Race/Ethnicity, United States

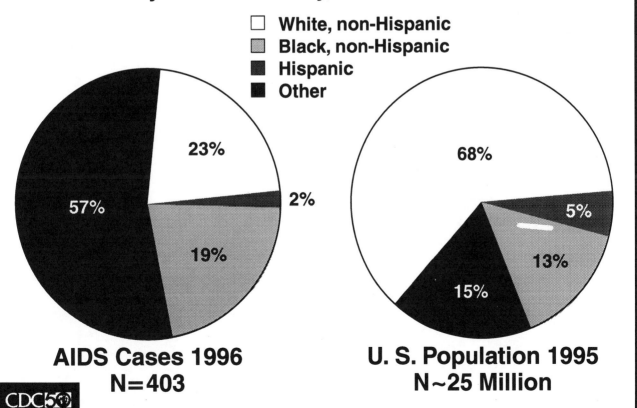

Record Sheet 1: Self-Assessment and Peer Feedback Checklist

Complete for each element of the campaign

How effective was the _____

in achieving the following goals:

Goal	Self-Assessment	Peer Assessment
Getting the attention of the audience		
Presenting accurate facts		
Appealing to emotions		
Conveying impressions		
Informing the audience about resources		
Integrating data from various sources		
Suggestions for improvement		

Guided by Performance, ©1998 Zephyr Press, Tucson, Arizona

Fractals
Classroom Implementation Guide

Curriculum Area: Mathematics

Products

Investigation for study team manual
Presentation at study team

Time: 2 weeks

Curriculum Notes

Please read the student task sheets carefully. Note any materials you will need for each task. Performance criteria are listed in the teacher checklist.

Fractal geometry is the focus of many innovative programs in mathematics education. You can obtain instruction from the following sources:

- The Math Forum website (http://forum.swarthmore.edu) lists more than one hundred online resources in this area (many sites also provide links to related sites and list additional print resources).
- The Geometer's Sketchpad (Key Curriculum Press 1995) affords students the opportunity to write scripts and generate fractals.
- The Fractal Microscope (NCSA 1997), an interactive tool for exploring fractals, can be downloaded from the National Center for Supercomputing Applications at http://www.ncsa.edu.

For an example for **step 2** that illustrates the integration of questions, prompts, and diagrams, students might want to access the variety of lesson plans available online (see The Math Forum). The fractals for this package are at mconnors@math.umass.edu. Please note that you must first obtain permission from Mary Ann Connors.

Performance Assessment Matrix

Package Title: Fractals

Curriculum Area: Mathematics

Package: Grade 8

Student: _____

Content Knowledge

Mathematics:
- Standard 1 (Problem solving)
- Standard 2 (Communication)
- Standard 3 (Reasoning)
- Standard 4 (Mathematical connections)
- Standard 8 (Patterns and functions)
- Standard 12 (Geometry)
- Standard 13 (Measurement)

Content Skills

Literacy	Mathematics	Science	Social Studies	Visual Arts
Reading	Problem solving	Defining questions	Acquiring information	Creating
for aesthetic response	Communication	Forming hypotheses	reading	conceptual skills
for information/understanding	Reasoning	Investigating	study skills	production skills
for critical analysis/evaluation	Connecting	Observing	reference skills	evaluation skills
Writing	Estimation	Monitoring	technical skills	application
for response/expression	Numeration	Measuring	Organizing/Using information	Responding
for social interaction	Computation	Keeping records	thinking skills	descriptive skills
for information/understanding	Data analysis	Transforming records	decision-making skills	analytical skills
for critical analysis/evaluation	Measurement	Collaborating	metacognitive skills	valuing skills
Listening	Patterning/Relating	Interpreting information	Relationships	application
for response/expression		Integrating information	personal skills	
for information/understanding			group interaction	
for critical analysis/evaluation			social/political participation	
Speaking			Historical thinking	
for response/expression			chronological thinking	
for social interaction			historical comprehension	
for information/understanding			analysis and interpretation	
for critical analysis/evaluation			historical research	
			issues and decisions	

Guided by Performance, ©1998 Zephyr Press, Tucson, Arizona

Performance Assessment Matrix

Performance Skills

Cognitive Strategies		Task Management Strategies		Student Role		Assessment Products		Evaluation Format	
Comparison		Analyzing the task		Museum curator		Portfolio		Student checklist (attached)	
Classification	▓	Establishing time lines		Reviewer		Publication	▓	Teacher checklist (attached)	▓
Induction		Staying productive		Engineer/Designer		Demonstration		Analytic scoring guide/ rubric (attached)	
Deduction		Meeting deadlines		Representative		Performance		Holistic scoring guide (attached)	
Error analysis		Accepting feedback	▓	Expert witness		Exhibition			
Constructing support		Working cooperatively		Character					
Abstracting		Making a contribution		Ad agency director					
Analyzing perspectives		Respecting others		Tour organizer					
Decision making		Accessing resources		Bank manager					
Investigation	▓	Striving for accuracy	▓	Psychologist/Sociologist					
Experimental inquiry		Striving for excellence		Archaeologist					
Problem solving	▓			Philosopher					
Invention				Historian					
				Writer/Editor					
				Teacher	▓				
				Job applicant					
				Speaker/Listener					

Anecdotal Observations

Teacher Checklist for "Fractals"

Performance Criteria	Excellent	Satisfactory	Needs Improvement
Step 1			
▪ Demonstrates understanding of fractals by selecting appropriate fractal image and aligning appropriate mathematical concepts and fractal properties with selection	_____	_____	_____
Step 2			
▪ Prepares logical sequence of investigative questions	_____	_____	_____
▪ Provides appropriate prompts, iterations, and diagrams in support of investigative questions	_____	_____	_____
Step 3			
▪ Submits complete planning sheet before conference	_____	_____	_____
▪ Demonstrates understanding of all terms, concepts, and problem-solving strategies relevant to the investigation	_____	_____	_____
▪ Presents the investigation in a logical, clear, and sequenced manner	_____	_____	_____
▪ Presents an accurate and well-reasoned solution to the investigations	_____	_____	_____
▪ Records feedback from the conference	_____	_____	_____
Step 4			
▪ Incorporates feedback into preparation of final draft	_____	_____	_____
▪ Prepares a complete and organized final draft that includes the questions, prompts, iterations, and diagrams necessary to conduct the investigation and allows space for students to work the problems and record solutions	_____	_____	_____
Step 5			
▪ Presents the investigation effectively to the study team; asks questions, provides prompts, and observes the team as they solve the problem on their own	_____	_____	_____
▪ Participates in a discussion of the investigation and solutions with the study team members	_____	_____	_____
▪ Demonstrates an understanding of all terms, concepts, and problem-solving strategies relevant to the investigation	_____	_____	_____
Step 6			
▪ Responds to the study team presentation by recording observations and making all appropriate changes to the investigation	_____	_____	_____
▪ Demonstrates an understanding of all terms, concepts, and problem-solving strategies relevant to the investigation	_____	_____	_____
▪ Submits planning sheet, solution sheet, study team materials, and reflection sheet by established deadlines	_____	_____	_____

Guided by Performance, ©1998 Zephyr Press, Tucson, Arizona

Fractals
Student Guide

I n this assessment package, you demonstrate your understanding of fractal geometry by developing an investigation for a study team manual and by using it to present an investigation at a study team meeting. Study teams are problem solving groups that work on investigations in mathematics; in each meeting, one student presents a problem that the whole group investigates. The group keeps track of problems and solutions in the study team manual.

Task: Investigation for Manual and Presentation at Meeting

1. Select a fractal image and a set of mathematical concepts and fractal properties as the focus of your investigation. Use the investigation planning sheet (see record sheet 1, page 139) to make your selections. If you don't have access to computer software, you might need to use triangle grid paper (see record sheet 2, page 140) to plan your investigation.

2. Using the planning sheet, design an investigation by writing a series of investigative questions, providing appropriate prompts, generating iterations, and developing the necessary diagrams. On a solution sheet, demonstrate your ability to answer the questions you've outlined.

3. As you design your investigation, you might need to make changes to your initial plans. Record these changes on the planning sheet. When you are satisfied with your investigation and with your ability to provide solutions, sign up for a conference by submitting the planning sheet and solution sheet for review. During the conference, present the investigation and your solutions; be prepared to record suggestions for improving the investigation.

4. Prepare a final draft of your investigation that incorporates all suggestions from the conference. Include questions, prompts, iterations, and diagrams you needed to conduct the investigation. In preparing your final draft, provide space for students to work the problems and to record their solutions; you might do so by attaching a solution sheet to the investigation or by providing space on the same page you used to present the investigation.

5. When it is your turn to present an investigation to the study team, provide a copy of the investigation to each participant. As you conduct the investigation with the study team, make sure that you ask questions or provide prompts that will help students solve the problems on their own. Do not provide answers or solutions to the team unless the group has exhausted all possible problem-solving strategies on their own. Observe the team as they work through your investigation, keeping track of how they respond to the questions you developed for the investigation. After the team has completed all the questions in the investigation, discuss the investigation and solutions with the team.

6. After the meeting, record your observations on the reflection sheet (see record sheet 3, page 141). If there are changes you would like to make to the investigation, note them before turning in your work. When you are satisfied with your investigation, submit the planning sheet, your solution sheet, all study team materials, and the reflection sheet for final review. Once approved, enter all your work into the study team manual.

Guided by Performance, ©1998 Zephyr Press, Tucson, Arizona

Record Sheet 1: Investigation Planning Sheet

Indicate which fractal images you will be working with in your investigation.		Indicate which mathematical concepts and fractal properties you will be working with in your investigation.

Record Sheet 2: Triangle Grid Paper

Guided by Performance, ©1998 Zephyr Press, Tucson, Arizona

Record Sheet 3: Reflection Sheet

Name: _____

Investigation: _____

Study Team Members: _____

_____

As team members worked through the investigation, they were effective in the following areas:	As team members worked through the investigation, they had difficulties in the following areas:
As I conducted the investigation, I was effective in the following areas:	As I conducted the investigation, I had difficulties in the following areas:
In doing this investigation, I think we learned more about the following mathematical concepts and fractal properties:	After doing this investigation, I think we still have questions about the following mathematical concepts and fractal properties:
If I were planning the investigation again, I would make the following modifications:	If I were conducting the investigation again, I would make the following modifications:

5

Performance Assessment Packages for Grade 11

Market Research
Classroom Implementation Guide

Curriculum Areas: Language Arts, Others
Products

Market research portfolio

Time: 1 semester
Curriculum Notes

Please read the student task sheets carefully. Note any materials you will need for each task. Performance criteria are listed in the teacher checklist.

Frigstad (1995) served as a guide in the development of this package. Another useful resource to accompany each step in this package is The American Marketing Association Marketing Toolbox, a series of publications that focus on stages of the market research process. You might want to restructure the package so that the portfolio components reflect the materials used at your school.

Integrate this package with content learning experiences, which will allow students to demonstrate mastery of multiple standards within the context of the market research process.

Parmerlee (1993e) contains useful instructional resources for students involved in **step 1** of this task.

Once students begin to make decisions about market segmentation in **step 2**, they might need to conduct research into the needs and characteristics of a specific market segment. If the curriculum does not provide targeted market information, students might need to assess materials designed for this purpose, such as Guber and Berry (1993) and Carter (1996). In addition, Parmerlee (1993c) contains useful instructional resources. In general, The American Marketing Association is a good source of information on particular marketing segments; you can write them for information at 250 S. Wacker Dr., Chicago, IL 60606, or call them at (312) 648-0536.

In addition to the general resources listed earlier, Breen (1989), Chisnail (1986), Cyr and Gray (1994), Edmunds (1996), and Pope (1993) are particularly suited for **steps 3 through 6**. Also useful for students involved in these steps is Parmerlee (1993b).

The format of the section of the portfolio created in **step 4** will depend on the customer research techniques individual students employ. You might want to make certain techniques mandatory and provide additional instruction in these techniques. For example, you might require students to use focus groups; a useful instruction resource for this purpose is Templeton (1994). You might want to emphasize the process of survey design and familiarize students with a software program designed for that purpose; Oasis Press's *The Survey Genie* is a good resource and is available from PSI Research, 300 N. Valley Dr., Grants Pass, OR 97526; (800) 228-2275. If you want to integrate online resources into the market research process, you'll find Sterne (1995) quite valuable.

For information for **step 5**, note that companies publish internal information such as press releases, advertising, and product literature that is readily available. They are required to file annual reports that are available to the public. You can also obtain information from secondary sources such as *Advertising Age, Barron's National and Financial Weekly, Business Week, Forbes, Fortune,* and *The Wall Street Transcript.* Students should also learn about the various directories that can be instrumental in the market research process, such as *Standard and Poor's Register of Corporations* and *Dun and Bradstreet Directories.* Frigstad (1995) contains an exhaustive list of secondary sources and contact information.

For **step 7**, Parmerlee works (1993a and 1993d) contain useful instructional resources.

Because the clarity and quality of the writing in the report in **step 8** would be important in an actual business context, drafting, revising, and editing are emphasized.

Resource List

The American Marketing Association Marketing Toolbox. 5 vols. Lincolnwood, IL: NTC Business.

Breen, G. E. 1989. *Do-it-yourself Marketing Research.* New York: McGraw-Hill.

Carter, D. M. 1996. *Keeping Score: An Insider Look at Sports Marketing.* Grants Pass, Ore.: Oasis Press, PSI Research.

Chisnail, P. M. 1986. *Marketing Research.* New York: McGraw-Hill.

Cyr, D. G., and D. A. Gray. 1994. *Marketing Your Product: A Planning Guide for Small Business.* North Vancouver, B.C.: Self-Counsel Press.

Edmunds, H. 1996. *The AMA Complete Guide to Marketing Research for Small Business.* Lincolnwood, Ill.: NTC Business.

Frigstad, D. B. 1995. *Know Your Market: How to Do Low-cost Market Research.* Grants Pass, Ore.: Oasis Press, PSI Research.

Guber, S. S., and J. Herry. 1993. *Marketing to and through Kids.* New York: Mcgraw-Hill.

Parmerlee, David. 1993a. *Developing Successful Marketing Strategies.* The American Marketing Association Marketing Toolbox, vol. 4. Lincolnwood, Ill.: NTC Business.

———. 1993b. *Evaluating Market Strengths and Weaknesses.* The American Marketing Association Marketing Toolbox, vol. 3. Lincolnwood, Ill.: NTC Business.

———. 1993c. *Identifying the Right Markets.* The American Marketing Association Marketing Toolbox, vol. 1. Lincolnwood, Ill.: NTC Business.

———. 1993d. *Preparing the Marketing Plan.* The American Marketing Association Marketing Toolbox, vol. 5. Lincolnwood, Ill.: NTC Business.

———. 1993e. *Selecting the Right Products and Services.* The American Marketing Association Marketing Toolbox, vol. 2. Lincolnwood, Ill.: NTC Business.

Pope, J. 1993. *Practical Marketing Research.* New York: AMACOM.

Sterne, J. 1995. *World Wide Web Marketing.* New York: John Wiley.

Templeton, J. F. 1994. *The Focus Group: A Strategic Guide to Organizing, Conducting, and Analyzing the Focus Groups Interview.* Chicago: Probus.

Performance Assessment Matrix

Package Title: Market Research

Curriculum Area: Language Arts, Others

Package: Grade 11

Student: _____

Content Knowledge

Language Arts: Standard 4 (Adjust use of spoken, written, and visual language for audience and purpose)

Standard 7 (Conduct research . . . gather, evaluate, and synthesize data, . . . communicate discoveries)

Standard 8 (Use a variety of technological and information sources to create and communicate knowledge)

Additional content areas will depend on the focus of the market research.

Content Skills

Literacy		Mathematics		Science		Social Studies		Visual Arts	
Reading		Problem solving		Defining questions		Acquiring information		Creating	
for aesthetic response		Communication		Forming hypotheses		*reading*		*conceptual skills*	
for information/understanding		Reasoning		Investigating		*study skills*		*production skills*	
for critical analysis/evaluation		Connecting		Observing		*reference skills*		*evaluation skills*	
Writing		Estimation		Monitoring		*technical skills*		*application*	
for response/expression		Numeration		Measuring		Organizing/Using information		Responding	
for social interaction		Computation		Keeping records		*thinking skills*		*descriptive skills*	
for information/understanding		Data analysis		Transforming records		*decision-making skills*		*analytical skills*	
for critical analysis/evaluation		Measurement		Collaborating		*metacognitive skills*		*valuing skills*	
Listening		Patterning/Relating		Interpreting information		Relationships		*application*	
for response/expression				Integrating information		*personal skills*			
for information/understanding						*group interaction*			
for critical analysis/evaluation						*social/political participation*			
Speaking						Historical thinking			
for response/expression						*chronological thinking*			
for social interaction						*historical comprehension*			
for information/understanding						*analysis and interpretation*			
for critical analysis/evaluation						*historical research*			
						issues and decisions			

Performance Assessment Matrix

Performance Skills

Cognitive Strategies		Task Management Strategies		Student Role		Assessment Products		Evaluation Format	
Comparison		Analyzing the task		Museum curator		Portfolio		Student checklist (attached)	
Classification		Establishing time lines		Reviewer		Publication		Teacher checklist (attached)	
Induction		Staying productive		Engineer/Designer		Demonstration		Analytic scoring guide/ rubric (attached)	
Deduction		Meeting deadlines		Representative		Performance		Holistic scoring guide (attached)	
Error analysis		Accepting feedback		Expert witness		Exhibition			
Constructing support		Working cooperatively		Character					
Abstracting		Making a contribution		Ad agency director					
Analyzing perspectives		Respecting others		Tour organizer					
Decision making		Accessing resources		Bank manager					
Investigation		Striving for accuracy		Psychologist/Sociologist					
Experimental inquiry		Striving for excellence		Archaeologist					
Problem solving				Philosopher					
Invention				Historian					
				Writer/Editor					
				Teacher					
				Job applicant					
				Speaker/Listener					
				Market analyst					

Anecdotal Observations

Guided by Performance, ©1998 Zephyr Press, Tucson, Arizona

Teacher Checklist for "Market Research"

Performance Criteria	Excellent	Satisfactory	Needs Improvement
Step 1			
▪ Identifies an appropriate product or service for market research	_____	_____	_____
▪ Describes the product or service	_____	_____	_____
▪ Provides a rationale for selection	_____	_____	_____
Step 2			
▪ Identifies appropriate geographic and end-user market segments	_____	_____	_____
▪ Uses information to support market segmentation decisions	_____	_____	_____
Step 3			
▪ Gathers and records data on the market potential for the service or product	_____	_____	_____
▪ Uses at least one technique to forecast the market potential for the service or product	_____	_____	_____
▪ Makes projections that are reasonable and supported by data	_____	_____	_____
▪ Presents information in an effective manner that is consistent with the forecasting technique employed	_____	_____	_____
Step 4			
▪ Develops a plan for customer research	_____	_____	_____
▪ Prepares drafts of data collection tools and makes decisions about customer sample prior to scheduling conference	_____	_____	_____
▪ Documents customer research process by providing			
• an overview of the data collection approach	_____	_____	_____
• examples of data collection methods used in the research process	_____	_____	_____
• a conference record sheet	_____	_____	_____
• representative examples of the data collected	_____	_____	_____
• written summary of findings and conclusions	_____	_____	_____
Step 5			
▪ Selects at least two companies that are situated in a competitive position in the marketplace	_____	_____	_____
▪ Gathers information through direct and indirect means	_____	_____	_____
▪ Completes a data sheet by finding accurate and complete information on each company in all four areas	_____	_____	_____
▪ Addresses ways in which the information obtained from competitor research might influence marketing decisions	_____	_____	_____
Step 6			
▪ Develops an effective marketing concept that is grounded in the results of market analysis, customer research, and competitor research	_____	_____	_____

Teacher Checklist for "Market Research"

Performance Criteria	Excellent	Satisfactory	Needs Improvement
■ Presents concept and strategy to a small group of peers; elicits feedback	_____	_____	_____
Step 7			
■ Accurately summarizes the market research process in a written report	_____	_____	_____
■ Uses conference effectively to make substantive revisions to the report	_____	_____	_____
■ Uses conferences effectively to edit the report	_____	_____	_____
■ Prepares a final market research report that includes			
• title page	_____	_____	_____
• table of contents	_____	_____	_____
• executive summary	_____	_____	_____
• introduction	_____	_____	_____
• body of report (research methods, market analysis results, customer research results, and competitor research results)	_____	_____	_____
• marketing recommendations	_____	_____	_____
• conclusions	_____	_____	_____
• appendixes	_____	_____	_____
Step 8			
■ Submits completed portfolio by established deadlines	_____	_____	_____

Guided by Performance, ©1998 Zephyr Press, Tucson, Arizona

Market Research
Student Guide

In this assessment package, you conduct research and prepare a marketing report for a specific product or service. To complete the package, you develop a market research portfolio by documenting your work in the following areas:

- identification of a product or service
- market segmentation
- market analysis
- customer research
- competitor research
- development of a marketing concept and marketing plan
- preparation of the market research report

Task: Market Research Portfolio

1. Identify a product or service. Depending on the products or services you are researching, you may use this assessment package in your business classes or in a variety of content areas (mathematics, arts, social sciences, sciences, language arts, family sciences, physical education, health, technology education, and foreign languages). You may conduct research on products (such as a foreign language prose and poetry publication, a telescope, a vegetarian burger) or services (tutoring, plasma storage, training) that are related to your work in a particular course. For your first entry in your portfolio, describe the product or service you select and provide a rationale (see example 1, page 152).

2. Identify the market segments that you are targeting and enter it in your portfolio (see example 2, page 152). Specify the *geographic segment* of the market you target. For example, in conducting market research on a new chicken wing recipe, you might target an area of the country, such as the southern or western states, or a type of community, such as college towns. Specify the *end-user segment* of the market. For example, in conducting research on a new form of facilitated mobility, you might target specific organizations such as nursing homes, professionals in a particular field such as health care workers, or a group of people such as senior citizens. Conduct initial research before you make decisions about market segmentation. Explain in your portfolio your approach to market segmentation and reasons for your decision.

3. Gather and record the data necessary to analyze the market (see example 3, page 153). Although you may use a variety of approaches, your portfolio must demonstrate at least one of the following forecasting techniques:

- **expert consensus**—interviewing experts and sales personnel in a field related to your product or service
- **time series analysis**—plotting past sales and projecting future trends using a time series graph
- **input-output models**—using interindustry sales ledgers
- **barometric forecasting**—using leading economic indicators that are available from the U.S. Department of Commerce
- **buyer intention surveys**—using industrial and consumer buyer surveys such as those published by the Bureau of Economic Analysis

Record the information in the fourth section of your portfolio.

4. Research the potential customers for your product or service. Document your ability to use at least two of the following customer research techniques:
   - end-user surveys
   - end-user interviews
   - focus groups
   - beta site testing
   - controlled test marketing
   - computer simulation

Begin by designing your data collection methods (such as the surveys and interview guides you will use) and selecting your customer sample. When you have prepared drafts of your data collection methods and made decisions about your customer sample, sign up for a conference before beginning your research. In your portfolio, include an overview of your data collection approach, examples of your data collection methods, a conference record, representative examples of the data collected (such as tapes of focus group meetings or completed end-user surveys), and a written summary of your findings and conclusions.

5. Research competitors who provide products or services similar to the one you have selected. Find out how competitive businesses are marketing their products and services. Identify at least two competitors. Prepare a data sheet on each company by assessing information *directly* from the company literature, by interviewing representatives of the company, by accessing company websites, or by visiting to the company. You may also access information *indirectly* through government files and publications. As you gather information, consider the categories you need to address to complete the data sheet.

The data sheet is organized into four areas. The first area of analysis concerns the company's *objectives?* What goals do you think the company hopes to achieve by using these marketing strategies. Whom are they trying to influence? What are they trying to achieve? The second area has to do with *marketing methods.* How does this company market their products or services? The third area has to do with the company's *capacity.* What is the company's financial position (profits, cash flow, cost structure)? How is the company organized? What is the size of the product line or the extent of the services the company provides? The fourth area of analysis concerns the *perceptions* others have of the company. Overall how is the company viewed? How is it viewed by those who work there? Using all available methods for gathering information, build a complete and accurate picture of each company in these four areas. Summarize reports of each of the competitors by indicating what you have learned that

Guided by Performance, ©1998 Zephyr Press, Tucson, Arizona

might influence your own marketing decisions.

6. Develop your marketing concept and marketing plan based upon the information you've collected. Present your concept and plans for marketing your product or service to a small group of your peers. You may use models, videos, slides, and computer graphics; documentation of your presentation for your portfolio will take the form of a photograph of your model, the video, the slides, and hard copies of the materials you produce using the graphics software. Include a presentation feedback form (see record sheet 1, page 154).

7. Develop a written market research report. Write a draft of your report that includes the following components:
    - title page
    - table of contents
    - executive summary
    - introduction (describes the product or service and the market segments)
    - body (research methods, market analysis results, customer research results, competitor research results)
    - marketing recommendations
    - conclusions
    - appendixes

Include graphs, charts, or diagrams where appropriate. Be clear, accurate, and complete. When you are satisfied with your draft, sign up for a revision conference with me or a peer. Be prepared to ask for and record feedback on the substance of your draft. Make revisions and proofread your report, then sign up for an editing conference. Be prepared to ask for and record feedback on the mechanics and style of your report. Incorporate editing suggestions into a final draft.

8. Submit the complete portfolio with labeled entries for a final review.

Example 1: Product or Service Selection

? Product or Service
"Brown Sugar and Ginger" BBQ Chickens Wings

Description of Product
These chicken wings are made using a recipe I developed in my food service course. They are marinated and cooked in a sweet and spicy sauce with a strong Asian flavor. They can be served alone, with extra dipping sauce, or accompanied by green onion sticks.

Reasons for My Selection

I'd like to market this idea for school cafeterias and mall food courts; the product appeals to young people.

I've been experimenting with the recipe in order to get the best balance of sweetness and spice.

I've been experimenting with how best to safely serve this product in larger quantities.

Example 2: Market Segmentation Strategy

Fits in well with regional cuisine preferences

Geographic Segments:
Western States
Southern States

Popular "taste" in these regions

"Brown Sugar and Ginger" BBQ Chicken Wings

Popular menu choice for young people

End-User Segments:
High school cafeterias and shopping mall food courts

Excellent option for fast food settings

Can be packaged in different quantities

Can easily be kept hot and served at proper temperature

Source of Information: Chicken Wing Central Website at http://bvsd.k12.co.us/~alums/wings.html

Guided by Performance, ©1998 Zephyr Press, Tucson, Arizona

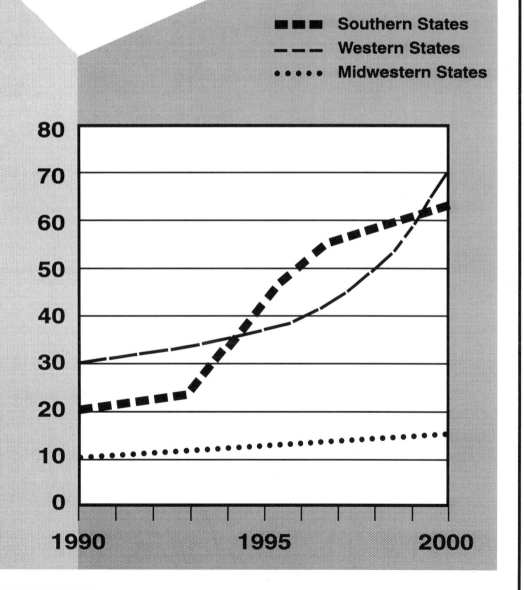

<u>Trend Projections:</u>

Chicken Wing Sales by Geographic Region
Five Competitors
Unit Sales in Millions

■ ■ ■ **Southern States**
— — — **Western States**
• • • • **Midwestern States**

Record Sheet 1: Presentation Feedback Form

Marketing Concept and Marketing Plan

After completing the left side of this form, fold the paper in half and give to an audience member before beginning your presentation. Make sure you and the audience member sign the feedback form.

Name _____ Date _____

Product or Service _____

Before your presentation, think about the following questions	Feedback from audience member
▶ What are your marketing objectives?	▶ What were the marketing objectives?
▶ What image do you want to convey?	▶ What image was conveyed?
▶ How will you convey this image?	▶ How was this image conveyed?
▶ What facts do you want to convey?	▶ What facts did you learn about the product or service?
▶ How will you convey these facts?	▶ How were these facts conveyed?
▶ What marketing strategies will you use?	▶ What marketing strategies were used?
▶ What media will you use?	▶ What media were used?
▶ How will you make your presentation effective?	▶ How effective was the presentation?
▶ Impressions (post-presentation):	▶ Suggestions:
Signature: _____	Signature: _____

Guided by Performance, ©1998 Zephyr Press, Tucson, Arizona

Procedural Writing in the Lab
Classroom Implementation Guide

Curriculum Areas: Language Arts, Science
Products

Analysis of procedural writing in laboratory experiments
Implementation and critique of two experiments
Written laboratory experiment

Time: 1 week
Curriculum Notes

Please read the student task sheets carefully. Note any materials you will need for each task. Performance criteria are listed in the teacher checklist.

Students will also be able to demonstrate standard level work in the sciences in conjunction with their work in this package. Provide a content focus in life science, earth science, or physical science. Provide materials consistent with the focus you choose.

Resources for this assessment package appear in the resource list; since the emphasis is on quality of writing, students may use science materials from elementary and middle grade levels (see example 1, page 163).

Many of the manuals you choose for **step 1** contain a combination of experiments in the life sciences, earth sciences, and physical sciences; when only one area is contained in the manual, it is clearly indicated in the title. In addition to written text, the manuals contain visual and graphic data that must be interpreted in order to complete the experiment effectively, which is an important component of procedural writing.

We assume that you will provide instruction in scientific writing before students participate in this assessment package. For example, students will have been introduced to the structure and elements of an experiment through the materials provided in their science curriculum. When presenting this package, adapt the package and use the same language that is currently being used in the science curriculum. For those teachers looking for instructional strategies that can be used prior to the implementation of this assessment package, the resource list provides books containing a wide range of useful ideas.

Rather than having each student conduct two different experiments in **step 3**, you might want to select two laboratory experiments for all students. If you select this option, each of the laboratory experiments should provide strong models of procedural writing and should be connected to the curriculum content. Although you may use laboratory experiments from your existing curricula, the resources listed would also be useful sources of model experiments. Even when the entire class completes the same experiments, individual students complete their own critiques of the author's procedural writing style.

In **step 6**, you and your students document the writing process through observations or conferences and by analyzing the final products and all rough drafts. If students will be using this package to demonstrate a standard level work in the sciences, you will need to generate additional performance criteria to assess the scientific content of the laboratory experiment.

Resource List

Manuals

Abruscato, J., and J. Hassard. 1991. *The Whole Cosmos Catalog of Science Activities*. Glenview, Ill.: Scott Foresman.

Beisenherz, P., and M. Dantonio. 1996. *Using the Learning Cycle to Teach Physical Science: A Hands-on Approach for the Middle Grades*. Portsmouth, N.H.: Heinemann.

Brown, R. 1987. *Two Hundred Illustrated Science Experiments for Children*. Blue Ridge Summit, Pa.: Tab.

———. 1988. *More Science for You: 112 Illustrated Experiments*. Blue Ridge Summit, Pa.: Tab.

Carr, J. 1992. *The Art of Science: A Practical Guide to Experiments, Observations, and Handling Data*. San Diego: High Text.

Challand, H. 1984. *Activities in Physical Sciences*. Chicago, Ill.: Childrens Press.

Cobb, V. 1985. *Chemically Active! Experiments You Can Do at Home*. New York: Harper and Row.

Ehrlich, R. 1990. *Turning the World Inside Out and 174 Other Simple Physics Demonstrations*. Princeton, N.J.: Princeton University Press.

Facts on File. 1992. *Nature Projects on File*. New York: Facts on File.

———. 1993. *Historical Science Experiments on File: Experiments, Demonstrations, and Projects for the School and Home*. New York: Facts on File.

Garder, R. 1989. *Energy Projects for Young Scientists*. New York: Franklin Watts.

Goodwin, P. 1991. *Physics Projects for Young Scientists*. New York: Franklin Watts.

Iritz, M. 1991. *Blue Ribbon Science Fair Projects*. Blue Ridge Summit, Pa.: Tab.

Kramer, A. 1989. *How to Make a Chemical Volcano and Other Mysterious Experiments*. New York: Franklin Watts.

Krishnan, C. 1990. *Physics Hands-on Activities*. Annapolis, Md.: Alpha.

Levy, S. 1990. *Physical Science Hands-on Activities*. Annapolis, Md.: Alpha.

Liem, T. 1981. *Invitations to Science Inquiry*. Lexington, Mass.: Ginn.

Lunetta, V., and S. Novick. 1982. *Inquiry and Problem Solving in the Physical Sciences: A Source Book*. Dubuque, Ia.: Kendall-Hunt.

Newton, D. 1991. *Science Technology Society Projects for Young Scientists*. New York: Franklin Watts.

Pilger, M. A. 1988. *Science Experiments Index for Young People*. Littleton, Colo.: Libraries Unlimited.

Rainis, K. 1989. *Nature Projects for Young Scientists*. New York: Franklin Watts.

Schneider, M. S. 1980. *Science Projects for the Intermediate Grades*. Carthage, Ill.: Fearon Teacher Aids.

Thomas Alva Edison Foundation. 1988. *The Thomas Edison Book of Easy and Incredible Experiments*. New York: John Wiley.

Tocci, S. 1989. *Biology Projects for Young Scientists*. New York: Franklin Watts.

Tolman, M., and J. Morton. 1986. *Physical Science Activities for Grades 2–8*. West Nyack, N.Y.: Parker.

VanDeman, B., and E. McDonald. 1980. *Nuts and Bolts: A Matter-of-fact Guide to Science Fair Projects*. Harwood Heights, Ill.: Science Man Press.

Wolfe, C. 1987. *Search: A Research Guide for Science Fairs and Independent Study*. Tucson, Ariz.: Zephyr Press.

Wood, C. *Physics for Kids: 49 Easy Experiments with Mechanics*. Blue Ridge Summit, Pa.: Tab.

Yoshika, R. 1987. *Thousands of Science Projects: Classified Titles of Exhibits Shown at Science Fairs and/or Produced as Projects for the Westinghouse Science Talent Search*. New York: Science Service.

Hands-On Activity Kits

AIMS (Activities Integrating Mathematics and Science). The AIMS Education Foundation, P.O. Box 8120, Fresno, CA 93747; (209) 255-4094

CHEM (Chemicals, Health, Environment, and Me). Lawrence Hall of Science, University of California at Berkeley; (415) 642-8718

FOSS (Full Option Science System). The Encyclopedia Britannica Education Corporation, 310 S. Michigan Avenue, Chicago, IL 60604; (800) 554-9862

GEMS (Great Exploration in Math and Science). Lawrence Hall of Science, University of California at Berkeley; (415) 642-7771

INSIGHTS (Improving Urban Middle School Science). Education Development Center, 55 Chapel Street, Newton, MA 02160; (800) 225-4276

STC (Science and Technology for Children). National Science Resources Center, Smithsonian Institute National Academy of Sciences, Arts, and Industries Building, Room 1201, Washington, DC, 20560; (800) 334-5551

TOPS (Task-Oriented Physical Science Learning Systems), 10970 S. Mulino Road, Canby, OR 97013

Instructional Resources

Brandt, W. 1971. "Practice in Critical Reading as a Method to Improve Scientific Writing." *Science Education* 55, 4: 451–55.

Burnham, C. 1992. *Improving Written Instructions for Procedural Tasks.* Berkeley, Calif.: The National Center for Research and Vocational Education.

Cannon, R. 1990. "Experiments with Writing to Teach Microbiology." *American Biology Teacher* 52, 3: 156–58.

Coggins, W. 1980. "A Hands-on Project for Teaching Instructions." *Technical Writing Teacher* 8, 1: 7–9.

Day, R. 1988. *How to Write and Publish a Scientific Paper.* Phoenix, Ariz.: Oryx Press.

Donin, J. 1992. "Student Strategies for Writing Instructions: Organizing Information and Text." *Written Communication* 9, 2: 209–36.

Giese, R. 1989. "Teaching Experiment Design to Beginning and Advanced Students: Procedure Writing—But This Ain't no English Class." *Science Activities* 26, 1: 24–27.

Gratz, R. 1990. "Improving Lab Report Quality by Model Analysis, Peer Review, and Revision." *The Journal of College Science Teaching* 19, 5: 292–95.

Jacobson, C. 1983. *Water, Water Everywhere, but . . . Notes for the Teacher: Report Writing Directions and Experiments.* Loveland, Colo.: Hawk Company.

Lang, T. 1988. "A Technical Writing Laboratory: The Puzzle Exercise." *Technical Writing Teacher* 15, 2: 132–37.

Mayer, B. 1988. "Science Writing Experiments." *Teachers and Writers Magazine* 19, 5: 6–10.

Mulcahy, P. 1988. "Writing Reader-based Instructions: Strategies to Build Coherence." *Technical Writing Teacher* 15, 3: 234–43.

Pechenik, J., and J. Tashir. 1991. "Instant Animals and Conceptual Loops: Teaching Experimental Design, Data Analysis, and Scientific Writing." *American Biology Teacher* 53, 4: 220–28.

Ross, F., and M. Jarosz. 1978. "Integrating Science Writing: A Biology Instructor and an English Teacher Get Together." *English Journal* 67, 4: 51–55.

Sheldon, D., and J. Penick. 1991. *Favorite Labs from Outstanding Teachers.* Reston, Va.: National Association of Biology Teachers.

Southland, S. 1988. "Bibliography on the Writing of Instructions." *Technical Communications* 35, 2: 101–104.

Totten, S., and C. Tinnin. 1988. "Incorporating Writing into the Science Curriculum: A Sample Activity." *Science Activities* 25, 4: 25–9.

Vargas, M. 1986. "Writing Skills for Science Labs." *Science Teacher* 53, 8: 29–33.

Walker, J. 1991. "A Student's Guide to Practical Write-ups." *Biochemical Education* 19, 1: 31–32.

Worsley, D., and B. Mayer. 1989. *The Art of Science Writing.* New York: Teachers' and Writers' Collaborative.

Wyatt, H. 1984. "Writing Tables and Graphs: Experience with Group Discussions in Microbiology Practical Work." *Journal of Biological Education* 18, 3: 239–45.

Performance Assessment Matrix

Package Title: Procedural Writing in the Lab

Curriculum Area: Language Arts, Science

Package: Grade 11

Student: _____

Content Knowledge

Language Arts: Standard 3 (Range of strategies to comprehend, interpret, and evaluate texts [textual features])

Standard 4 (Adjust use of written language for audience and purpose)

Standard 5 (Range of strategies to write for a variety of audiences and purposes)

Science standards vary depending on curriculum focus

Content Skills

Literacy		Mathematics		Science		Social Studies		Visual Arts	
Reading		Problem solving		Defining questions		Acquiring information		Creating	
for aesthetic response		Communication		Forming hypotheses		reading		conceptual skills	
for information/understanding		Reasoning		Investigating		study skills		production skills	
for critical analysis/evaluation		Connecting		Observing		reference skills		evaluation skills	
Writing		Estimation		Monitoring		technical skills		application	
for response/expression		Numeration		Measuring		Organizing/Using information		Responding	
for social interaction		Computation		Keeping records		thinking skills		descriptive skills	
for information/understanding		Data analysis		Transforming records		decision-making skills		analytical skills	
for critical analysis/evaluation		Measurement		Collaborating		metacognitive skills		valuing skills	
Listening		Patterning/Relating		Interpreting information		Relationships		application	
for response/expression				Integrating information		personal skills			
for information/understanding						group interaction			
for critical analysis/evaluation						social/political participation			
Speaking						Historical thinking			
for response/expression						chronological thinking			
for social interaction						historical comprehension			
for information/understanding						analysis and interpretation			
for critical analysis/evaluation						historical research			
						issues and decisions			

Guided by Performance, ©1998 Zephyr Press, Tucson, Arizona

Performance Assessment Matrix

Performance Skills

Cognitive Strategies		Task Management Strategies		Student Role		Assessment Products		Evaluation Format	
Comparison	▓	Analyzing the task		Museum curator		Portfolio		Student checklist (attached)	▓
Classification		Establishing time lines		Reviewer	▓	Publication		Teacher checklist (attached)	▓
Induction		Staying productive		Engineer/Designer		Demonstration		Analytic scoring guide/ rubric (attached)	
Deduction		Meeting deadlines		Representative		Performance		Holistic scoring guide (attached)	
Error analysis		Accepting feedback		Expert witness		Exhibition			
Constructing support		Working cooperatively		Character					
Abstracting		Making a contribution		Ad agency director					
Analyzing perspectives		Respecting others		Tour organizer					
Decision making		Accessing resources	▓	Bank manager					
Investigation		Striving for accuracy	▓	Psychologist/Sociologist					
Experimental inquiry	▓	Striving for excellence		Archaeologist					
Problem solving				Philosopher					
Invention				Historian					
				Writer/Editor	▓				
				Teacher					
				Job applicant					
				Speaker/Listener					

Anecdotal Observations

Teacher Checklist for "Procedural Writing in the Lab"

Performance Criteria	Excellent	Satisfactory	Needs Improvement
Step 2			
▪ Accurately records observations about the procedural writing in ten laboratory experiments	_____	_____	_____
▪ Draws logical conclusions about the effectiveness of the procedural writing in ten laboratory experiments	_____	_____	_____
Step 3			
▪ Provides a strong rationale for the selection of two laboratory experiments based upon the effectiveness of the procedural writing	_____	_____	_____
Step 4			
▪ Accurately applies instructions when conducting two laboratory experiments	_____	_____	_____
▪ Accurately uses listed materials when conducting two laboratory experiments	_____	_____	_____
▪ Accurately follows safety procedures when conducting two laboratory experiments	_____	_____	_____
▪ Thoughtfully critiques the procedural writing style of the author(s) after conducting two laboratory experiments	_____	_____	_____
Step 5			
Includes			
▪ a clear description of the background knowledge required in the experiment	_____	_____	_____
▪ a definition of the problem being investigated	_____	_____	_____
▪ a statement of the hypothesis being tested	_____	_____	_____
▪ appropriate technical terms used to describe the materials needed	_____	_____	_____
▪ sequenced procedures and steps that are part of the methodology and are listed using a numbered, bulleted, or outlined format	_____	_____	_____
▪ procedures for data collection	_____	_____	_____
▪ visual and graphic aids that support the text	_____	_____	_____
▪ a glossary of technical terms used	_____	_____	_____
▪ precise wording	_____	_____	_____
▪ objective writing style	_____	_____	_____

Guided by Performance, ©1998 Zephyr Press, Tucson, Arizona

Procedural Writing in the Lab
Student Guide

In this assessment package, you demonstrate your understanding of written procedures. When you use or write laboratory experiments in science class, use your procedural reading and writing skills to make sense of scientific information. To demonstrate your skills, you analyze the procedural writing used in a variety of laboratory experiments, apply these procedures to complete two laboratory experiments, and use your skills to write your own laboratory experiment.

Task: Laboratory Experiment

1. I will identify a focus for your reading and will provide laboratory manuals for you to use.
2. Using at least two of the lab manuals, read at least ten laboratory experiments very carefully. Pay attention to the author's procedural writing style. Answer the following questions as you read each experiment:
    - How does the author structure each experiment?
    - When and how effectively does the author use written text to describe the elements of an experiment (that is, background, problem, hypothesis, materials, methodology, and procedures for data collection)?
    - When and how effectively does the author use visual and graphic aids to describe the elements of an experiment?
    - When and how effectively does the author use bullets, numbers, or an outline to list procedures and steps?
    - In what ways and how effectively does the author use precise wording?
    - In what ways and how effectively does the author define technical terms?
    - In what ways and how effectively does the author use an objective writing style?
    - What else does the author do to make the writing clear and effective?
    - Do you think you could conduct this experiment successfully? Why or why not?

    Use a chart to keep track of your observations and conclusions about each of the laboratory experiments you read (see example 1, page 163).
3. Choose two of the laboratory experiments that you feel are clearly and effectively written. Prepare a short rationale explaining your reasons for selecting these two experiments. Sign up for a progress conference with me. Be prepared to discuss your selected experiments and your rationale.
4. After I have approved your selections, conduct each experiment using the instructions provided, the materials indicated, and the safety procedures described for each experiment. Pay special attention to the instructions. After you have conducted each experiment, complete a critique of the author's procedural writing style (see record sheet 1, page 164).

5. After completing an experiment, a scientist is often left with questions that require additional investigation. Using what you have learned about effective procedural writing, prepare a laboratory experiment that you could use to investigate one of the questions that you were left with after conducting the experiments in step 4. Make sure you

- provide a clear description of the background knowledge required in the experiment
- define the problem being investigated
- state the hypothesis the user will be testing
- include appropriate technical terms to describe the materials needed
- sequence the procedures and steps that are part of the methodology using a numbered, bulleted, or outlined format
- describe procedures for data collection
- include visual and graphic aids to support your text
- include a glossary of technical terms you use
- use precise wording and objective style throughout

6. When you have completed a first draft, self-assess your draft using the checklist for procedural writing (see record sheet 2, page 165). Make any changes indicated by your self-assessment. When you are ready, sign up for a progress conference with me. I will make revision and editing suggestions. When you have responded to these suggestions, prepare your final draft. Submit all of your rough drafts and a final draft. I might request that you conduct this experiment or that you make it available for other students in your science class to use.

Guided by Performance, ©1998 Zephyr Press, Tucson, Arizona

Example 1: Laboratory Experiments (Observations and Conclusions)

Complete one chart for each experiment.

LABORATORY MANUAL (SOURCE)
Beisenherz, P., & Dantonio, M. (1996). *Using the Learning Cycle to Teach Physical Science: A Hands-on Approach for the Middle Grades.* Portsmouth, N.H.: Heinemann.

EXPERIMENT
Activity 5A: Which liquid contains the most acid?

Questions	Observations	Conclusions
How does the author structure the experiment?	The author starts with background information and materials. Questions are bold; procedures are bulleted. There are lots of charts and diagrams throughout.	I think the use of the visuals is effective. The bold questions, which are also in boxes, are a little distracting since they come in the middle of the procedure.
When and how effectively does the author use written text to describe the elements of an experiment (i.e., background, problem, hypothesis, materials, methodology, and procedures for data collection)?	The author writes a lot of text in the section on background information. The hypothesis is stated as a problem or question. Materials, methods, and procedures are listed—minimum number of words.	The author is very good at listing materials and steps in a few words and phrases. Sentences are used only in the background information section.
When and how effectively does the author use visuals/graphics to describe the elements of an experiment?	Most of the steps are matched up with a diagram; the diagram is labeled. Charts are included for data collection.	I think the diagrams are helpful and they make things clear. The labels help me understand the terms. Charts are useful because I might not know how to set it up without an example.
When and how effectively does the author use bullets, numbers, or an outline to list procedures and steps?		
In what ways and how effectively does the author use precise wording?		
In what ways and how effectively does the author define technical terms?		
In what ways and how effectively does the author use an objective writing style?		
What else does the author do to make his/her writing clear and effective?		
Do you think you could conduct this experiment successfully? Why or why not?		

Record Sheet 1: Critique of Procedural Writing

Complete one chart for each experiment.

EXPERIMENT		
As you conduct the experiment, evaluate the writing in each of these areas:	**Effective and clear**	**Confusing and needs to be improved**
Overall structure of experiment		
Elements of experiment		
Visual and graphic aids		
Bullets, numbers, or outline		
Precise wording		
Definition of technical terms		
Objective writing style		
Other		

Guided by Performance, ©1998 Zephyr Press, Tucson, Arizona

Record Sheet 2: Checklist for Procedural Writing

Did I . . . ?

Provide a clear description of the background knowledge required in the experiment?	
Define the problem being investigated?	
State the hypothesis I will be testing?	
Include the technical terms needed to describe my materials?	
Sequence the procedures and steps using numbers, bullets, or an outline?	
Describe procedures for data collection?	
Include visual and graphic aids to support the text?	
Include a glossary of technical terms used?	
Use precise wording?	
Use an objective writing style?	
Revision Suggestions	
Editing Suggestions	

Leonardo's Legacy
Classroom Implementation Guide

Curriculum Area: Visual Arts, Science, History

Products

Portfolio that documents critical inquiry in visual arts, life science, physical science, and earth science
Artifact analysis sheets
Critical essay
Synthesizing activity

Time: 6 weeks

Curriculum Notes

Please read the student task sheets carefully. Note any materials you will need for each task. Performance criteria are listed in the teacher checklist.

Inspiration for this assessment package came from an exhibit at the Museum of Science, Boston. The exhibit, entitled *Leonardo da Vinci: Scientist, Inventor, Artist,* was on display at the museum from March 3 through September 1, 1997. Corbis (1996) provides an excellent overview and source of information throughout the package.

Task 1

For instructional purposes in **step 2**, you might want to refer to Wolff and Geahigan (1997), which describes the process and strategies involved in critical inquiry in great detail.

As general references, such as those students are to find in **step 3**, Wolff and Geahigan (1997) suggest consulting such sources as biographies and autobiographies of artists, correspondence, critical reviews, monographs on the artist, monographs about a particular art form, and general works of history, sociology, and literature that deal with the time period in which the work was produced. You might also refer to Fehr (1994).

We assume that students will have attained a level of conceptual and perceptual skill in the visual arts that will enable genuine experimentation in **step 4**.

For critical analyses such as the one students do in **step 5**, Wolff and Geahigan (1997) suggest that students read professional criticism and that teachers model critical response as a foundation for writing their own critical essays. Error analysis requires students to discuss the ways in which common fallacies, faulty logic, biases, and inaccurate information lead to errors in judgement. For a complete discussion of error analysis, see Marzano et al. (1992).

When possible, the discussions in **step 6** should include other students in the school, parents, and community members.

Task 2

For use in **step 4,** many of the publications listed on the resource list contain extended bibliographies that relate to each area of experimentation; these include general scientific references and history of science texts.

An excellent example of a parallel time line for **step 7** is in Reti (1974).

Resource List

Bramly, S. 1991. *Discovering the Life of Leonardo da Vinci: A Biography.* New York: HarperCollins.

Clark, K. 1988. *Leonardo da Vinci.* New York: Viking-Penguin.

Cooper, M. 1965. *The Inventions of Leonardo da Vinci.* New York: Macmillan.

Corbis. 1996. *Leonardo da Vinci.* Bellevue, Wash.: Corbis.

Farago, C. 1996. *Leonardo da Vinci: Codex Leicester, A Masterpiece of Science.* New York: American Museum of Natural History.

Fehr, D. 1994. "From Theory to Practice: Applying the Historical Context of Art Criticism." *Art Education* 46, 1: 53–58.

Gibbs-Smith, C. 1978. *The Inventions of Leonardo da Vinci.* New York: Charles Scribner's Sons.

Hart, T. 1994. *Famous Children: Leonardo da Vinci.* Hauppauge, N.Y.: Barron's Educational Series.

Kemp, M. 1981. *Leonardo da Vinci: The Marvelous Works of Nature and Man.* Cambridge: Harvard University Press.

Krull, K. 1995. *Lives of the Artists: Masterpieces, Messes (and What the Neighbors Thought).* San Diego: Harcourt, Brace.

Leonardo da Vinci: Special Collector's Edition. 1996. Bellevue, Wash.: Corbis.

Letze, O., and T. Buchsteiner, eds. 1997. *Leonardo da Vinci: Scientist, Inventor, Artist.* Tübingen, Germany: Institut für Kulturaustausch.

Marzano, R., D. Pickering, D. Arrendondo, G. Blackburn, R. Brandt, and C. Moffet. 1992. *Dimensions of Learning: Teacher's Manual.* Alexandria, Va.: ASCD.

McLanathan, R. 1966. *Images of the Universe: Leonardo da Vinci—The Artist as Scientist.* Garden City, N.Y.: Doubleday.

McLanathan, R., and R. Mühlberger. 1990. *What Makes a Leonardo a Leonardo?* New York: Viking, The Metropolitan Museum of Art.

Philipson, M., ed. 1966. *Leonardo da Vinci: Aspects of the Renaissance Genius.* New York: George Braziller.

Pierre, M. 1987. *The Renaissance.* Morristown, N.J.: Silver Burdett.

Provensen, A., and M. Provensen. 1984. *Leonardo da Vinci.* New York: Viking.

Reti, L., ed. 1974. *The Unknown Leonardo.* New York: McGraw-Hill.

Richter, J. P. 1970. *The Notebooks of Leonardo da Vinci.* New York: Dover.

Romei, F. 1994. *Masters of Art: Leonardo da Vinci—Artist, Inventor, and Scientist of the Renaissance.* New York: Peter Bedrick.

Santi, B. 1990. *Leonardo da Vinci.* Italy: SCALA, Istituto Fotografico.

Skira-Venturi, R. 1993. *A Weekend with Leonardo da Vinci.* New York: Rizzoli.

Stanley, D. 1996. *Leonardo da Vinci.* New York: Morrow Junior.

Turner, A. R. 1993. *Inventing Leonardo.* New York: Knopf.

Venezia, M. 1989. *Getting to Know the World's Greatest Artists: Da Vinci.* Chicago: Childrens Press.

Wallace, R. 1966. *The World of Leonardo, 1452–1519.* New York: Time.

Wolff, T. F., and G. Geahigan. 1997. *Art Criticism and Education.* Urbana, Ill.: University of Illinois Press.

Performance Assessment Matrix

Package Title: Leonardo's Legacy

Curriculum Area: Visual Arts, Sciences, History

Package: Grade 11

Student: _____

Content Knowledge

Visual Arts: Media, techniques, and processes; subject matter, symbols, and ideas; relations to history and cultures; characteristics and merits of work

Science: *Science as Inquiry* (Abilities necessary to do scientific inquiry)
Unifying Concepts and Processes (Systems, order, and organization; evidence, models, and explanation)
Physical Science (Structure and properties of matter; motions and forces; interactions of energy and matter)
Life Science (Interdependence of organisms; matter, energy, and organization in living systems; behavior of organisms)
Earth and Space Science (Energy in the earth system; geochemical cycles; origin and evolution of the earth and universe)
History and Nature of Science (Science as a human endeavor; nature of scientific knowledge; historical perspectives)

History: World History, Era 6 (Standard 2B: The Renaissance)

Content Skills

Literacy	Mathematics	Science	Social Studies	Visual Arts
Reading	Problem solving	Defining questions	Acquiring information	Creating
for aesthetic response	Communication	Forming hypotheses	reading	conceptual skills
for information/understanding	Reasoning	Investigating	study skills	production skills
for critical analysis/evaluation	Connecting	Observing	reference skills	evaluation skills
Writing	Estimation	Monitoring	technical skills	application
for response/expression	Numeration	Measuring	Organizing/Using information	Responding
for social interaction	Computation	Keeping records	thinking skills	descriptive skills
for information/understanding	Data analysis	Transforming records	decision-making skills	analytical skills
for critical analysis/evaluation	Measurement	Collaborating	metacognitive skills	valuing skills
Listening	Patterning/Relating	Interpreting information	Relationships	application
for response/expression		Integrating information	personal skills	
for information/understanding			group interaction	
for critical analysis/evaluation			social/political participation	
Speaking			Historical thinking	
for response/expression			chronological thinking	
for social interaction			historical comprehension	
for information/understanding			analysis and interpretation	
for critical analysis/evaluation			historical research	
			issues and decisions	

Guided by Performance, ©1998 Zephyr Press, Tucson, Arizona

Performance Assessment Matrix

Performance Skills

Cognitive Strategies	Task Management Strategies	Student Role	Assessment Products	Evaluation Format
Comparison	Analyzing the task	Museum curator	Portfolio	Student checklist (attached)
Classification	Establishing time lines	Reviewer	Publication	Teacher checklist (attached)
Induction	Staying productive	Engineer/Designer	Demonstration	Analytic scoring guide/ rubric (attached)
Deduction	Meeting deadlines	Representative	Performance	Holistic scoring guide (attached)
Error analysis	Accepting feedback	Expert witness	Exhibition	
Constructing support	Working cooperatively	Character		
Abstracting	Making a contribution	Ad agency director		
Analyzing perspectives	Respecting others	Tour organizer		
Decision making	Accessing resources	Bank manager		
Investigation	Striving for accuracy	Psychologist/Sociologist		
Experimental inquiry	Striving for excellence	Archaeologist		
Problem solving		Philosopher		
Invention		Historian		
		Writer/Editor		
		Teacher		
		Job applicant		
		Speaker/Listener		

Anecdotal Observations

Teacher Checklist for "Leonardo's Legacy"

Performance Criteria	Excellent	Satisfactory	Needs Improvement
Task 1			
Step 1			
▪ Accesses appropriate general references	____	____	____
▪ Selects an appropriate area of experimentation	____	____	____
▪ Identifies a sufficient number of artifacts to investigate an area of experimentation	____	____	____
Step 2			
▪ Responds to each artifact from three different perspectives (emotive, associative, evaluative)	____	____	____
Step 3			
▪ Gathers information and draws inferences regarding the artistic intentions of the artist	____	____	____
▪ Gathers biographical information and draws inferences regarding the influence of personal history on the artist's work	____	____	____
▪ Gathers contextual information and draws inferences regarding the social, cultural and historical influences on the artist's work	____	____	____
▪ Completes an artifact analysis sheet for each artifact	____	____	____
Step 4			
▪ Designs an artistic investigation directly related to an area of artistic experimentation	____	____	____
▪ Demonstrates an understanding of the connections between Leonardo's work and own experimentation	____	____	____
▪ Achieves goals of experimentation by taking risks and by engaging in genuine exploration	____	____	____
▪ Reflects on own experimentation by keeping a running commentary	____	____	____
Step 5			
▪ Produces an essay in which the following goals are achieved:			
• defines the area of experimentation and the body of work	____	____	____
• states the explicit standards used to evaluate the body of work	____	____	____
• draws upon knowledge of artistic intentions, biographical information, and contextual information to develop standards	____	____	____
• uses these standards to evaluate each artifact and to make comparisons between artifacts	____	____	____
• argues for positive attributes in the work and provides evidence	____	____	____
• argues for negative attributes in the work and, when appropriate, conducts an error analysis	____	____	____
• summarizes own impressions of the artist's experimentation	____	____	____
Step 6			
▪ Prepares for a small group discussion by developing a series of questions designed to elicit emotive, associative, and evaluative responses	____	____	____
▪ Conducts the small group discussion effectively	____	____	____
▪ Includes videotape or audiotape in portfolio	____	____	____
Step 7			
▪ Writes an addendum to the critical essay that addresses responses from small group discussion	____	____	____

Guided by Performance, ©1998 Zephyr Press, Tucson, Arizona

Teacher Checklist for "Leonardo's Legacy"

Performance Criteria	Excellent	Satisfactory	Needs Improvement
Task 2 (_____Science)			
Step 1			
■ Accesses appropriate general references	____	____	____
■ Selects areas of experimentation that address a content standard in the science	____	____	____
Step 2			
■ Identifies a sufficient number of artifacts to investigate each area of experimentation	____	____	____
Step 3			
■ Examines each artifact and records questions, hypotheses, methodology, measurement techniques, and record-keeping strategies that shaped the scientist's inquiry	____	____	____
Step 4			
■ Gathers information and draws inferences regarding the scientific accuracy of the experimentation	____	____	____
■ Gathers contextual information and draws inferences regarding social, cultural, and historical influences on the area of experimentation	____	____	____
■ Gathers historical information and draws inferences regarding developments and improvements in the area of experimentation	____	____	____
■ Completes an artifact analysis sheet for each artifact	____	____	____
Step 5			
■ Designs an experimental inquiry that includes			
• a research question or hypothesis	____	____	____
• methodology	____	____	____
• measurement techniques	____	____	____
• documentation of experimentation	____	____	____
■ Conducts the inquiry successfully and provides documentation	____	____	____
Step 6			
■ Produces an essay in which the following goals are achieved:			
• defines the areas of experimentation in the science and the specific artifacts being analyzed	____	____	____
• states the explicit standards used to evaluate the artifacts	____	____	____
• develops standards-based scientific accuracy, contextual knowledge of the time period, and knowledge of historical developments that have led to improvements in the area of experimentation	____	____	____
• uses the standards to evaluate each artifact and to make comparisons between artifacts	____	____	____
• argues for positive attributes in the work and provides evidence	____	____	____
• argues for negative attributes in the work and, when appropriate, conducts an analysis of errors in the work	____	____	____
• summarizes own impressions of experimentation in each area	____	____	____
Step 7			
■ Effectively synthesizes information on a parallel time line	____	____	____
■ Accurately displays information on a parallel time line; includes Leonardo's inventions and major developments in the science	____	____	____
■ Uses visual display strategies to create a parallel time line that effectively communicates information	____	____	____

Guided by Performance, ©1998 Zephyr Press, Tucson, Arizona

Leonardo's Legacy
Student Guide

Leonardo da Vinci was a true "Renaissance man"—genius, scientist, artist, and student of human nature. Leonardo came to understand the natural world through the processes of observing, reasoning, and experimenting. He is credited with the following quotation: "Open your eyes . . . you have only to see things properly to understand." In this assessment package, you look closely at his contributions to the arts and to the sciences, place his work in a historical context, understand the boundaries of knowledge that shaped Leonardo's understanding of the world, and experiment with the same kinds of principles using modern tools and materials. Your goal in the visual arts, life science, physical science, and earth science is to conduct a critical inquiry into an aspect of Leonardo's work in each area and demonstrate how our understanding in each of these areas has evolved over time.

Task 1: Critical Inquiry into Art

1. Find general research materials on the life of Leonardo da Vinci. Look carefully for specific artifacts that illustrate a contribution to the visual arts. Leonardo experimented with techniques, media, and subject matter that were considered new and innovative during the period in which he worked. For example, his work illustrates experimentation with perspective, contrapposto, chiarascuro, and sfumato. In this assessment package, focus on one technique, medium, or subject of Leonardo's experimentation. If you were to focus on perspective, for example, you might select prints of Leonardo's *Annunciation* (ca. 1475) and *The Virgin of the Rocks* (ca. 1483–5). As you look for specific contributions, keep in mind that not all of Leonardo's experiments were successful and not all of his innovations have stood the test of time. For example, Leonardo experimented with an oil-tempera mix on his famous fresco, *The Last Supper* (ca. 1495–497). Although experimentation in this medium proved difficult, Leonardo learned something from the process and, as a result, he contributed to our understanding of the medium. As you collect these artifacts, keep your focus consistent. Remember that you are looking for specific examples of work that illustrate a particular area of experimentation.

2. Analyze the artifacts you have collected and record your initial observations and personal response (see record sheet 1, page 176). Look at the work from three perspectives: emotive, associative, and evaluative. Present your artifact analysis sheets in a portfolio.

3. Find general references that will provide you with more information about the area you are investigating. Specifically, gather information from sources that will help you make informed judgments about Leonardo's artistic intentions, that will provide you with biographical information on the life of Leonardo, and that will provide you with contextual knowledge of

the time period (see record sheet 1, page 176). Add this information to your artifact analysis sheets; you may also want to add general notes to your portfolio.

4. Design an artistic investigation of your own into Leonardo's area of experimentation. Working with our previous example, you might explore various strategies for achieving a sense of perspective in painting. In his time, Leonardo abandoned many of the conventions associated with landscape portrayal in order to achieve a sense of distance, depth, and dimension in his painting. How have these conventions changed over time? In your own work, experiment with these conventions and also with the abandonment of these conventions. Before you begin, sign up for a conference with me to get approval of your choice. As you experiment, keep examples or photographs of your work in your portfolio and keep a running reflective commentary describing your experimentation.

5. You have sufficient background knowledge and direct experience to make critical judgements about Leonardo's work. Drawing upon the information contained in your portfolio, write a critical essay in which you achieve the following goals:

    ■ define the area of experimentation and the body of work (specific artifacts) that you are analyzing
    ■ state the explicit standards that you use to evaluate the body of work by drawing upon your knowledge of Leonardo's artistic intentions, biographical information, and contextual information
    ■ use these standards to evaluate each artifact and to make comparisons among these artifacts
    ■ state what you think are positive attributes in the work and provide evidence
    ■ state what you think are negative attributes in the work and, when appropriate, conduct an error analysis
    ■ summarize your own impressions of Leonardo's experimentation in this area

6. Structure a small group discussion with others in your class. The purpose of the discussion is to synthesize your findings and impressions, draw conclusions about your area of investigation, and gather others' personal responses to the artist's work. Develop a series of questions that will engage the group in emotive, associative, and evaluative response. Present your artifacts to the group and play the role of facilitator by asking questions and eliciting responses. Videotape or audiotape your discussion; include a copy in your portfolio.

7. Prepare an addendum to your critical essay in which you consider the body of work in light of your small group discussion. When appropriate, include direct quotations from the discussion to support your observations and arguments.

8. Submit your portfolio (including your artifact analysis sheets, essay, video- or audiotape, addendum, and notes) for final review.

Task 2: Critical Inquiry into Life Science, Physical Science, and Earth Science

In this task, you repeat the process of critical inquiry. However, your focus will be on Leonardo's experimentation in the sciences (life, physical, and earth) and your analysis will utilize scientific principles, concepts, and materials.

1. Select an area of experimentation in life science that relates to one of the following content standards: interdependence of organisms; matter, energy, and organization in living systems;

or behavior of organisms. Select an area of experimentation in physical science that relates to one of the following content standards: structure and properties of matter; motions and forces; or interactions of energy and matter. Select an area of experimentation in earth sciences that relates to one of the following content standards: energy in the Earth system; geochemical cycles; origin and evolution of Earth and the universe.

2. Find general references to collect artifacts of experimentation (see task 1, step 1, and resource list); these might include specific inventions or explications of theory. In the life sciences, Leonardo experimented in the areas of anatomical structure and the functioning of body systems. He made contributions in the areas of skeletal structure and embryonic development. He developed the cross-section as a tool in anatomical study and, to our knowledge, he was the first person to draw the spine as a curved series of vertebrae. In the physical sciences, Leonardo experimented in aeronautics, military science, hydraulics, mechanics, vehicular science, and architecture. Examples of inventions he was working on include coin stamping machines, wire strength testers, optical lens grinders, hygrometers, paddle boats, turbine wheels, sewage canals, matchlock firing devices, bridges, siege ladders, army tanks, flying machines, helicopters, submarines, robots, and diving suits. In the earth sciences, his theories addressed cosmological and astronomical phenomenon. He hypothesized about the influence of gravity on the flow of water, the composition and movement of the moon, and the physical geography of Earth's surface. As you collect artifacts, keep your focus consistent. Remember that you are looking for specific examples of work that illustrate a particular area of experimentation, one example for each of the sciences.

3. Analyze the artifacts that you have collected and record your initial observations (see record sheet 2, page 177). Examine each artifact from the perspective of the experimentation that might have yielded its creation. In some cases, Leonardo has left behind concrete evidence of his experimentation; however, in some cases, you must infer what experiments resulted in the invention or theory. Specifically, look for the questions that generated the inquiry, the hypotheses that appeared to be guiding Leonardo's work, the investigative and observational methodology he used, the measurement techniques he used, and the records he kept of his work. Present your artifact analysis sheets in a portfolio.

4. Find general references that will provide you with more information about each area you are investigating. Specifically, gather information from sources that will help you make informed judgments about the scientific accuracy of Leonardo's experimentation, that will provide you with contextual knowledge of the time period, and that will provide you with information on historical developments that have led to improvements in this area of experimentation (see record sheet 2, page 177). Add this information to your artifact analysis sheets.

5. Design an experimental inquiry of your own in the life, physical, and earth sciences. Design an experiment that includes a research question or hypothesis, methodology, measurement techniques, and records that document your experimentation. You may draw upon existing or published laboratory experiments that investigate these concepts and achieve your objectives. For example, you might investigate Leonardo's experimentation with timekeeping principles and inventions (hour glasses, sundials, water clocks, mechanical wheel clocks, hydraulic clocks, and weighted clocks) by conducting an experiment in chronometry. Before you begin, sign up for a conference with me to get approval on each experimental design. As you conduct each experiment, keep examples of your work in a portfolio and

Guided by Performance, ©1998 Zephyr Press, Tucson, Arizona

include all records that document your experimentation. Utilize the same process for investigation in the other two sciences.

6. Drawing upon the information in your portfolio, write a critical essay in which you achieve the following:

   - define the area of experimentation and the specific artifacts (inventions and explications of theory) that you are analyzing
   - state the explicit standards you are using to evaluate the artifacts based upon information you obtained regarding scientific accuracy, contextual knowledge of the time period, and historical developments that have lead to improvements in this area of experimentation
   - use these standards to evaluate each artifact and to make comparisons between artifacts
   - state what you think are positive attributes in the work and provide evidence
   - state what you think are negative attributes in the work and, when appropriate, conduct an error analysis
   - summarize your impressions of Leonardo's experimentation in this area

   To begin, write one essay for each science (life, physical, and earth); in your final draft, combine these into one essay that achieves all the goals for each area.

7. Create a parallel time line to display the history of experimentation in the life, physical, and earth sciences you've identified. The purpose of the time line is to synthesize your findings and draw conclusions about your area of investigation. Begin with Leonardo's inventions and theories and include the major developments in each science that led to modern science in that field; include a copy of the time line in your portfolio.

8. Submit your portfolio (including your artifact analysis sheets, essay, parallel time line, and notes) for final review.

Record Sheet 1: Artifact Analysis in the Visual Arts

Enlarge to ledger size

Artifact (list work of art and year of production here)

Sources (list source you found the work in and sources you might have used to gather background information)

Page (list page number on which work of art is found)

Emotive Response What emotions do you feel as you examine this work of art?	Associative Response How is this work of art associated with other works, ideas, or thoughts?	Evaluative Response What qualities do you appreciate or dislike in this work of art?

Artistic Intentions What do you think the artist was trying to achieve in the work?	Biographical Information How is the artist's life reflected in this work?	Contextual Knowledge What social, cultural, and historical influences shaped the artist's work?

Guided by Performance, ©1998 Zephyr Press, Tucson, Arizona

Record Sheet 2: Artifact Analysis in the _____ Science

Artifact (list theory, invention, or other artifact here)

Sources (list source you found artifact in and sources you might have used to gather background information)

Page (list page number on which work of art is found)

What *research questions* and *hypotheses* guided your inquiry?	What *observational* and *investigative methodologies* did you employ?	What *measurement techniques* and *record-keeping strategies* did you use?

Scientific Accuracy Based upon what we know today in this area of experimentation, how accurate was Leonardo?	**Contextual Knowledge** How did the time period (social, cultural, and historical influence) shape Leonardo's experimentation in this area?	**Historical Developments** Over time, what major developments and improvements have occurred in this area of experimentation?

The Heroine's Journey
Classroom Implementation Guide

Curriculum Area: Language Arts, Social Studies
Products

Portfolio (vocabulary words, comparison grid, retelling)
Museum exhibit

Time: 2 weeks

Curriculum Notes

Please read the student task sheets carefully. Note any materials you will need for each task. Performance criteria are listed in the teacher checklist.

You can easily expand this package to include nonfiction selections. Students examine contemporary and historical biographies for evidence of the heroine's journey pattern. You can obtain an excellent selection of nonfiction materials from the National Women's History Project, 7738 Bell Rd., Windsor, CA 95492-8518. Call (707) 838-6000 for a catalog, or access their website at http://www.nwhp.org for a list of materials and other women's organizations. Their catalog serves as an excellent bibliography, representing multiple publishers. A bibliography of media resources can be obtained from the Kresge Center at Lesley College by calling (800) 999-1959; request the "Images of Women: Yesterday and Today" videotape list.

You can also expand this package to include a writing component. Students write and illustrate a heroine's journey pattern book for an audience of younger readers or write an anthology of heroine's journey narratives.

The five selections listed in **step 1** are used to raise issues and prompt discussion; the stories, illustrations, and perspectives are particularly compelling. You might wish to substitute other sources from the resource list or from your own curriculum. The questions listed in example 1 (page 185) were generated by students who had read and discussed the selections.

In **step 3**, students read the fifth chapter of Campbell (1988). It provides a more in-depth description of the hero's adventure and illustrative examples that students can use to supplement the summary contained in this package. The television series based upon the book is also available on video from PBS, Mystic Fire Video; check your public library. Obviously, the use of the framework to analyze the hero's adventure is well documented; there are few examples of the framework applied to women characters. Even so, using the framework with stories containing male characters is an option.

Johnson and Louis (1990) explain and describe comparison grids for **step 5**. The retelling assessment strategy in **step 6** is described in greater detail in Brown and Cambourne (1987). See also: Harp (1996).

Many museums have excellent examples of museum exhibits that could be used as models for **step 8**. For example, in the Twin Cities metropolitan area, the Children's Museum in St. Paul has an exhibit entitled *Unpacking on the Prairie: Jewish Women's Experiences in the Upper Midwest.* In addition, many libraries and bookstores prepare displays for Women's History Month. Finally, you can obtain sample display materials from the National Women's History Project, 7738 Bell Road, Windsor, CA 95492-8518. Call 707-838-6000 for a catalog. Access their website at http://www.nwhp.org for a listing of materials and other women's organizations.

Resource List

For Students

Bosma, B. 1987. *Fairy Tales, Fables, Legends, and Myths.* New York: Teachers College Press.

Campbell, Joseph. 1988. *The Power of Myth.* New York: Doubleday.

Climo, S. 1989. *The Egyptian Cinderella.* New York: Crowell.

Dahl, R. 1983. *Roald Dahl's Revolting Rhymes.* New York: Bantam.

Dundes, A., ed. 1983. *Cinderella: A Casebook.* New York: Wildman Press.

Hooks, W. H. 1987. *Moss Gown.* Boston: Houghton Mifflin.

Huck, C. 1989. *Princess Furball.* New York: Greenwillow.

Louie, A. 1982. *Yeh-Shen: A Cinderella Story from China.* New York: Philomel.

Lurie, A., ed. 1980. *Clever Gretchen and Other Forgotten Folktales.* New York: Crowell.

Martin, R. 1992. *The Rough-Faced Girl.* New York: Scholastic.

McCarty, T. 1981. *The Skull in the Snow.* New York: Delacorte.

Minard, R. 1975. *Womenfolk and Fairy Tales.* Boston: Houghton Mifflin.

Phelps, E. J., ed. 1978. *Tatterhood and Other Tales.* Old Westbury, N.Y.: Feminist Press.

———. 1981. *The Maid of the North: Feminist Folktales from around the World.* New York: Holt.

Riordan, J. 1984. *The Woman in the Moon and Other Tales of Forgotten Heroines.* New York: Dial.

Schimmel, N. 1982. *Just Enough to Make a Story.* Berkeley, Calif.: Sisters' Choice Press.

———. 1992. *Active Heroines in Folktales for Children.* Berkeley, Calif.: Sister's Choice Press.
    A comprehensive bibliography of multicultural tales available through Sisters' Choice Press, 2027 Parker Street, Berkeley, CA 94704.

Smith, R. 1981. *Mythologies of the World.* Urbana, Ill.: National Council of Teachers of English.

Steptoe, J. 1987. *Mufaro's Beautiful Daughters.* New York: Lothrop, Lee, and Shepard.

Vuong, L. D. 1982. *The Brocaded Slipper and Other Vietnamese Tales.* New York: Addison Wesley.

Weigle, M. 1982. *Spiders and Spinsters: Women and Mythology.* Albuquerque, N.M.: University of New Mexico Press.

Williams, J. 1973. *Petronella.* New York: Parents' Magazine Press.

Yolen, J., ed. 1977a. *The Hundredth Dove and Other Tales.* New York: Crowell.

———. 1977b. *The Moon Ribbon and Other Tales.* New York: Crowell.

———. 1986. *Favorite Folktales from around the World.* New York: Pantheon.

Zipes, J., trans. 1987. *The Complete Fairytales of the Brothers Grimm.* Toronto: Bantam

For Teachers

Bettleheim, B. 1976. *The Uses of Enchantment: The Meaning and Importance of Fairy Tales.* New York: Knopf.

Brown, H., and B. Cambourne. 1987. *Read and Retell.* Portsmouth, N.H.: Heinemann.

Dowling, C. 1981. *The Cinderella Complex: Women's Hidden Fear of Independence.* New York: Simon and Schuster.

Harp, B. 1996. *The Handbook of Literacy Assessment and Evaluation.* Norwood, Mass.: Christopher-Gordon.

Johnson, T. D., and D. R. Lovis. 1990. *Bringing It All Together: A Program for Literacy.* Portsmouth, N.H.: Heinemann.

Yolen, J. 1981. *Touch Magic: Fantasy, Faerie, and Folklore in the Literature of Childhood.* New York: Philomel.

Zipes, J. 1979. *Breaking the Magic Spell: Radical Theories of Folk and Fairy Tales.* London: Heinemann.

———. 1983. *The Trials and Tribulations of Little Red Riding Hood.* London: Heinemann.

Performance Assessment Matrix

Package Title: The Heroine's Journey

Curriculum Area: Language Arts, Social Studies

Package: Grade 11

Student: _____

Content Knowledge

Language Arts: Standard 1 (read a wide range of texts to build an understanding of texts, of themselves, and of culture)
Standard 2 (Literature from many periods and genres, and understanding human experience)
Standard 3 (Apply wide range of strategies to comprehend, interpret, and evaluate texts)
Standard 6 (Apply knowledge of . . . genre to create, critique, and discuss print and nonprint text)
Standard 7 (Conduct research; generate questions; gather data; communicate discoveries)
Standard 9 (Respect for diversity in language use, patterns, and dialects across cultures)

Social Studies: Standard 1 (Culture as in integrated whole; functions and interactions of literature)
Standard 4 (Individual development and identity: compare and evaluate the impact of stereotyping, conformity, and other behaviors)

Content Skills

Literacy		Mathematics	Science	Social Studies		Visual Arts	
Reading		Problem solving	Defining questions	Acquiring information		Creating	
for aesthetic response	▓	Communication	Forming hypotheses	reading	▓	conceptual skills	
for information/understanding	▓	Reasoning	Investigating	study skills		production skills	▓
for critical analysis/evaluation	▓	Connecting	Observing	reference skills		evaluation skills	
Writing		Estimation	Monitoring	technical skills		application	
for response/expression		Numeration	Measuring	Organizing/Using information		Responding	
for social interaction		Computation	Keeping records	thinking skills		descriptive skills	
for information/understanding		Data analysis	Transforming records	decision-making skills		analytical skills	
for critical analysis/evaluation	▓	Measurement	Collaborating	metacognitive skills		valuing skills	
Listening		Patterning/Relating	Interpreting information	Relationships		application	
for response/expression			Integrating information	personal skills			
for information/understanding				group interaction			
for critical analysis/evaluation	▓			social/political participation			
Speaking				Historical thinking			
for response/expression				chronological thinking			
for social interaction				historical comprehension			
for information/understanding				analysis and interpretation			
for critical analysis/evaluation				historical research			
				issues and decisions			

Guided by Performance, ©1998 Zephyr Press, Tucson, Arizona

Performance Assessment Matrix

Performance Skills

Cognitive Strategies	Task Management Strategies	Student Role	Assessment Products	Evaluation Format
Comparison	Analyzing the task	Museum curator	Portfolio	Student checklist (attached)
Classification	Establishing time lines	Reviewer	Publication	Teacher checklist (attached)
Induction	Staying productive	Engineer/Designer	Demonstration	Analytic scoring guide/ rubric (attached)
Deduction	Meeting deadlines	Representative	Performance	Holistic scoring guide (attached)
Error analysis	Accepting feedback	Expert witness	Exhibition	
Constructing support	Working cooperatively	Character		
Abstracting	Making a contribution	Ad agency director		
Analyzing perspectives	Respecting others	Tour organizer		
Decision making	Accessing resources	Bank manager		
Investigation	Striving for accuracy	Psychologist/Sociologist		
Experimental inquiry	Striving for excellence	Archaeologist		
Problem solving		Philosopher		
Invention		Historian		
		Writer/Editor		
		Teacher		
		Job applicant		
		Speaker/Listener		

Anecdotal Observations

Teacher Checklist for "The Heroine's Journey"

Performance Criteria	Excellent	Satisfactory	Needs Improvement
Step 1			
■ Generates a series of questions related to the themes and images in the initial readings	_____	_____	_____
Step 2			
■ Shares questions and participates in group discussion	_____	_____	_____
Step 4			
■ Selects at least ten selections that represent at least four cultural traditions	_____	_____	_____
■ Reads, views, or listens to these selections independently	_____	_____	_____
Step 5			
■ Develops a record of vocabulary words used to create an image of the female character in each selection	_____	_____	_____
■ Uses a strategy to demonstrate understanding of the words	_____	_____	_____
Step 6			
■ Notes events that correspond or conflict with the heroine's journey pattern on a comparison grid for each selection	_____	_____	_____
■ Evaluates each selection using the heroine's journey pattern	_____	_____	_____
Step 7			
■ Demonstrates understanding of story structure by using heroine's journey framework to outline events	_____	_____	_____
■ Incorporates all stages of heroine's journey framework into written retelling	_____	_____	_____
■ Accurately and completely retells in writing, including character, setting, appropriate details, and sequence of events	_____	_____	_____
Step 8			
■ Completes and submits all activities related to ten reading, viewing, and listening selections	_____	_____	_____
Step 9			
■ Draws conclusions about female image in traditional literature	_____	_____	_____
■ Supports conclusions with critical examples from reading, viewing, or listening	_____	_____	_____
■ Uses display board and interpretive guide to convey and support conclusions effectively	_____	_____	_____

Guided by Performance, ©1998 Zephyr Press, Tucson, Arizona

The Heroine's Journey
Student Guide

I n this assessment package, you interpret images used to portray women and girls in traditional literature (legends, myths, fairy tales, and folktales) from a variety of cultural traditions.

Task: Portfolio and Museum Exhibit

1. Read the following short selections, paying careful attention to the illustrations:

    American Association of University Women. 1992. *How Schools Shortchange Girls*. Annapolis Junction, Md.: American Association of University Women. (Read selections.)

    Hastings, Selina. 1985. *Sir Gawain and the Loathly Lady*. New York: Mulberry.

    Lurie, Alison. 1990. *Don't Tell the Grown-ups: Subversive Children's Literature*. Boston: Little Brown. (Read selections.)

    Perrault, Charles. 1969. "Cinderella." In *Perrault's Fairy Tales*. Illus. by Gustave Dore. New York: Dover.

    Perrault, Charles. 1988. *Cinderella*. Trans. and illus. by Diane Goode. New York: Knopf.

    List questions you have regarding the images of women in traditional literature.

2. Meet with a small group of students to respond to these readings. Share your questions and discuss them as a group. Record your questions on a wall chart (see example 1, page 185). Use these questions to guide your examination of the literature.

3. As you examine the literature, use an analytic framework to compare, contrast, and evaluate a wide range of literature selections based upon criteria. We will be using a framework described by Joseph Campbell in *The Power of Myth*. In "The Hero's Adventure," Campbell describes a prevalent story pattern in the traditional literature of a variety of cultures. Although he states that both males and females are often written about in this way, he refers to a variety of traditional and contemporary male hero images whose stories were told using this pattern (Prometheus, Don Quixote, Buddha, Lancelot, and Luke Skywalker). Using this framework, examine the image of girls and women in traditional literature.

4. With your questions and analytic framework as a guide, examine at least ten literature selections by reading, viewing, and listening to them. These selections must represent at least four different cultural traditions. As you read, view, or listen, complete several activities. Keep these activities in a portfolio.

5. Keep an ongoing record of the vocabulary words that are used to create an image of the female characters. Choose a strategy to show that you understand the meaning of these words: categorize the descriptive words, sketch or otherwise illustrate the descriptive words, or illustrate the relationships among words by using a semantic map.

6. Using a comparison grid (see example 2, page 186), record the events that correspond or conflict with stages in the heroine's journey. Evaluate each selection using the heroine's journey pattern.

7. Retell at least one selection in writing using the heroine's journey framework (see example 3, page 187).

8. Submit the vocabulary words, comparison grid, and retelling for review.

9. Drawing upon the work you have done, construct a museum exhibit based upon your interpretation of the female image in traditional literature. Include a display board (see example 4, page 188) that presents your conclusions about the image of women in traditional literature and that uses critical examples to illustrate the points you are making. Include a title, text, and graphics. Prepare an interpretive guide for the display. Include more detailed examples, articles, references, and readings related to your display board in the guide. Given the content of the museum exhibit, libraries or bookstores would make excellent display locations. Other locations dealing with women's studies or women's issues would provide good display locations. I will help you identify an audience and location for your exhibit.

The following questions are representative examples

Our Questions

▶ Are all women in traditional tales passive (Snow White waiting for her prince to come)? When women are active, what do they do?

▶ Are women primarily depicted in subservient roles or are they also engaged in productive work?

▶ Why are women victimized by the men in these tales (body parts cut off, forced into marriages)?

▶ What does it mean to be beautiful? Is beautiful more important than strong or smart?

▶ Are most of the women unresourceful? Do they have others (fairy godmothers) to solve their problems, or do they try to solve them on their own?

▶ When women have power or strength, are they always evil, ugly hags?

▶ Are women portrayed differently in stories from different cultures?

▶ Do women ever save the day? Do they ever make it on their own?

▶ Do women do everything in life just so they can get a boyfriend or a husband?

▶ Are women ever the heroes in these stories?

▶ Are the images in these stories a reflection of how society views women?

▶ Did women tell these stories—or did women tell other versions of these stories?

Example 2: Comparison Grid

The Heroine's Journey
Comparison Grid

✔ Corresponds with Stages of Heroine's Journey ☹ Conflicts with Stages of Heroine's Journey

Stages	Story 1: "Unanana and the Elephant"			Story 2:			Story 3:		
	Story Events	✔	☹	**Story Events**	✔	☹	**Story Events**	✔	☹
The Call	When her children are kidnapped, Unanana must rescue them.	✔							
Preparation	She prepares beans to feed her children and brings a knife for the elephant.	✔							
Crossing the Threshold	She follows the elephant's tracks into the bush.	✔							
Road of Trials	Animals she meets along the way point her toward the elephant. It is hot and dusty; she is tired and hungry.	✔							
Saving Experience	She is swallowed whole by the elephant. She finds her children, feeds them, and uses the knife to carve her way out of the elephant.	✔							
Changes	All of those she sets free from the elephant reward her.	✔							
The Return	The little cousin welcomes them home.	✔							
Sharing	They have a feast . . . of roasted elephant meat.	✔							
Evaluation	This story is true to the heroine's journey pattern. Unanana takes action and solves her problems independently.	✔							

Guided by Performance, ©1998 Zephyr Press, Tucson, Arizona

Example 3: Retelling

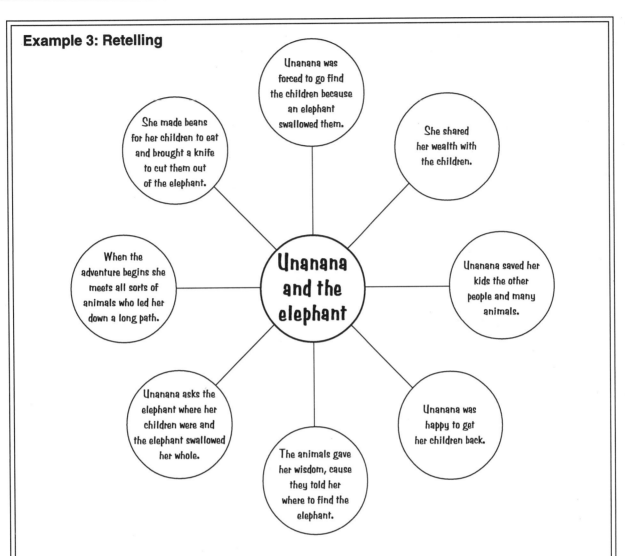

Unanana was forced to go find the children because an elephant swallowed them.

She made beans for her children to eat and brought a knife to cut them out of the elephant.

She shared her wealth with the children.

When the adventure begins she meets all sorts of animals who led her down a long path.

Unanana and the elephant

Unanana saved her kids the other people and many animals.

Unanana asks the elephant where her children were and the elephant swallowed her whole.

The animals gave her wisdom, cause they told her where to find the elephant.

Unanana was happy to get her children back.

Unanana and the elephant

Unanana and the elephant is about a woman who had two beautiful children. One day Unanana went out to gather fire-wood and she left the two children with their cousin. While Unanana was gone three animals came up to the cousin and asked whose children they were, and each time the cousin would reply Unanana. The one special animal that came up to Unanana was a one-tusked elephant, and when the cousin replied Unanana to his question the elephant said, "Well, I shall take them with me" and he swallowed them whole. The cousin didn't know what to do about it so she waited until Unanana came home. As soon as Unanana came home the cousin told her what happened so Unanana packed some beans for her

children and a knife in case she needed it.

Unanana was on her way when she met three animals, and each animal told her she could find the elephant where there are high trees and white stones. So Unanana followed the path until she came to the elephant.

There she asked the elephant two times if he had eaten her children and both times he said no. And the third time Unanana said Where are my children, and the elephant got mad and swallowed up Unanana.

After a few days the elephant died and Unanana cut a hole through the elephant as a door and everyone inside was free.

Example 4: Museum Exhibit Display Board

Princess Furball

(Story goes here.)

Yeh Shen

(Story goes here.)

Rough-Face Girl

(Story goes here.)

Move Over, Cinderella!!

(Story goes here.)

Variations of this story appear in cultures around the world. Many of the characters in these stories are resourceful and smart. Many are strong and brave. Many possess inner beauty. On this tour of the world . . . Cinderella is our guide!

Guided by Performance, ©1998 Zephyr Press, Tucson, Arizona

Teaching Kit
Classroom Implementation Guide

Curriculum Areas: Language Arts
Product

Teaching kit for conflict resolution, problem solving, and mediation

Time: 1 week

Curriculum Notes

Please read the student task sheets carefully. Note any materials you will need for each task. Performance criteria are listed in the teacher checklist.

Depending on the curriculum used in the district, you might have presented one or more models for conflict resolution, problem solving, and mediation. If students select from among several appropriate models, review and identify options for students before they select. If students have been introduced to only one model, they do not need to make a selection in **step 1**; instead, move to **step 2**.

For **step 1**, if a model or models have not been identified, you need to select an appropriate model before using this assessment package. Bodine, Crawford, and Schrumpt (1994) is an excellent instructional resource for this purpose. The program guide and student manual can be ordered by calling (217) 352-3273.

You might want to schedule periodic progress check conferences at various times throughout **step 4**.

Resource List

Bodine, R. J., D. K. Crawford, and F. Schrumpt. 1994. *Creating the Peaceable School: A Comprehensive Program for Teaching Conflict Resolution.* Champaign, Ill.: Research Press.

Bullyproof: A Teacher's Guide on Teasing and Bullying for Use with Fourth and Fifth Grade Students. 1996. Wellesley, Mass.: Wellesley College Center for Research on Women.

Performance Assessment Matrix

Package Title: Teaching Kit

Curriculum Area: Language Arts

Package: Grade 11

Student: _____

Content Knowledge

Language Arts: Standard 4 (Adjust use of spoken, written, and visual language for audience and purpose)

Standard 5 (Employ a wide range of writing strategies and use writing process elements to communicate)

Standard 9 (Develop an understanding of and respect for diversity in language use and patterns across social roles)

Standard 12 (Students use language to accomplish their own purposes.)

Content Skills

Literacy		Mathematics		Science		Social Studies		Visual Arts	
Reading		Problem solving		Defining questions		Acquiring information		Creating	
for aesthetic response		Communication		Forming hypotheses		*reading*		*conceptual skills*	
for information/understanding		Reasoning		Investigating		*study skills*		*production skills*	
for critical analysis/evaluation		Connecting		Observing		*reference skills*		*evaluation skills*	
Writing		Estimation		Monitoring		*technical skills*		*application*	
for response/expression		Numeration		Measuring		Organizing/Using information		Responding	
for social interaction		Computation		Keeping records		*thinking skills*		*descriptive skills*	
for information/understanding		Data analysis		Transforming records		*decision-making skills*		*analytical skills*	
for critical analysis/evaluation		Measurement		Collaborating		*metacognitive skills*		*valuing skills*	
Listening		Patterning/Relating		Interpreting information		Relationships		*application*	
for response/expression				Integrating information		*personal skills*			
for information/understanding						*group interaction*			
for critical analysis/evaluation						*social/political participation*			
Speaking						Historical thinking			
for response/expression						*chronological thinking*			
for social interaction						*historical comprehension*			
for information/understanding						*analysis and interpretation*			
for critical analysis/evaluation						*historical research*			
						issues and decisions			

Guided by Performance, ©1998 Zephyr Press, Tucson, Arizona

Performance Assessment Matrix

Performance Skills

Cognitive Strategies	Task Management Strategies	Student Role	Assessment Products	Evaluation Format
Comparison	Analyzing the task	Museum curator	Portfolio	Student checklist (attached)
Classification	Establishing time lines	Reviewer	Publication	Teacher checklist (attached)
Induction	Staying productive	Engineer/Designer	Demonstration	Analytic scoring guide/ rubric (attached)
Deduction	Meeting deadlines	Representative	Performance	Holistic scoring guide (attached)
Error analysis	Accepting feedback	Expert witness	Exhibition	
Constructing support	Working cooperatively	Character		
Abstracting	Making a contribution	Ad agency director		
Analyzing perspectives	Respecting others	Tour organizer		
Decision making	Accessing resources	Bank manager		
Investigation	Striving for accuracy	Psychologist/Sociologist		
Experimental inquiry	Striving for excellence	Archaeologist		
Problem solving		Philosopher		
Invention		Historian		
		Writer/Editor		
		Teacher		
		Job applicant		
		Speaker/Listener		

Anecdotal Observations

Teacher Checklist for "Teaching Kit"

Performance Criteria	Excellent	Satisfactory	Needs Improvement
Step 1			
▪ Works cooperatively with group members to reach consensus and select appropriate model	____	____	____
Step 2			
▪ Contributes to group development of teaching kit by working on a scenario, teaching posters or handouts, and teaching activities	____	____	____
▪ Demonstrates understanding of problem-solving model by developing appropriate scenarios	____	____	____
▪ Demonstrates understanding of the problem-solving model by including all steps on teaching posters or handouts	____	____	____
▪ Demonstrates understanding of the problem-solving model by designing activities for use with each scenario and with each step of model	____	____	____
▪ Acts responsibly in completing work as planned by group	____	____	____
Step 4			
▪ Practices using teaching kit within the group before using it with focus groups	____	____	____
▪ Thoughtfully records observations and goals based upon practice session	____	____	____
Step 5			
▪ Actively participates in two pilot tests with two focus groups	____	____	____
▪ Thoughtfully records observations and goals based upon focus group experiences	____	____	____
Step 6			
▪ Summarizes observations in a way that demonstrates understanding of			
• respect for diversity in interaction and communication	____	____	____
• ways to adjust communication on the basis of feedback	____	____	____
• ways to express feeling, tone, mood, and vocabulary appropriate to the situation	____	____	____
▪ Summarizes observations in a way that improves teaching kit	____	____	____

Guided by Performance, ©1998 Zephyr Press, Tucson, Arizona

Teaching Kit
Student Guide

We have learned a variety of approaches for conflict resolution, problem solving, and mediation. In this assessment package, you work in a group to prepare a teaching kit to use with younger students. You pilot your teaching kit with at least two focus groups. You refine and modify your teaching kit based upon what you have learned.

Task: Teaching Kit

1. Working with a small group of your peers, select a model for conflict resolution, problem solving, or mediation that you feel is important for others to learn. Although you may have different opinions about the various models available to you, your group needs to come to a consensus and select a model that you feel would be most useful for others to learn.

2. Develop a teaching kit with the following components to present this model to an audience of younger students:

   - at least two scenarios that present a conflict for group discussion
   - posters or handouts that outline various steps in the model
   - activities to teach each step

   For example, you might develop two scenarios. One might focus on a student who has been spreading rumors about another student; the second might focus on a student who catches another students cheating on a test. Using sample scenarios we have used in class, write your own examples. Develop posters or handouts that outline the steps in conflict resolution that you will teach to a group as they work through the scenarios. For example, if you are using the "Peaceable School" model, your posters might include the following:

      a. Agree to problem solve.
      b. Gather points of view.
      c. Focus on interests.
      d. Create win-win options.
      e. Establish criteria to evaluate options.
      f. Evaluate options.
      g. Create an agreement.

   Identify activities that could be used in the teaching kit. Again, using samples that you have seen in class, design your own activities for each step of the conflict resolution model that could be used with one or both scenarios. An example of a strategy that could be used with the first scenario to teach the skill of gathering points of view would be to role-play an "I Was . . . /I Feel . . . " conversation between the two students and a teacher.

3. Decide with your group how to divide the work and create a plan for completing the work. Sign up for a progress check when you have completed this step.

4. When you have designed your teaching kit, practice using it by working through the scenarios, using the poster, handouts, and activities as a group. Before you practice with one another, review the communication checklist (see record sheet 1, page 195). After you have practiced with one another, complete the communication checklist. Each individual must complete a checklist.

5. Pilot your teaching kit with two different focus groups. I will help you identify an appropriate audience of younger students. As you use the kit, decide which members of your small group will present the scenarios, introduce the steps of the process, and conduct the activities with the focus group. When you are not responsible for teaching, observe the interaction of your group members with focus group members. Prior to each focus group, review the communication checklist. After each focus group, complete the communication checklist. Again, students complete individual checklists.

6. Summarize your observations as a group using the summary sheet (see record sheet 2, page 196); refine and modify your teaching kit as appropriate.

7. After the pilot, submit your teaching kit, any refinements or modifications you've made, the communication checklists completed by each member of your group, and the summary sheet.

Guided by Performance, ©1998 Zephyr Press, Tucson, Arizona

Record Sheet 1: Communication Checklist

Interpersonal Communication Goals	Practice Session		Focus Group 1		Focus Group 2	
How have we ...	Observations	Goals	Observations	Goals	Observations	Goals
Shown respect for differences in gender, age, culture, and points of view during our use of the teaching kit?						
Adjusted our communication based on verbal and nonverbal feedback?						
Expressed appropriate feeling, tone, mood, and vocabulary for the situation?						

Record Sheet 2: Summary Sheet

Interpersonal Communication Goals	Scenarios		Posters or Handouts		Teaching Activities	
How does our teaching kit help us to . . .	Observations	Suggested Changes	Observations	Suggested Changes	Observations	Suggested Changes
Show respect for differences in gender, age, culture, and points of view during our use of the teaching kit?						
Adjust our communication based on verbal and nonverbal feedback?						
Express appropriate feeling, tone, mood, and vocabulary for the situation?						

Guided by Performance, ©1998 Zephyr Press, Tucson, Arizona

Biomedical Ethics

Classroom Implementation Guide

Curriculum Areas: Health and Fitness, Science, Language Arts

Products

Preparation of executive summary and visual aids for testimony before simulated medical ethics panel

Time: 3 weeks

Curriculum Notes

Please read the student task sheets carefully. Note any materials you will need for each task. Performance criteria are listed in the rubric.

The following resources provide useful introductions, historical overviews, and contemporary viewpoints. In addition, they are written for teenage readers: Gorovitz (1982), Hyde and Forsyth (1990), Jussim (1991), Koop (1992), Pringle (1989), and Weiss (1985). In addition, the Opposing Viewpoints Series from Greenhaven Press in San Diego includes the following relevant titles: "Euthanasia," "Abortion," "Biomedical Ethics," "Death and Dying," and "The Health Crisis." Review these materials to ensure they comply with district policies regarding the use of instructional materials.

Using the school library computer, the public library computer, or the Internet, all students conduct a keyword search in **step 2** for books and periodicals on their topic within medical ethics. This search will yield a great deal of useful information. For example, a keyword search on this term for books in the Dakota County, Minnesota, Public Library yielded fifty-seven titles and a variety of other options for additional searches using more specific keyword descriptors; a keyword search on periodicals yielded a similar wealth of resources. Again, you might want to access these materials to ensure compliance with school district policies and to determine which materials are most appropriate for an adolescent audience.

Whenever possible, in **step 9** students present to an authentic panel that includes adults who work in the health professions. When hearing testimony, the panel evaluates the student's presentation based upon the performance criteria in this package. Panel members should be able to affirm, challenge, and extend the content of the student's testimony, visual aids, and executive summary. If members of the panel feel the student has not been effective in an area covered by the performance criteria, they ask the student direct questions or require an addendum to the executive summary. If it is not possible to invite professionals to participate on the panel, provide panel members with a list of questions that they might ask students.

Resource List

Gorovitz, S. 1982. *Doctor's Dilemmas: Moral Conflict and Medical Care.* Oxford: Oxford University Press.

Hyde, M. S., and E. H. Forsyth. 1990. *Medical Dilemmas.* New York: G. P. Putnam.

Jussim, D. 1991. *Medical Ethics: Moral and Legal Conflict in Health Care.* Englewood Cliffs, N.J.: Julian Messner.

Koop, C. E. 1992. *Let's Talk: Honest Conversation on Critical Issues.* Grand Rapids, Mich.: Zondervan.

Pringle, L. 1989. *The Animal Rights Controversy.* San Diego: Harcourt Brace Jovanovich.

Weiss, A. E. 1985. *Bioethics: Dilemmas in Modern Medicine.* Hillside, N.J.: Enslow.

Performance Assessment Matrix

Package Title: Biomedical Ethics

Curriculum Area: Health and Fitness, Science, Language Arts

Package: Grade 11

Student: _____

Content Knowledge

Health:	Standard 1 (Health Services, Products, and Information)
	Standard 2 (Factors affecting individual and community health)
Science:	Standard 18 (Interactions of science, technology, and society)
Language Arts:	Standard 1 (Read to acquire information)
	Standard 4 (Adjust use of spoken, written, and visual language for audience and purpose)
	Standard 5 (Conduct research on issues)

Content Skills

Literacy		Mathematics	Science		Social Studies		Visual Arts	
Reading		Problem solving	Defining questions		Acquiring information		Creating	
for aesthetic response		Communication	Forming hypotheses		reading	▓	conceptual skills	
for information/understanding	▓	Reasoning	Investigating		study skills		production skills	
for critical analysis/evaluation		Connecting	Observing		reference skills		evaluation skills	
Writing		Estimation	Monitoring		technical skills		application	
for response/expression		Numeration	Measuring		Organizing/Using information		Responding	
for social interaction		Computation	Keeping records		thinking skills		descriptive skills	▓
for information/understanding	▓	Data analysis	Transforming records		decision-making skills		analytical skills	
for critical analysis/evaluation		Measurement	Collaborating		metacognitive skills		valuing skills	
Listening		Patterning/Relating	Interpreting information	▓	Relationships		application	
for response/expression			Integrating information		personal skills			
for information/understanding	▓				group interaction			
for critical analysis/evaluation					social/political participation	▓		
Speaking					Historical thinking			
for response/expression					chronological thinking			
for social interaction					historical comprehension	▓		
for information/understanding	▓				analysis and interpretation			
for critical analysis/evaluation					historical research	▓		
					issues and decisions	▓		

198

Performance Assessment Matrix

Performance Skills

Cognitive Strategies	Task Management Strategies	Student Role	Assessment Products	Evaluation Format
Comparison	Analyzing the task	Museum curator	Portfolio	Student checklist (attached)
Classification	Establishing time lines	Reviewer	Publication	Teacher checklist (attached)
Induction	Staying productive	Engineer/Designer	Demonstration	Analytic scoring guide/ rubric (attached)
Deduction	Meeting deadlines	Representative	Performance	Holistic scoring guide (attached)
Error analysis	Accepting feedback	Expert witness	Exhibition	
Constructing support	Working cooperatively	Character		
Abstracting	Making a contribution	Ad agency director		
Analyzing perspectives	Respecting others	Tour organizer		
Decision making	Accessing resources	Bank manager		
Investigation	Striving for accuracy	Psychologist/Sociologist		
Experimental inquiry	Striving for excellence	Archaeologist		
Problem solving		Philosopher		
Invention		Historian		
		Writer/Editor		
		Teacher		
		Job applicant		
		Speaker/Listener		

Anecdotal Observations

Rubric for "Biomedical Ethics"

Component of Performance	Excellent Level of Performance	Satisfactory Level of Performance	Needs Improvement Level of Performance
Step 2	Accesses information on the issue; provides evidence of having used more than one general resource and of having found more than five relevant articles with current publication dates	Accesses information on the issue; provides evidence of having used at least one general resource and of having found at least five relevant articles with current publication dates	Accesses information on the issue; provides evidence of having used less than one general resource and of having found less than five relevant articles with current publication dates
Step 3	Selects and prepares to defend a position based upon complex information	Selects and prepares to defend a position based upon information	Has some difficulty selecting and preparing to defend a position based upon information
Step 4	Provides strong evidence of the following: • ability to create a complete and accurate time line of historical events associated with controversy • ability to effectively summarize origin and sources of controversy • ability to create a chart that thoroughly outlines at least two positions on the issue • thorough and thoughtful understanding of values, beliefs, and emotions associated with positions • ability to select and describe a situation that effectively illustrates the impact of the issue • ability to identify a complete list of resources for education and involvement	Provides evidence of the following: • ability to create a time line of historical events associated with controversy • ability to summarize origin and sources of controversy • ability to create a chart that outlines at least two positions on the issue • understanding of values, beliefs, and emotions associated with positions • ability to select and describe a situation that effectively illustrates the impact of the issue • ability to identify resources for education and involvement	Fails to provide evidence of one or more of the following: • ability to create time line of historical events associated with controversy • ability to summarize origin and sources of controversy • ability to create a chart that outlines at least two positions on the issue • understanding of values, beliefs, and emotions associated with positions • ability to select and describe a situation that effectively illustrates the impact of the issue • ability to identify resources for education and involvement
Step 5	Selects appropriate visual aids and uses them effectively	Selects appropriate visual aids and uses them effectively	Has difficulty selecting appropriate visual aids and using them effectively

Rubric for "Biomedical Ethics"

Component of Performance	Excellent Level of Performance	Satisfactory Level of Performance	Needs Improvement Level of Performance
Step 6	Provides strong evidence of the following: • ability to effectively summarize findings in approximately ten minutes • ability to thoroughly identify historical events and scientific facts that provide historical perspective on issue • ability to clearly summarize origin and sources of controversy • extensive knowledge of various positions on issue • thorough and thoughtful understanding of values, beliefs, and emotions associated with positions • thorough and thoughtful understanding of implications and responsibilities associated with issue Selects appropriate visual aids and uses them effectively	Provides strong evidence of the following: • ability to summarize findings in approximately ten minutes • ability to identify historical events and scientific facts that provide historical perspective on issue • ability to summarize origin and sources of controversy • knowledge of various positions on issue • understanding of values, beliefs, and emotions associated with positions • understanding of implications and responsibilities associated with issue Selects appropriate visual aids and uses them effectively	Fails to provide evidence of one or more of the following: • ability to summarize findings in approximately ten minutes • ability to identify historical events and scientific facts that provide historical perspective on issue • ability to summarize origin and sources of controversy • knowledge of various positions on issue • understanding of values, beliefs, and emotions associated with positions • understanding of implications and responsibilities associated with issue Has difficulty selecting appropriate visual aids and using them effectively
Step 8	Thoroughly prepares for progress checks Responds to feedback and addresses questions raised in a way that demonstrates a thorough understanding of the interaction	Prepares for progress checks Responds to feedback and addresses questions raised	Does not adequately prepare for progress checks Has difficulty responding to feedback and addressing questions raised
Step 9	Addresses questions raised by panel at time of testimony or by preparing addendum in a way that demonstrates a thorough understanding of the ethical issues	Addresses questions raised by panel at time of testimony or by preparing addendum	Has difficulty addressing questions raised by panel at time of testimony or by preparing addendum

Biomedical Ethics
Student Guide

I n this assessment package, you examine medical ethics issues, choose an issue, take a position, and defend that position. To complete the package, prepare oral testimony for a simulated medical ethics panel, write an executive summary to distribute to members of the panel, and prepare visual aids.

Task: Preparation of Executive Summary and Visual Aids for Testimony before Simulated Medical Ethics Panel

1. I will provide you with general resources and a list of possible topics in medical ethics; these might include equal access to medical care, doctor/patient confidentiality, human experimentation, organ donation, genetic engineering, managed health care, patient rights, euthanasia and the right to die, abortion and the right to life, and animal rights and research. Read through some of these resources and select a topic for further research.

2. Using the available resources, gather information on your topic. Although the general resources you used in step 1 contain useful background information, these topics are of current interest and you will need to find numerous current magazine and newspaper articles. Find at least five sources of information on your topic that have been published in the last three years. To find this information, access popular medical journals (*American Medical News, American Health, Modern Healthcare, Private Practice, Nexus*), current issue magazines (*Newsweek, People*), and newspapers.

3. Select and prepare to defend a position as if you were an expert witness on the issue. Prepare to testify before a simulated medical ethics panel. Prepare the following: oral testimony, an executive summary to distribute to panel members, and visual aids.

4. Develop a six-page executive summary in the following format:

Title Page:	Include the issue, your name, the role you will be playing, and the date of your testimony.
Historical Perspective:	Include a time line of historical events associated with the issue.
Controversy:	Summarize how, why, and when the issue became controversial; list individuals and organizations that have been involved in the controversy.
Positions:	Prepare a chart that outlines at least two positions on the issue and lists the values, beliefs, and emotions associated with each position.

<dl>
<dt>Case Study:</dt>
<dd>Describe a specific situation that illustrates the impact of the issue. The situation should be an actual example of a personal story, legal case, or documented medical incident that you discovered during your initial research.</dd>
<dt>Resources:</dt>
<dd>Prepare a chart that lists resources a citizen might use to find out more and get involved. These resources might include individuals, organizations, and readings on the issue.</dd>
</dl>

5. Make overheads, posters, photographs, or models of anything that you have included in your executive summary or will address in your oral testimony. Since you will need to limit yourself to two visual aids, select items that will have the most impact on the panel.

6. Plan a ten-minute oral testimony. During your speech, make several points. Follow this format:

<dl>
<dt>Introduction:</dt>
<dd>Adopt a role associated with the issue and consistent with your position (that is, doctor, patient, parent of an organ donor, attorney, animal rights activist). Clearly and briefly state your position on the issue. Inform the panel that you will provide historical perspectives on the issue, identify the origins and sources of controversy, identify various positions on the issue, and discuss the implications.</dd>
<dt>Historical Perspective:</dt>
<dd>Define the issue and tell the panel about the historical events associated with the issue, and the major medical discoveries, patient histories, court cases, and scientific facts that relate to the issue.</dd>
<dt>Controversy:</dt>
<dd>Tell the panel how, when, and why the issue became controversial. Identify the sources of controversy (proponents, opponents, advocates, and organizations).</dd>
<dt>Positions:</dt>
<dd>Identify at least two major positions on the issue. Tell the panel what you believe to be the values, beliefs, and emotions associated with these various positions.</dd>
<dt>Implications:</dt>
<dd>Describe why you feel the issue is important and provide an example of a situation that illustrates the impact of the issue. With respect to the issue, describe the responsibilities of an involved citizenry and describe various actions that citizens could take.</dd>
<dt>Conclusion:</dt>
<dd>Restate your position, distribute your executive summary, and encourage panel members to ask questions about the issue.</dd>
</dl>

7. Prepare note cards for your oral testimony and decide how you will use the visual aids during your presentation. Practice your presentation several times before scheduling your testimony before the medical ethics panel.

8. I will schedule progress checks with you at several stages in the process (when you select your issue; gather information; select your position; and prepare your executive summary, visual aids, and oral testimony). For each progress check, be prepared to discuss the work you have completed to date. After each progress check, be prepared to respond to suggestions and to address questions that I raised.

9. Present your oral testimony before the panel and submit your executive summary to the panel for final review. If members of the panel have questions, they may ask you to address them on the spot or submit an addendum to your executive summary.

Grant Proposal
Classroom Implementation Guide

Curriculum Areas: Social Studies, Civics
Products

>   Portfolio that contains individual reflections
>   Team-generated grant proposal
>   Self-evaluation

Time: ongoing throughout semester
Curriculum Notes

Please read the student task sheets carefully. Note any materials you will need for each task. Performance criteria are listed in the teacher checklist.

Lewis (1991) is an excellent source of ideas, examples of student projects, and teaching strategies for this task. See especially the proposal form (163) and grant application checklist (164).

The action plan in **step 3** should focus on what the individual student could do to prepare for the grant writing team project. The action plan should focus on strategies for gathering information such as the following: background of the problem, issue, or situation; potential sources of funding in the area; and grant writing process. For background information, students access print information and contact individuals involved with the issue. For information about potential sources of funding, students access the following reference sources at their local library to obtain donor profiles:

>   *Taft Corporate Giving Directory* (The Taft Group, 1992)
>   *National Directory of Non-Profit Organizations* (The Taft Group, 1992)
>   *The Foundation Grants Index* (The Foundation Center, 1991)
>   *Grants for Children and Youth* (The Foundation Center, 1992)
>   *National Data Book of Foundations* (The Foundation Center, 1992)
>   *The Catalog of Federal Domestic Assistance* (U.S. Government Printing Office, annual publication)

For information about the grant writing process, students access materials that provide outlines and strategies for grant writing, such as Brewer, Achilles, and Fuhriman (1995), Jasso (1996), and Ruskin and Achilles (1995). You might also access these resources for **step 5**. Encourage students to prepare a proposal for a funding source with a history of giving to such projects at the proposed level of need and that is receptive to student-initiated grant proposals. Such information is readily obtainable in donor profiles. If the entire class is working on the same issue, teams can develop their own projects and approach their own potential sources of funding.

Although an example self-evaluation tool for **step 9** is included with the package, we strongly encourage you to develop a tool with students that reflects the context of the classroom, the projects, and the proposals.

Resource List

Brewer, E. W., C. M. Achilles, and J. R. Fuhriman. 1995. *Finding Funding: Grant Writing and Project Management from Start to Finish.* Thousand Oaks, Calif.: Corwin Press.

Jasso, G. 1996. *Finding Corporate Resources: Maximizing School/ Business Partnerships.* Thousand Oaks, Calif.: Corwin Press.

Lewis, B. 1991. *The Kid's Guide to Social Action: How to Solve the Social Problems You Choose—and Turn Creative Thinking into Positive Action.* Minneapolis, Minn.: Free Spirit. (400 First Ave. N., Ste. 616, Minneapolis, MN 55401; (612) 338-2068.)

Ruskin, K. B., and C. M. Achilles. 1995. *Grant Writing, Fundraising, and Partnerships: Strategies That Work!* Thousand Oaks, Calif. Corwin Press.

Performance Assessment Matrix

Package Title: Grant Proposal

Curriculum Area: Social Studies, Civics

Package: Grade 11

Student: _____

Content Knowledge

Social Studies: IV (Individual development and identify: H—Work independently and cooperatively to accomplish goals)

(Production, distribution, and consumption: H—Economic concepts and social development issues; J—Analysis of an issue and economic planning)

Civics: V (Roles of citizens in a democracy: E—How can citizens take part in civic life?)

Content Skills

Literacy		Mathematics	Science	Social Studies		Visual Arts	
Reading		Problem solving	Defining questions	Acquiring information		Creating	
for aesthetic response		Communication	Forming hypotheses	reading		conceptual skills	
for information/understanding		Reasoning	Investigating	study skills		production skills	
for critical analysis/evaluation		Connecting	Observing	reference skills		evaluation skills	
Writing		Estimation	Monitoring	technical skills		application	
for response/expression		Numeration	Measuring	Organizing/Using information		Responding	
for social interaction		Computation	Keeping records	thinking skills		descriptive skills	
for information/understanding		Data analysis	Transforming records	decision-making skills		analytical skills	
for critical analysis/evaluation		Measurement	Collaborating	metacognitive skills		valuing skills	
Listening		Patterning/Relating	Interpreting information	Relationships		application	
for response/expression			Integrating information	personal skills			
for information/understanding				group interaction			
for critical analysis/evaluation				social/political participation			
Speaking				Historical thinking			
for response/expression				chronological thinking			
for social interaction				historical comprehension			
for information/understanding				analysis and interpretation			
for critical analysis/evaluation				historical research			
				issues and decisions			

Guided by Performance, ©1998 Zephyr Press, Tucson, Arizona

Performance Assessment Matrix

Performance Skills

Cognitive Strategies	Task Management Strategies	Student Role	Assessment Products	Evaluation Format
Comparison	Analyzing the task	Museum curator	Portfolio	Student checklist (attached)
Classification	Establishing time lines	Reviewer	Publication	Teacher checklist (attached)
Induction	Staying productive	Engineer/Designer	Demonstration	Analytic scoring guide/ rubric (attached)
Deduction	Meeting deadlines	Representative	Performance	Holistic scoring guide (attached)
Error analysis	Accepting feedback	Expert witness	Exhibition	
Constructing support	Working cooperatively	Character		
Abstracting	Making a contribution	Ad agency director		
Analyzing perspectives	Respecting others	Tour organizer		
Decision making	Accessing resources	Bank manager		
Investigation	Striving for accuracy	Psychologist/Sociologist		
Experimental inquiry	Striving for excellence	Archaeologist		
Problem solving		Philosopher		
Invention		Historian		
		Writer/Editor		
		Teacher		
		Job applicant		
		Speaker/Listener		
		Grant writer		

Anecdotal Observations

Teacher Checklist for "Grant Proposal"

Performance Criteria	Excellent	Satisfactory	Needs Improvement
Step 2			
■ Defines the issue in a manner that reflects understanding	_____	_____	_____
■ Identifies manageable goals with respect to the issue	_____	_____	_____
■ Considers ways to marshal personal resources to address the issue	_____	_____	_____
■ Identifies the need for additional contributions from human and nonhuman sources	_____	_____	_____
■ Generates reasonable options or solutions and associates these with the consequences	_____	_____	_____
■ Identifies at least one way of assessing effectiveness or impact	_____	_____	_____
■ Develops an action plan that prepares for team grant proposal	_____	_____	_____
■ Implements action plan in time allotted	_____	_____	_____
Step 3			
■ Prepares for initial team meeting; is ready to share individual findings	_____	_____	_____
■ Actively participates in initial team meeting	_____	_____	_____
■ Shares with team information regarding problem definitions, personal resources, additional resources, options or solutions, and consequences	_____	_____	_____
Step 4			
■ Helps team select one option or solution	_____	_____	_____
■ Helps team describe project based on that option	_____	_____	_____
■ Contributes to completion of team progress sheet	_____	_____	_____
Step 6			
■ Contributes to the assignment of team roles and work	_____	_____	_____
■ Contributes to team flow chart or schedule	_____	_____	_____
Step 7			
■ Contributes to grant proposal by completing all assigned work by deadlines	_____	_____	_____
■ Contributes to consolidation of individual work into finished project	_____	_____	_____
Step 8			
■ Contributes to submission of proposal to funding source	_____	_____	_____
Step 9			
■ Completes self-evaluation in a thoughtful manner	_____	_____	_____
■ Shares impressions with team in a productive manner	_____	_____	_____
Step 10			
■ Contributes to submission of all required work by deadlines	_____	_____	_____

Guided by Performance, ©1998 Zephyr Press, Tucson, Arizona

Grant Proposal
Student Guide

In this assessment package, you work independently and as part of a team to write a grant proposal. You demonstrate your ability to manage resources effectively as you work to meet an individual goal and to produce a completed proposal with your team.

Task: Portfolio, Grant Proposal, and Self-Evaluation

1. I'll provide a focus for your grant-writing activities. As a class, identify issues in our school or local community that could be addressed. For example, you might discover that our town library must close on weekends due to a lack of funding. You investigate what would be required to write a grant proposal to staff the library with student interns and fund one professional librarian on weekends. Or you might find that a local nature center is having trouble with their land preservation and restoration activities due to neighboring residents' allowing their dogs to use the land freely. You investigate what would be required to write a grant proposal to support a public relations program, a community education effort, and the posting of signs along the borders of the nature center. I might decide that the entire class will focus on the same issue or that you may identify several issues.

2. Consider what potential contribution you could make to resolving the issue. Using a reflection sheet to record your responses (see record sheet 1, page 211), answer the following:

   - What is your definition of the issue?
   - What are your goals with respect to the issue? What would you like to achieve? What role do you think you can play in achieving a solution?
   - How and to what extent are you willing to contribute time, money, energy, or skills to solve the problem? How and to what extent will these resources need to come from human and nonhuman resources?
   - What do you see as potential options or solutions? What might be the consequences of each of these?
   - How will you know if you have been effective in achieving the desired impact?
   - What will you do (action plan) to prepare for your work on the grant writing team?

   Meet with me for a progress conference before implementing your action plan.

3. After you have implemented your personal action plan, I will put you in teams of four. During your initial meeting, share definitions of the issue. Next identify all potential resources that each team member brings to the team. Then share your ideas regarding additional resources, options or solutions, and consequences. Record these responses on a wall chart.

4. During your second meeting, consider the information you shared during your first meeting. Select one of the options or solutions proposed by a group member, develop this option or solution into a planned project, and generate a grant proposal to support implementation. Working as a group, select one of the proposed options or solutions, describe a project based upon that option or solution, identify the resources that would relate to this project, and list the human and nonhuman resources required for your project; record all information on a planning sheet (see record sheet 2, page 212). I will schedule a progress conference with your group when you have completed this step.

5. The individual work you did will be useful in the work you complete as a group. Use information on the background of the problem, potential sources of funding, and the grant writing process to proceed with your grant writing project. Compare the available resources with your anticipated needs for the project. Your grant proposal will supplement your own resources and address your anticipated needs; know what you will be asking for in the grant proposal. Next, determine how to get the needed resources. Although you might have some ideas based upon individual research, I will help you select a potential funding source.

6. After reviewing the components of a grant proposal (see record sheet 3, page 213), create a flow chart or schedule that describes how the task will be structured and indicates the specific work assigned to each team member (see record sheet 4, page 214). Schedule periodic meetings as a group to support one another's work and to ensure that all group members are meeting established goals and deadlines.

7. When each member has completed the individual work, meet to put the proposal together. One team member is responsible for making sure that the whole proposal makes sense. When your team has completed a draft of your proposal, submit it for suggestions and editing. I might request a progress conference with your group at any point during this process.

8. Make all necessary revisions or corrections to your proposal. Submit your grant proposal to the potential funding source; be sure to conform to any guidelines provided by your particular funding source.

9. Using the self-evaluation (see record sheet 5, page 215), evaluate your role in the group and the effectiveness of the team's management of resources. Meet to share your impressions.

10. In a portfolio, submit reflection sheets, a copy of your proposal, and the self-evaluations for all members of your team.

Guided by Performance, ©1998 Zephyr Press, Tucson, Arizona

Record Sheet 1: Individual Reflection Sheet

Definition of the Issue

Personal Goals
▶
▶
▶

Personal Contributions	Time	Money	Energy	Skills
Other Contributions				
Potential Options or Solutions				
	▼	▼	▼	▼
Potential Consequences				

Action Plan		
What?	References to Read	People to Talk To
❑ Find background information ❑ Find information on funders ❑ Find information on grant writing		

Record Sheet 2: Planning Sheet

Team Members

Problem, Issue, or Situation

Selected Option or Solution

Proposed Project

Personal Resources (List for each team member)				

Additional Resources Required for Project

Guided by Performance, ©1998 Zephyr Press, Tucson, Arizona

Record Sheet 3: General Components of a Grant Proposal

Questions to Ask	Information to Include
Why are we preparing this proposal?	Background information on the issue; available resources; needs and importance
What are we trying to fund?	Description of project, goals, general overview of activities
How will be achieve our goals?	Goals; activities required for each; nonhuman resource requirements
Who will we involve?	Roles of individuals; personal resources; roles that need to be filled; human resources needed
When will we implement our project?	Time lines and schedule
How much will the project cost and what level of funding are we requesting?	Budget; comparison of available resources with needs
How will we know if our project works?	Evaluation of project (photographing activities, collecting documents, conducting surveys, and recording observations)

Record Sheet 4: Flow Chart

Questions to Ask	Information to Include	Person(s) Responsible	Date Due
Preparation What specific guidelines, requirements, and time lines does the funder require?	All guidelines, requirements, and time lines		
TEAM MEETING:	What do we need to know?	All	
Proposal Writing Why are we preparing this proposal?	Background information on the issue; available resources, needs, and importance		
What are we trying to fund?	Description of project, goals; general overview of activities		
How will we achieve our goals?	Goals; activities required for each; nonhuman resource requirements		
Who will be involved?	Roles of individuals; personal resources; roles that will need to be filled; human resources that will be needed		
When will we implement our project?	Time lines and schedule of activities		
How much will the project cost and what level of funding are we requesting?	Budget; comparison of available resources with needs		
How will we know if our project works?	Evaluation of the project (photographing activities, collecting documents, conducting surveys, and recording observations)		
TEAM MEETING:	How are we doing on each piece of the proposal?	All	
Coordination How do the parts of our proposal fit together?	All proposal pieces put together in one form (check to make sure things make sense); questions clarified with individuals		
Revisions What suggestions does our teacher have for improving the proposal?	Necessary revisions or corrections		
Mailing How many copies will need to be mailed? Where do we send the proposal?	Prepared copies for team members, teacher, and foundation (as required). Addressed envelope		
TEAM MEETING:	How did we do (self-evaluation)?	All	
Final Evaluation Who will prepare materials to submit to our teacher?	Copy of proposal and self-evaluations for final evaluation		

Guided by Performance, ©1998 Zephyr Press, Tucson, Arizona

Record Sheet 5: Self-Evaluation

Criteria	Was I effective in this area? Why or why not?	Was our group effective in this area? Why or why not?
Adequate preparation for team meetings		
Appropriate definition of an issue		
Appropriate description of a project		
Accurate identification of personal resources		
Accurate identification of needed human and nonhuman resources		
Effective development of grant proposal as means of acquiring necessary resources		
Completion of assigned tasks and assignments		
Meeting of established deadlines		
Productive contributions to all team meetings and group processes		
On-time mailing and delivery of a final product		
Other areas:		

HyperCard Stack
Classroom Implementation Guide

Curriculum Areas: Technology, Science
Products

Documentation of skill development
Documentation of process
Demonstration

Time: 3 weeks
Curriculum Notes

Please read the student task sheets carefully. Note any materials you will need for each task. Performance criteria are listed in the teacher checklist.

This assessment package requires students to demonstrate an understanding of computer technology through the development of a multimedia presentation. The package enables students to report the findings of an inquiry through the development of a HyperCard stack.

Because the content of this package can vary depending upon the nature of the inquiry in which students are engaged, this assessment package must be combined with a content area learning experience or one of the other assessment packages in this volume, or imbedded within the context of a particular course.

Resource List

There are many online resources available to students in this area; these contain the most comprehensive and up-to-date information available.

HyperCard Workshop Page
URL: http://lightning.stvital.winnipeg.mb.ca/hcstuff/hcworkshop.html

Welcome to HyperCard
URL: http://hypercard.apple.com/

HyperCard Heaven—What's HyperCard?
URL: http://members.aol.com/hcheaven/hypercard.html

HyperCard: Teach Yourself HyperCard
URL: http://www.chepd.mq.edu.au/boomerang/teachhc/

HyperCard 2.3.5
URL: http://mike.info.apple.com/productinfo/datasheets/as/hypercard2.3.5.htm

HyperCard 3.0
URL: http://www.chepd.mq.edu.au/boomerang/teachhc/hc3.html

HyperCard Bibliography and Stackography
URL: http://lightning.stvital.winnipeg.mb.ca/hcstuff/TeachHC/books.htm

Teach Yourself HyperCard—Index
URL: http://lightning.stvital.winnipeg.mb.ca/hcstuff/TeachHC/index.html

HyperCard and Sound
URL: http://lightning.stvital.winnipeg.mb.ca/hcstuff/TeachHC/hcsound/hcsound.html

HyperCard Menus
URL: http://lightning.stvital.winnipeg.mb.ca/hcstuff/TeachHC/menu/menu.html

XCMD's for HyperCard and Sound
URL: http://lightning.stvital.winnipeg.mb.ca/hcstuff/TeachHC/hcsound/hcsound2.html

Sam's Page/HyperCard
URL: http://www.cuug.ab.ca:8001/~johnstos/hypercd.html

Hyper
URL: http://rezso.sote.hu/users/andras/Ehyper.htm

HyperCard and Music
URL: http://lightning.stvital.winnipeg.mb.ca/hcstuff/TeachHC/hcsound/hcmusic.html

Colouring Cards Fields and Buttons
URL: http://lightning.stvital.winnipeg.mb.ca/hcstuff/TeachHC/hccol/objects.html

HyperCard Bibliography and Stackography
URL: http://199.176.205.211/HCMS/TeachHC/books.html

In addition, the following books are excellent sources of information on using HyperCard, developing stacks, and working with HyperTalk:

Beekman, G. 1996. *HyperCard 2.3 in a Hurry: The Fast Track to Multimedia.* Wadsworth and Peachpit Press.

Winkler, D., S. Kamins, and J. DeVoto. 1994. *HyperTalk 2.2: The Book.* New York: Random House.

Performance Assessment Matrix

Package Title: HyperCard Stack

Curriculum Area: Science, Technology

Package: Grade 11

Student: _____

Content Knowledge

The standards will vary depending on how the package is implemented; implementation might also affect the standards indicated in this chart.

Content Skills

Literacy		Mathematics	Science	Social Studies		Visual Arts	
Reading		Problem solving	Defining questions	Acquiring information		Creating	
for aesthetic response		Communication	Forming hypotheses	*reading*		*conceptual skills*	
for information/understanding	▓	Reasoning	Investigating	*study skills*		*production skills*	
for critical analysis/evaluation		Connecting	Observing	*reference skills*		*evaluation skills*	
Writing		Estimation	Monitoring	*technical skills*	▓	*application*	▓
for response/expression		Numeration	Measuring	Organizing/Using information		Responding	
for social interaction		Computation	Keeping records	*thinking skills*		*descriptive skills*	
for information/understanding		Data analysis	Transforming records	*decision-making skills*		*analytical skills*	
for critical analysis/evaluation		Measurement	Collaborating	*metacognitive skills*		*valuing skills*	
Listening		Patterning/Relating	Interpreting information	Relationships		*application*	
for response/expression			Integrating information	*personal skills*			
for information/understanding				*group interaction*			
for critical analysis/evaluation	▓			*social/political participation*			
Speaking				Historical thinking			
for response/expression				*chronological thinking*			
for social interaction				*historical comprehension*			
for information/understanding	▓			*analysis and interpretation*			
for critical analysis/evaluation	▓			*historical research*			
				issues and decisions			

Guided by Performance, ©1998 Zephyr Press, Tucson, Arizona

Performance Assessment Matrix

Performance Skills

Cognitive Strategies		Task Management Strategies		Student Role		Assessment Products		Evaluation Format	
Comparison		Analyzing the task	▨	Museum curator		Portfolio		Student checklist (attached)	
Classification		Establishing time lines	▨	Reviewer		Publication		Teacher checklist (attached)	▨
Induction		Staying productive		Engineer/Designer	▨	Demonstration		Analytic scoring guide/ rubric (attached)	
Deduction		Meeting deadlines	▨	Representative		Performance		Holistic scoring guide (attached)	
Error analysis	▨	Accepting feedback	▨	Expert witness		Exhibition			
Constructing support		Working cooperatively		Character					
Abstracting		Making a contribution		Ad agency director					
Analyzing perspectives		Respecting others		Tour organizer					
Decision making	▨	Accessing resources		Bank manager					
Investigation		Striving for accuracy	▨	Psychologist/Sociologist					
Experimental inquiry		Striving for excellence		Archaeologist					
Problem solving	▨			Philosopher					
Invention				Historian					
				Writer/Editor					
				Teacher					
				Job applicant					
				Speaker/Listener					

Anecdotal Observations

Teacher Checklist for "HyperCard Stack"

Performance Criteria	Excellent	Satisfactory	Needs Improvement
Task 1			
■ Provides evidence of participation in a tutorial by documentation in a portfolio	_____	_____	_____
■ Includes at least three work samples in the portfolio (commands, script from sample stack from tutorial, sample stack of own creation)	_____	_____	_____
■ Prepares adequately for conference with teacher and peers	_____	_____	_____
■ Participates actively in conference with teacher and peers	_____	_____	_____
■ Responds to conference by articulating new learning in section of portfolio	_____	_____	_____
■ Submits completed portfolio on time	_____	_____	_____
Task 2			
■ Demonstrates understanding of process by generating manageable plan focused on clear objectives	_____	_____	_____
■ Demonstrates ability to script a field using HyperTalk	_____	_____	_____
■ Demonstrates ability to script a button using HyperTalk	_____	_____	_____
■ Demonstrates ability to add sound and music using HyperTalk	_____	_____	_____
■ Demonstrates ability to create a menu using HyperTalk	_____	_____	_____
■ Demonstrates ability to debug script by finding problems and accessing resources	_____	_____	_____
■ Prepares for each conference by providing documentation and generating questions	_____	_____	_____
Task 3			
■ Accurately completes scripting at a level that enables a successful demonstration of the HyperCard stack	_____	_____	_____
■ Provides oral commentary that illustrates understanding of			
• goals of presentation	_____	_____	_____
• extent to which goals were achieved	_____	_____	_____
• problems encountered and solved	_____	_____	_____
• own learning throughout process	_____	_____	_____
• own questions about process	_____	_____	_____
■ Submits work for final review with all appropriate revisions	_____	_____	_____

Guided by Performance, ©1998 Zephyr Press, Tucson, Arizona

HyperCard Stack
Student Guide

Task 1: Documentation of Skill Development

1. To begin working with HyperCard, demonstrate a basic skill level. Prepare a documentation portfolio that illustrates your growing fluency with HyperCard and your developing understanding of HyperTalk. Using one of the online tutorial programs or another tutorial that I provide, prepare the following work samples:

   a. glossary of basic scripting commands (see example 1, page 223), with source listed

   b. script from a sample stack downloaded from a website or contained in a tutorial

   c. ministack of your own creation (requiring you to open HyperCard, select "New Stack" from the file menu, give the stack a name by selecting "Stack Info" from the Objects menu, select "Background," "Tools," and "Patterns" from the menu, add a field, and add at least two buttons)

2. As you go through the procedures necessary to access this information, you naturally have a variety of questions about scripting. In addition to the work samples, include in your portfolio a sheet that outlines these questions, including those about the glossary, downloading a sample stack, and creating a ministack.

3. Sign up for a conference with me and with a small group of your peers. In this group conference, present your portfolio and discuss the questions. Be prepared to participate in this conference by having all of your materials ready, play an active role in the conference by ensuring that your questions are discussed, and respond to the conference by including a "notes" section in your portfolio that reflects knowledge you gained through the discussion.

4. Submit your documentation portfolio for final review.

Task 2: Documentation of Process

1. Working on a project of your own, prepare a HyperCard stack to present information on your topic to an audience. Provide documentation of the steps you took along the way. After each of the following steps, sign up for a conference with me as indicated; for each conference, be prepared with the required documentation and your questions.

2. Generate a rough plan of your project. Identify several objectives you would like to achieve. Using a large sheet of paper, sketch out the information you would like to include and how you envision presenting that information. Keeping your overall objectives in mind, sketch out where and how your presentation will address broad categories of information. Outline

where you will be including graphics, sound, and music. Once you have completed your plan, sign up for a conference.

3. Script your stack. Although you might want a conference periodically throughout this process, sign up for at least one conference to provide evidence of having completed the following functions:

    a. scripting a field

    b. scripting a button

    c. adding sound and music

    d. creating a menu

For your conference, select or highlight portions of your script that illustrate these functions (see example 2, page 224).

4. After these conferences, debug your stack to present the final product. Find problems in the stack and access the resources necessary to solve those problems. To provide evidence of this process, I will need to observe you engaged in some form of debugging. When you are ready for this observation, sign up for a conference.

Task 3: Demonstration

1. If you have achieved a satisfactory level of performance on the preceding tasks, demonstrate your work by presenting your HyperCard stack to an audience. As you present the stack, provide a commentary that includes the following:

    a. the goals you were trying to achieve through the presentation

    b. your own assessment of the extent to which these goals were achieved

    c. problems you encountered and solved along the way

    d. your learning throughout the process

    e. questions you have about the process

2. Encourage the audience to respond to your presentation with comments and questions; ask the group to give you specific feedback on ways to strengthen the communicative capacity of your presentation. Record audience feedback.

3. Before submitting your work for a final review, make any necessary or desired changes to the script. You might have uncovered some additional bugs in your script as you presented it to your audience or you might want to respond to specific suggestions from your audience.

Guided by Performance, ©1998 Zephyr Press, Tucson, Arizona

Example 1: Glossary

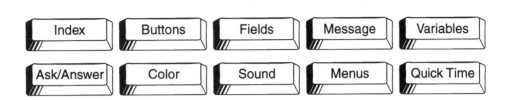

Index	Buttons	Fields	Message	Variables
Ask/Answer	Color	Sound	Menus	Quick Time

Commands
Reference Index

Add <source> to <container>
Add <number> to [<chunk> of]<container>

Answer <question> with [<reply> [or <reply 2> [or <reply 3>]]]
Answer file [<promptText>] [of type <fileType>]
Answer program [<promptText>] [of type <processType>]

arrowKey <direction>

Ask <question> [with <defaultAnswer>]
Ask password [clear] <question> [with <defaultAnswer>]

Beep <number>

Choose <toolname> tool
browse, lasso, line, bucket, regular polygon, button, pencil, spray, oval, field, brush, rectangle, curve,
polygon, select, eraser, round rect, text
Choose tool <toolnumber>

Click at <location>
Click at <location> with [<key> [, <key2> [, <key3>]]]

Close file <fileName>
Close printing
Close window <windowName>

CommandKeyDown <char>

ControlKey <keyNumber>

Example 2: Scripting Excerpts

Scripting a Field
```
on mouseUp
   select the clickLine
      put word 2 of the clickLine into lino
   do line lino of cd fld 1
end mouseUp
```

Sound & Music
```
on mouseUp
  play "imagine"
end mouseUp
```

```
speak "once upon a time" with female voice
speak "once upon a time" with male voice
speak "once upon a time" with voice otis
```

Guided by Performance, ©1998 Zephyr Press, Tucson, Arizona

Decades Project
Classroom Implementation Guide

Curriculum Areas: Language Arts, Social Studies
Products

> Research question
> Essay
> Biographical sketch
> Analytic paper
> Annotated bibliography
> Collage
> Photograph and written analysis
> Text for nonfiction book

Time: 4 weeks

Curriculum Notes

Please read the student task sheets carefully. Note any materials you will need for each task. Performance criteria are listed in the teacher checklist.

This assessment package requires eleventh grade students to analyze the sociopolitical developments during a selected twentieth-century American decade through the lenses of history, literature, technology, and the arts. As historians, students are asked to assemble a portfolio of work that reflects their conclusions about the American dream during the decade they have selected.

Suggested texts for task 1 are Fyson (1991), Layman (1996), and Sharman (1991). For task 2, students may refer to *The New York Times* for the selected decade. *Dictionary of American Biography* is a good resource for task 3. For task 4, *The New York Times Book Review* is available on microfiche in most libraries.

Resource List

Fyson, N. L. 1991. *Portrait of a Decade*. London: B. T. Batsford.
Layman, R. 1996. *The American Decades*. Detroit: Gale Research.
Sharman, M. 1991. *Take Ten Years: 1900; The First Decade*. Austin, Tex.: Steck-Vaughn.

Performance Assessment Matrix

Package Title: Decades Project

Curriculum Area: Language Arts, Social Studies

Package: Grade 11

Student: _____

Content Knowledge

Language Arts: Standard 2 (Students read a wide range of literature from many periods in many genres to build an understanding of the many dimensions of human experience)

Social Studies: Standard 1 (Culture); Standard 2 (Time, continuity and change); Standard 4 (Individual development and identity); Standard 6 (Power, authority, and governance); Standard 8 (Science, technology, and society)

Content Skills

Literacy		Mathematics	Science	Social Studies		Visual Arts	
Reading		Problem solving	Defining questions	Acquiring information		Creating	
for aesthetic response		Communication	Forming hypotheses	*reading*		*conceptual skills*	
for information/understanding	▒	Reasoning	Investigating	*study skills*		*production skills*	
for critical analysis/evaluation	▒	Connecting	Observing	*reference skills*		*evaluation skills*	
Writing		Estimation	Monitoring	*technical skills*		*application*	
for response/expression		Numeration	Measuring	Organizing/Using information		Responding	
for social interaction		Computation	Keeping records	*thinking skills*	▒	*descriptive skills*	
for information/understanding		Data analysis	Transforming records	*decision-making skills*		*analytical skills*	
for critical analysis/evaluation		Measurement	Collaborating	*metacognitive skills*		*valuing skills*	
Listening		Patterning/Relating	Interpreting information	Relationships		*application*	
for response/expression			Integrating information	*personal skills*			
for information/understanding				*group interaction*	▒		
for critical analysis/evaluation				*social/political participation*			
Speaking				Historical thinking			
for response/expression				*chronological thinking*			
for social interaction				*historical comprehension*	▒		
for information/understanding				*analysis and interpretation*			
for critical analysis/evaluation				*historical research*	▒		
				issues and decisions			

Guided by Performance, ©1998 Zephyr Press, Tucson, Arizona

Performance Assessment Matrix

Performance Skills

Cognitive Strategies		Task Management Strategies		Student Role		Assessment Products		Evaluation Format	
Comparison		Analyzing the task	▓	Museum curator		Portfolio	▓	Student checklist (attached)	
Classification		Establishing time lines		Reviewer		Publication		Teacher checklist (attached)	▓
Induction		Staying productive		Engineer/Designer		Demonstration		Analytic scoring guide/ rubric (attached)	
Deduction	▓	Meeting deadlines		Representative		Performance		Holistic scoring guide (attached)	
Error analysis		Accepting feedback		Expert witness		Exhibition			
Constructing support	▓	Working cooperatively		Character					
Abstracting		Making a contribution		Ad agency director					
Analyzing perspectives		Respecting others		Tour organizer					
Decision making		Accessing resources		Bank manager					
Investigation	▓	Striving for accuracy		Psychologist/Sociologist					
Experimental inquiry		Striving for excellence		Archaeologist					
Problem solving				Philosopher					
Invention				Historian	▓				
				Writer/Editor					
				Teacher					
				Job applicant					
				Speaker/Listener					
				Researcher					

Anecdotal Observations

Teacher Checklist for "Decades Project"

Performance Criteria	Excellent	Satisfactory	Needs Improvement
Task 1			
▪ Formulates a question about a historical event or conflict related to the selected decade	____	____	____
Task 2			
▪ In a persuasive essay, investigates, interprets, and analyzes historical and cultural viewpoints related to important events; employs critical judgment	____	____	____
Task 3			
▪ Gathers information to analyze the contributions of important people	____	____	____
▪ Summarizes information effectively in a brief biographical sketch that establishes an individual's important contribution to shaping public opinion	____	____	____
Task 4			
▪ Reads fiction that establishes an understanding of the human experience	____	____	____
▪ Analyzes fiction that establishes an understanding of the human experience and the cultural expressions of an era	____	____	____
▪ Systematically employs critical inquiry to reinterpret the past	____	____	____
Task 5			
▪ Draws inferences from collected samples of primary data	____	____	____
Task 6			
▪ Selects, describes, and interprets works of art in a historical or cultural framework	____	____	____
▪ Applies understanding of culture as an integrated whole that explains the interaction of the arts, beliefs, values, and behavior patterns	____	____	____
Task 7			
▪ Identifies and describes historical examples of the interaction of science and society in cultural settings	____	____	____
or			
▪ Evaluates the role of technology in communications and information processing that shape cultural beliefs	____	____	____
Task 8			
▪ Compares representations of the historical period to authentic cultural expression	____	____	____
▪ Applies an understanding of culture as an integrated whole that explains the functions and interactions of literature, the arts, traditions, beliefs, values, and behavior patterns	____	____	____
▪ Interprets the key ideals of the democratic republican form of government	____	____	____

Guided by Performance, ©1998 Zephyr Press, Tucson, Arizona

Decades Project
Student Guide

Task 1: Research Question

1. Select a decade to study. Select a major event or conflict that illustrates the reality or myth of the "American dream."

2. Write a question that frames an inquiry into this event or conflict. For example, if you select the internment of Japanese Americans in World War II, your question might read, "In what ways did the Bill of Rights protect the freedoms of Japanese Americans living in the United States during the 1940s?"

3. After you have written a draft of a question, submit it.

Task 2: Essay

1. Write a two- to three-page essay that defines the American dream in the context of your selected decade. Cite the work of principal thinkers, authors, artists, and political leaders of the selected decade.

Task 3: Biography

1. Select an important thinker, artist, leader, or author from your decade. Research your choice fully.

2. Write a two- to three-page biography to provide evidence that establishes the importance of this person's role in shaping contemporary public opinion. Specifically, what events did this person influence or cause that shaped public opinion about the American dream, thereby establishing this person's place in history?

Task 4: Analytic Writing

1. Select a work of fiction (a novel, short story, or play) that had a major influence on the public during the decade you are studying.

2. In one page or less, summarize this work, then provide evidence that describes and establishes how this work shaped public opinion. You might use reviews in newspapers or periodicals. Cite at least one secondary source that confirms the importance of this piece of fiction.

Task 5: Annotated Bibliography

1. Create an annotated bibliography of the decade's ten best-selling works of nonfiction. Select one day (for example, the first Sunday in July) from each year of the decade, then check *The New York Times Book Review* for that date to find the best-selling book.

2. Draw from book reviews to write a short paragraph on each work. What conclusions can you draw about the concerns people had throughout that decade?

Task 6: Collage

1. Artists often make powerful social and political statements through their work. Select one medium of artistic expression (for example, photographs, drawings, paintings, movies, television or radio shows, plays) that portrays the myth or reality of the American dream during your selected decade.

2. Create a collage with representative samples of artists' works.

Task 7: Architectural Study or Technology Artifact

1. Select one photograph of either one piece of architecture erected during the decade you are studying or one piece of technology that was considered state of the art for that decade.

2. Write a one- to two-page analysis of how your selection reflects the American dream.

Task 8: Final Synthesis

1. This final task requires you to think about all you have learned about ways people viewed the American dream in your selected decade. What conclusions can you draw about the American dream in this decade? Evaluate the chapter in your history text that describes this decade. How has the text represented this decade? Has the text captured the culture of the decade?

2. Rewrite the chapter of your textbook that deals with this decade of twentieth-century American history. What do you feel should be added to the text to give other students a more complete picture of the decade and the myth or reality of the American dream? Your answers to these questions will be reflected in the body of the new chapter of the text.

3. Write an editor's introduction to the chapter that explains to the reader what has been changed from the "earlier" edition of this text (that is, your real textbook) and how this version reflects improvements over the earlier version. How has the revised chapter more effectively communicated the realization, or lack of realization, of the key American ideals embedded in the concept of the American dream?

Guided by Performance, ©1998 Zephyr Press, Tucson, Arizona

Fast Food Quality: A Statistics Problem

Classroom Implementation Guide

Curriculum Areas: Mathematics, Language Arts

Products

> Written research question
> Written research design
> Written analysis and report

Time: 2 weeks

Curriculum Notes

Please read the student task sheets carefully. Note any materials you will need for each task. Performance criteria are listed in the teacher checklist.

This assessment package requires students to collect statistical data on the consistency of fast food service at two competing fast food outlets. Students use descriptive research methodology to determine which of two fast food competitors provides food in the shortest period of time. Students design a research question, collect data randomly, analyze the data, and use measures of central tendency (mean, mode, range, standard deviation). Students write about their findings and present the evidence collected to support their conclusions. Tasks 1 and 2 are done in the first week; tasks 3 and 4 in the second.

Resource List

> Mertens, D. 1998. *Research Methods in Education and Psychology*. London: Sage.
> Triola, Mario. 1995. *Elementary Statistics*. Boston: Addison-Wesley.

by Gerald Brown and Robert J. Monson

Performance Assessment Matrix

Package Title: Fast Food Quality

Curriculum Area: Mathematics, Language Arts

Package: Grade 11

Student: _____

Content Knowledge

Mathematics: Standard 10 (Statistics)

Language Arts: Standard 7 (Students conduct research on issues of interest. They communicate their discoveries in ways that suit their purpose and audience.)

Content Skills

Literacy		Mathematics		Science		Social Studies		Visual Arts	
Reading		Problem solving		Defining questions		Acquiring information		Creating	
for aesthetic response		Communication		Forming hypotheses		reading		conceptual skills	
for information/understanding		Reasoning		Investigating		study skills		production skills	
for critical analysis/evaluation		Connecting		Observing		reference skills		evaluation skills	
Writing		Estimation		Monitoring		technical skills		application	
for response/expression		Numeration		Measuring		Organizing/Using information		Responding	
for social interaction		Computation		Keeping records		thinking skills		descriptive skills	
for information/understanding		Data analysis		Transforming records		decision-making skills		analytical skills	
for critical analysis/evaluation		Measurement		Collaborating		metacognitive skills		valuing skills	
Listening		Patterning/Relating		Interpreting information		Relationships		application	
for response/expression				Integrating information		personal skills			
for information/understanding						group interaction			
for critical analysis/evaluation						social/political participation			
Speaking						Historical thinking			
for response/expression						chronological thinking			
for social interaction						historical comprehension			
for information/understanding						analysis and interpretation			
for critical analysis/evaluation						historical research			
						issues and decisions			

Guided by Performance, ©1998 Zephyr Press, Tucson, Arizona

Performance Assessment Matrix

Performance Skills

Cognitive Strategies	Task Management Strategies	Student Role	Assessment Products	Evaluation Format	
Comparison	Analyzing the task	Museum curator	Portfolio	Student checklist (attached)	
Classification	Establishing time lines	Reviewer	Publication	Teacher checklist (attached)	
Induction	Staying productive	Engineer/Designer	Demonstration	Analytic scoring guide/ rubric (attached)	
Deduction	Meeting deadlines	Representative	Performance	Holistic scoring guide (attached)	
Error analysis	Accepting feedback	Expert witness	Exhibition		
Constructing support	Working cooperatively	Character			
Abstracting	Making a contribution	Ad agency director			
Analyzing perspectives	Respecting others	Tour organizer			
Decision making	Accessing resources	Bank manager			
Investigation	Striving for accuracy	Psychologist/Sociologist			
Experimental inquiry	Striving for excellence	Archaeologist			
Problem solving		Philosopher			
Invention		Historian			
		Writer/Editor			
		Teacher			
		Job applicant			
		Speaker/Listener			
		Researcher			

Anecdotal Observations

Teacher Checklist for "Fast Food Quality: A Statistics Problem"

Performance Criteria	Excellent	Satisfactory	Needs Improvement
Task 1			
■ Develops a topic into a clear statement of a research problem with subproblems	_____	_____	_____
Task 2			
■ Employs sampling strategies and recognizes their role in statistical claims	_____	_____	_____
■ Designs and conducts investigation	_____	_____	_____
Task 3			
■ Analyzes the effects of data transformations on measures of central tendency and variability	_____	_____	_____
■ Transforms data to aid in data interpretation and prediction	_____	_____	_____
■ Tests hypothesis (if generated) using appropriate mean and standard of deviation	_____	_____	_____
■ Communicates discoveries in ways that suit purpose and audience	_____	_____	_____

Guided by Performance, ©1998 Zephyr Press, Tucson, Arizona

Fast Food Quality: A Statistics Problem
Student Guide

After learning the statistical tools of the mean, range, mode, and standard deviation, demonstrate a working knowledge of them in the context of a real-life problem that has some relevance and usefulness. One of the components of free market competition is the ability of one company to deliver products of consistently higher quality at a price attractive to consumers. One context for understanding these principles is the fast food marketplace.

Task 1: Research Question

1. Pair with one partner or two at the most. Select two fast food competitors that deliver roughly the same product (for example, two hamburger chains).

2. Develop a research question that invites the collection of quantitative data that can be statistically manipulated. Include a description of the collection process (see example 1, page 237). For example, which hamburger franchise, X or Y, delivers orders to customers at the drive-up window in the shortest amount of time? Make the question specific enough to guide data collection.

Task 2: Research Design

1. Develop a plan to collect data that will answer the research question. Identify the key issues (variables) that will influence the outcome of the question (drive-up window or counter, size of the order, day and time of day for data collection, and so on).

2. Delineate the steps needed to collect the data that are relevant to the research question. Will it be possible to collect these data? How much time will it take? How many researchers do you need? What materials will you need to collect the data? What type of permission will you need to have before collecting the data? What specific methodologies will you need to collect the required data? Answer all these questions before submitting the research question and design proposal for reaction and suggestions.

3. Write a two- to three-page plan that outlines the components of your research design (see example 2, page 238).

Task 3: Gathering and Analyzing Data and Reporting Findings

1. Gather the raw data that will eventually enable you to draw conclusions and write a report (see example 3, page 239). You might wish to collect data in teams, with each member assigned a specific task. A calendar will be helpful. We suggest that the data collection phase begin on the weekend following week 1. You need to get permission before you begin collecting data. A review and advice session with me could facilitate this work and avoid problems.

2. Format the data in a way that will speed up summarization and analysis (see example 4, page 240). Create a summary form onto which raw data can be recorded and later summarized.

3. Record the *range* of data collected, and calculate the *mean* and the *standard deviation*. Be sure to note the size of the sample. Show the formulas and statistical calculations you used.

4. Write the final report in the third person; the audience for this report is the managers of the fast food outlets from which you collected your data. Include the rationale for the study, the research questions, a summary of the research design, the summarized data (including the actual sample size and a description of the variables that were directly related to the question, your conclusions, and any recommendations). Do not exceed ten pages.

Guided by Performance, ©1998 Zephyr Press, Tucson, Arizona

How Fast Is "Fast Food"?

by Jennie Lassey and Jill Bruder

Jennie Lassey and Jill Bruder took a simple random sample of 10 customers per hour for three days at the local McDonalds. The sample was an SRS because the customers entering the restaurant were unaware of the test and entered at random times in the afternoon. About every second customer was timed from the time they stood in line to the time they received their food (time intervals). Not only were the customers unaware of the tests, but it was also a blind experiment for the workers. Because we are students, we were only able to time the midafternoon to dinner shifts. During our testing, there were three shifts; 3-4 P.M., 4-5 P.M., 5-6 P.M. We continued our test for three days, Saturday, Monday, and Wednesday (notice that the days are not consecutive, therefore more random). Each half-hour we made sure to time only 5 customers; we did this because it is important that the data reflects the time intervals of the whole hour instead of just the first 10-15 minutes of the hour. All of the time intervals were recorded in seconds.

The importance of this test was to discover if fast food is "fast." To the average fast-food customer it may be beneficial to know if they are receiving good/fast service for his/her food at different times of the day. At McDonalds we spoke to the manager on duty; she informed us that the mean time for a person to wait for their food is 180 seconds (3 minutes).

Example 2: Research Design

Validation

1. Simple Random Sample (as explained in research question and description)
2. Normal distributions
   We designed three graphs by combining the three hour shifts of Saturday, Monday, and Wednesday. See graphs on following pages, all graphs are almost normal. This is acceptable because of large sample sizes (30) and also when examining the graphs, you can trace the outline of a bell-shaped curve.
3. $N > 10n$ N represents the population of McDonalds customers.
       n represents the sample sizes.
   $N > 300$ when $n = 30$.
   $N > 100$ when $n = 10$.

Statistical Methods Employed

I. F-test

An F-test tests whether or not there is difference among two or more means. We calculated the combination of each hourly shift from all three days.

a. $H_o: u_1 = u_2 = u_3$
   H_a: means are not equal (difference between means)

u_1 is the mean time interval of the hours 3:00 to 4:00 P.M. taken from all three days
u_2 is the mean time interval of the hours 4:00 to 5:00 P.M. taken from all three days
u_3 is the mean time interval of the hours 5:00 to 6:00 P.M. taken from all three days

II. T-test

We performed three T-tests against the expected time it should take for a customer to receive his/her food.

a. $H_o: u_1 \leq 180$ seconds
   $H_a: u_1 > 180$ seconds

u_1 is the mean time interval of the hours 3:00 to 4:00 P.M. taken from all three days.

b. $H_o: u_2 \leq 180$ seconds
   $H_a: u_2 > 180$ seconds

u_2 is the mean time interval of the hours 4:00 to 5:00 P.M. taken from all three days.

c. $H_o: u_3 \leq 180$ seconds
   $H_a: u_3 > 180$ seconds

u_3 is the mean time interval of the hours 5:00 to 6:00 P.M. taken from all three days.

Guided by Performance, ©1998 Zephyr Press, Tucson, Arizona

Example 3: Gathering Data (Representative Sample)

Saturday 3:00-4:00 P.M	**Monday** 3:00-4:00 P.M.	**Sunday** 3:00-4:00 P.M.
65	93	77
45	105	178
33	39	151
140	99	60
105	53	152
34	135	32
79	107	110
61	160	65
80	108	63
70	75	123

4:00-5:00 P.M.	4:00-5:00 P.M.	4:00-5:00 P.M.
223	144	123
178	88	117
108	206	135
211	63	120
184	55	75
143	179	61
70	165	105
185	216	285
135	147	105
108	161	115

Data of all three days put together:

$\bar{x}$ = sample mean   n = sample size   s = standard deviation of the sample

3–4 P.M.

$\bar{x}$ = 89.9 seconds
n = 30 customers
s = 40.6 seconds

4–5 P.M.

$\bar{x}$ = 140.3 seconds
n = 30 customers
s = 55.3 seconds

Example 4: Analysis of Data and Report of Findings

III. T-Test

a. 1. After comparing the sample mean from each hour shift to the given mean time for a customer to wait to receive their food, we calculated the total sample mean from all three days of all three time shifts. We tested the total sample mean against the given mean to find whether or not McDonalds was satisfying their quota standard time (overall).

2. H_o: $u_{total} \leq 180$ seconds
    H_a: $u_{total} > 180$ seconds

3. $\alpha = .05$

4. See data sheet

5. $t = \dfrac{x - M_{total}}{\dfrac{s}{\sqrt{n}}}$ $\qquad$ $t = \dfrac{171.1 - 180}{\dfrac{80.97}{\sqrt{90}}}$ $\qquad$ $t = -1.04$

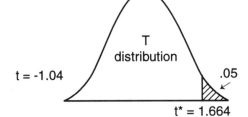

6. We received a t score of -1.04, therefore accepting the null hypothesis that u_{total} is less than or equal to 180 seconds. We did this by examining the upper bound of the graph which was 1.664, with degrees of freedom 89. Our t score did not lie in the area of rejection, therefore there is statistically significant evidence supporting H_o. We also received a P value of greater than .25, this is more evidence that we fail to reject H_o.

Conclusion of Total sample mean T-test:

After calculating the total sample mean it is evident that McDonalds, in fact, is serving their customers within three minutes or less. So, to answer the question of "How fast is 'Fast Food,'" we would have to conclude that it is fast enough.

Guided by Performance, ©1998 Zephyr Press, Tucson, Arizona

6
Final Thoughts and Reflections

Working with performance assessment packages is a learning experience. We've tried to design assessment packages as a forum for describing, examining, evaluating, and improving student performance in key curriculum areas. We've encouraged individual teachers to use the model packages or to implement the package design process in order to build their own assessment packages; in doing so, they will be able to use performance as a guide for their own instructional planning. In addition, when teachers use assessment packages to promote reflection, collaboration, interaction, and action planning with other professionals at their school or in their district, great potential exists for achieving educational improvement targeted at specific areas of student performance. However, we've also learned a great deal about the kinds of support that teachers need in order to focus effectively on student performance.

Edward Chittendon (1991) suggests that teachers adopt three stances with respect to their student assessment practices—keeping track, checking up, and finding out. We believe that each of these stances is also associated with specific assessment tools and should be the primary responsibility of people who play different roles in the school environment (see figure 6-1).

School administrators are concerned with keeping track. They need data on student performance for the purposes of program evaluation and accountability. The tools used to keep track should conform to specifications for technical adequacy.

In contrast, teachers are concerned primarily with finding out; they want to implement assessments in the context of their classrooms in order to inform instruction and improve their practice. The tools used for finding out should conform to specifications for practical adequacy.

In contrast, specialists in the school environment are concerned with the need to check up on students who need support in order to perform at high or satisfactory levels. The assessments they use for individual assessment should conform to specifications for diagnostic adequacy.

Like Chittendon (1991), we believe that the primary concern of classroom teachers should be finding out—a stance that is quite possibly "the most critical to successful teaching" (30). By finding out, teachers discover things that can shape educational decisions. When they use performance assessment packages, teachers are using a tool uniquely designed for the purpose of finding out. However, they can easily get distracted from this purpose by the demands of accountability testing or by the demands of diagnosing students with special learning needs. In order to focus effectively on student performance, teachers need to be allowed to experiment with finding out assessments in their own classrooms and need opportunities to collaborate with other teachers engaged in this kind of experimentation.

Thoughtful experimentation with performance assessment packages provides teachers with a variety of opportunities for professional development (see table 6-1). As we've worked with various schools to use the model performance packages, to adapt the model packages, and to build new packages based upon the models, we've found that they provide a powerful focus for professional development and allow for a variety of professional development planning options. Each of these options has the potential for yielding different outcomes for the teachers involved.

Without opportunities to examine samples of student work, it is hard for teachers to develop the capacity to implement educational improvements. While it is possible for individual teachers to engage

Figure 6-1: Stances toward assessment: Purpose, distinctions, and design considerations

Keeping Track

Large-scale Performance Assessment
Program Evaluation and Accountability

"Tight specifications, common, detailed scoring rubrics, and operational definitions of domain . . ."

—Linn and Baker (1996)

Technical Adequacy

▶ Efficiency (Time, Cost)
▶ Comparability (Functional Task Equivalence)
▶ Fairness (Tasks, Scoring)
▶ Opportunity to Learn (Debra P. v. Turlington)
▶ Generalizability, Reliability, and Transfer
  • Variability Due to Task/Increase in Tasks
  • Individual Performance vs. Matrix Sampling
  • Task Specification or Item Shell Analysis
▶ Cognitive Complexity
▶ Content Quality
▶ Content Coverage
▶ Validity (Construct, Ecological, Consequential)

Finding Out

Classroom-based Assessment
Whole Class, Small Group, and Individual
Inform Instruction and Improve Practice

" . . . intense engagement of staff in collaboratively defining, redefining, testing, and activating their own constructed and contextualized understanding of what is worth knowing and how it can be assessed."

—Darling-Hammond and Ancess (1996)

Practical Adequacy

▶ Valid (Construct, Ecological, Consequential)
▶ Credible and Useful (Practitioner Oriented)
▶ Flexible (Student Options, Teacher Options)
▶ Standards and Curriculum Alignment
▶ Learner Centered (Feedback, Self-Assessment)
▶ School-based Inquiry (Design through Interpretation)
▶ Professional Development
▶ Reporting to Parents
▶ Structured Responsiveness

Checking Up

Specialized Assessment
Individual Diagnosis and Intervention

"The repertoire of procedures was designed for children having the most difficulty . . . considering each child, teachers had to select carefully and sensitively from this repertoire."

—Lyons, Pinnell, and DeFord (1993)

Diagnostic Adequacy

▶ Developmental Benchmarks
▶ Range of Acceptable Performance
▶ Generalizability—Domain Specific
▶ Exploratory Options
  • Learning Style
  • Language Diversity
  • Background Knowledge
  • Instructional Support
  • Special Needs
▶ Interactive Assessment Formats

Table 6-1: Professional Development Planning Options

Activities	Structures	Outcomes
Implementing model assessment packages	Pilot testing Small group processing	■ Develop assessment literacy in teachers ■ Increase comparability of results ■ Collaborate to analyze student work ■ Identify areas for curriculum support
Adapting model assessment packages	Grade-level teams Working groups	■ Generate new ideas and approaches ■ Greater alignment with curriculum ■ Respond to student characteristics ■ Identify areas for curriculum support
Building new assessment packages	Grade-level teams Working groups	■ Capitalize on teacher creativity ■ Align more closely with curriculum ■ Develop greater understanding of process ■ Identify areas for curriculum support
Developing class profiles	Individual trajectories Cross-case analyses Longitudinal tracking Reliability studies	■ Improve overall quality of packages ■ Develop common assessment language ■ Develop common learning expectations ■ Identify areas for curriculum support
Analyzing patterns of student performance	Grade-level teams Working groups	■ Improve opportunity to learn for students ■ Address areas for curriculum support ■ Respond to individual student needs ■ Increase access to resources
Developing a program matrix	K–12 representative teams Working groups	■ Ensure opportunity to learn for students ■ Address areas for curriculum support ■ Lay foundation for curriculum evaluation ■ Outline system accountability process
Mentoring	Individual partnerships	■ Recognize expertise ■ Encourage innovation and excellence ■ Disseminate effective practices ■ Value collegial exchanges

in thoughtful experimentation on their own, it is so much more powerful when done in collaboration with others who share responsibility for student performance.

On the most basic level, performance assessment packages provide teachers with strategies for understanding and documenting student performance. However, by implementing the process we've described and by using performance assessment packages on a more comprehensive level, teachers can take steps to improve student learning and to strengthen the curriculum in their schools. In or-

der to be successful, teachers need to find out about student learning through assessment and they need to use that information to make informed educational decisions in their classrooms. Administrators can support these efforts by enabling teachers to focus more closely on the kinds of assessments that inform instructional practice and by providing opportunities for collaborative professional development. In order to strengthen the bridges between student learning, curriculum, and assessment, the entire school community needs to become guided by student performance.

◆◆

Appendix

Content knowledge standards were drawn from the following publications and are referenced in the cover sheet that accompanies each performance assessment package:

Center for Civic Education. 1994. *National Standards for Civics and Government.* Calabasas, Calif.: Center for Civic Education.

Consortium of National Arts Education Associations. 1994. *National Standards for Art Education: What Every Young American Should Know and Be Able to Do in the Arts.* Reston, Va.: Music Educators National Conference.

International Reading Association and the National Council of Teachers of English. 1996. *Standards for the English Language Arts.* Newark, Del.: International Reading Association.

Joint Committee on Health Education Standards. 1995. *National Health Education Standards: Achieving Health Literacy.* Reston, Va.: Association for the Advancement of Health Education.

National Association for Sport and Physical Education. 1992. *Outcomes of Quality Physical Education Programs.* Reston, Va.: National Association for Sport and Physical Education.

National Center for History in the Schools. 1996. *National Standards for History.* Los Angeles: National Center for History in the Schools.

National Council for the Social Studies. 1994. *Expectations of Excellence: Curriculum Standards for Social Studies.* Washington, D.C.: National Council for the Social Studies.

National Council of Teachers of Mathematics. 1989. *Curriculum and Evaluation Standards for School Mathematics.* Reston, Va.: National Council of Teachers of Mathematics.

National Research Council. 1996. *National Science Education Standards.* Washington, D.C.: National Academy Press.

Bibliography

Armstrong, T. 1994. *Multiple Intelligences in the Classroom*. Alexandria, Va.: Association for Supervision and Curriculum Development.

Caine, R. N., and G. Caine. 1997. *Education on the Edge of Possibility*. Alexandria, Va.: Association for Supervision and Curriculum Development.

Chittendon, E. 1991. "Authentic Assessment, Evaluation, and Documentation of Student Performance." In V. Perrone, ed., *Expanding Student Assessment*. Alexandria, Va.: Association for Supervision and Curriculum Development, 22–31.

Darling-Hammond, L., and J. Ancess. 1996. "Authentic Assessment and School Development." In J. B. Baron and D. P. Wolf, eds. *Performance-Based Student Assessment: Challenges and Possibilities*. Chicago: National Society for Study of Education. 521–83.

Department of Labor. 1991. *What Work Requires of Schools: A SCANS Report for America 2000*. Washington, D.C.: Government Printing Office.

Fabio, R. Y. 1994. *Outcomes in Process: Setting Standards for Language Use*. Portsmouth, N.H.: Heinemann.

Gandal, M. 1996. *Making Standards Matter 1996: An Annual Fifty-State Report on Efforts to Raise Academic Standards*. Washington, D.C.: American Federation of Teachers.

Gardner, H. 1983. *Frames of Mind: The Theory of Multiple Intelligences*. New York: Basic.

Geography Education Standards Project. 1994. *Geography for Life: National Geography Standards*. Washington, D.C.: National Geographic Research and Exploration.

Hogan, K. 1991. *Eco-Inquiry: An Ecology Program for Grades 5 and 6*. New York: Institute of Ecosystem Studies.

Linn, R. L. 1993. "Educational Assessment: Expanded Expectations and Challenges." *Educational Evaluation and Policy Analysis* 15, 1: 1–16.

Lyons, C. A., G. S. Pinnell, and D. E. DeFord. 1993. *Partners in Learning: Teachers and Children in Learning Recovery*. New York: Teacher's College Press.

Marzano, R. J., and J. S. Kendall. 1996. *A Comprehensive Guide to Designing Standards-Based Districts, Schools, and Classrooms*. Aurora, Colo.: Mid-Continent Regional Educational Laboratory (McREL).

Marzano, R. J., D. Pickering, and J. McTighe. 1993. *Assessing Student Outcomes: Performance Assessment Using the Dimensions of Learning Model*. Alexandria, Va.: Association for Supervision and Curriculum Development.

Massachusetts State Department of Education. 1997. *Massachusetts English Language Arts Curriculum Framework*. Boston: Massachusetts State Department of Education.

Minnesota Department of Children, Families, and Learning. 1996. *High Standards in the Profile of Learning*. St. Paul, Minn.: Minnesota Department of Children, Families, and Learning.

National Art Education Association. 1994. *NAEP Visual Arts Assessment and Exercise Specifications*. Reston, Va.: NAEA.

National Center for History in the Schools. 1996. *National Standards for History*. Los Angeles: NCHS.

National Council for the Social Studies. 1994. *Expectations of Excellence: Curriculum Standards for Social Studies*. Washington, D.C.: NCSS.

National Council of Teachers of Mathematics. 1989. *Curriculum and Evaluation Standards for School Mathematics*. Reston, Va.: NCTM.

National Research Council. 1996. *National Science Education Standards*. Washington, D.C.: National Academy Press.

Wiggins, G. P. 1993. *Assessing Student Performance: Exploring the Purpose and Limits of Testing*. San Francisco: Jossey-Bass.

Notes

Notes

Improve Classroom Success Using These Proven MI Assessment Techniques

MULTIPLE INTELLIGENCE APPROACHES TO ASSESSMENT
Solving the Assessment Conundrum
by David Lazear
foreword by Grant Wiggins
Grades K–12+

Here are more than 1,000 specific ideas to help you accurately assess students' academic progress. Learn how to create intelligence profiles based on your observations. You'll also find practical prescriptive ideas on how to teach to varying intelligences.

1039-W . . . $39

THE RUBRICS WAY
Using MI to Assess Understanding
by David Lazear
Grades K–12+

If you've been waiting for the right assessment tool, you don't have to wait any longer. Bring authentic assessment into your classroom with this multimodal approach. For all 8 intelligences you'll find—

- Content rubrics—adaptable to any content in your curriculum
- Basic, complex, and higher-order intelligence rubrics—related to performance
- Questions to ask yourself when assessing student understanding
- Questions to ask your students to confirm their understanding

Performance assessment guidelines will help you create your own rubrics that are authentic, intelligence fair, and brain compatible.

1092-W . . . $39

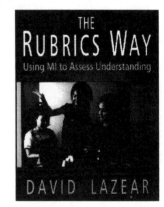

SQUARE PEGS
Building Success in School and Life through MI
by Jean Bowen, Carol King, and Marianne Hawkins
Grades 4–12

Teach your students learning skills they'll use throughout life. An MI book that goes beyond the classroom! You'll find this resource set up in an easy-to-use format. With numerous reproducible activity sheets, teacher resource sheets, wall posters, and cartoons, your students learn how to—

- Take control of their attitudes, thoughts, and feelings
- Develop strategies for applying each intelligence to a variety of curricular areas
- Develop general life skills (focus, organization, communication)

1079-W . . . $36

It's easy to put MI strategies into your daily lessons with these handy resources

TAP YOUR MULTIPLE INTELLIGENCES
Posters for the Classroom
text by David Lazear, illustrations by Nancy Margulies, M.A.
Grades 3–12
Help your students learn about all their intelligences with full-size color posters. This handy set of 8 colorful posters will remind your students to use all their intelligences—including the naturalist! Each poster reinforces a specific intelligence.
8 full-color, 11" x 17" posters.
1811-W . . . $27

A DAILY DOSE
Integrating MI into Your Curriculum
by Bonita DeAmicis
Grades 3–6
Where do you begin to bring MI into your classroom? Get started right now with this easy-to-use guide. You'll be linking each intelligence to your curriculum in convenient daily doses—even if you have no experience with MI. Follow the step-by-step lessons or apply the flexible MI-based strategies immediately to your own curriculum. Integrate each intelligence into—

- Literature
- Social studies
- Science
- Math

1081-W . . . $30